30TH ANNIVERSARY EDITION

CHURCH & NONPROFIT

TAX & FINANCIAL GUIDE

2021
FOR 2020 TAX RETURNS

Easy to use—
cutting through the
complexity of taxes and finance.

MICHAEL MARTIN

Appreciation

This guide is a successor edition of a guide originally authored by Dan Busby. The availability of this guide today would not be possible were it not for Dan's original authorship of it and his improvements to it over the years. ECFA is most grateful for Dan's vision in creating this resource and for his contribution of its content to ECFA for publication of subsequent editions.

2021 Church and Nonprofit Tax and Financial Guide
Copyright © 2020 by ECFA (Evangelical Council for Financial Accountability)

Requests for information should be addressed to:
ECFA, 440 West Jubal Early Drive, Suite 100, Winchester, VA 22601

ISBN 978-1-949365-28-3

Publisher's note: This guide is published in recognition of the need for clarification of tax and other laws for churches and nonprofit organizations. Every effort has been made to publish a timely, accurate, and authoritative guide. The publisher, author, and reviewers do not assume any legal responsibility for the accuracy of the text or any other contents.

Readers are cautioned that this book is sold with the understanding that the publisher is not rendering legal, accounting, or other professional service. Organizations with specific tax problems should seek the professional advice of a tax accountant or lawyer.

References to IRS forms and tax rates are derived from preliminary proofs of 2020 forms or 2019 forms. Some adaptation for changes may be necessary. These materials should be used solely as a guide in filling out 2020 tax and information returns. To obtain the final forms, schedules, and tables for filing returns and forms, contact the IRS or a public library.

The Internal Revenue Code does not use the word "nonprofit." The Code refers to nonprofits as "exempt organizations." Certain state statutes use the term "not-for-profit." A not-for-profit organization under state law may or may not be tax-exempt under federal law. In this book, the term "nonprofit" refers to nonprofit organizations that are exempt from federal income tax.

Any internet addresses (websites, blogs, etc.) and telephone numbers in this book are offered as a resource. They are not intended in any way to be or imply an endorsement by ECFA, nor does ECFA vouch for the content of these sites and numbers for the life of this book.

With the exception of the sample board resolutions, checklists, charts, and procedures, no part of this publication may be reproduced, stored in a retrieval system, or transmitted in any form or by any means—electronic, mechanical, photocopy, recording, or any other—except for brief quotations in printed reviews, without the prior permission of the publisher.

Printed in the United States of America

Contents

How to Use this Church and Nonprofit Tax & Financial Guide

This is the 30th anniversary edition of the *Church and Nonprofit Tax & Financial Guide*! As with earlier editions, this Guide, now published by ECFAPress, includes the latest tax forms from the IRS, the impact of Capitol Hill legislation, the effect of court decisions, and more.

But this 30th anniversary edition of the Guide is not just another book—it is your gateway to ECFA's incredible and FREE online resources for churches and ministries.

- You may have a printed copy of the book in your hands. Or you may have accessed our book webpage (*www.ECFA.church/TaxBooks/ChurchNPGuide*), and you are viewing the book online.

- If you are viewing the book online, you may have already clicked on some of the links embedded in the book which open the world of ECFA's online catalog of 50 eBooks and over 700 Knowledge Center documents.

- Listening and watching may be your preferred learning style. If so, there are a series of short videos on our website that highlight the key takeaways from the guide.

You get the picture—here at ECFA, we want to serve you. We do this by helping you understand the basics of church and nonprofit taxes and finance through a variety of learning formats.

Our prayer is that God will use this guide to help you to be the best possible steward of your God-given resources and free you to focus on ministry!

Michael Martin, JD, CPA
ECFA President

New Bonus Videos for Churches and Nonprofits

From author: Michael Martin, ECFA President

- **Chapter 1 – Financial Integrity Foundations**

  Video: 4 Keys to Faithful Administration of Church Finances

- **Chapter 2 – Tax Exemption**

  Video: Does Your Church or Ministry Actually Owe Taxes? Maybe So

- **Chapter 3 – Compensating Employees**

  Video: 9 Compensation Steps of Excellence

- **Chapter 4 – Employer Reporting**

  Video: To Be or Not to Be (An Employee) . . . That Is the Question

- **Chapter 5 – Information Reporting**

  Video: 7 Information Reporting Forms Your Church or Ministry May Have
  to File

- **Chapter 6 – Financial Management and Reporting**

  Video: How to Prevent and Detect Fraud

- **Chapter 7 – Charitable Gifts**

  Video: The Key Elements of a Charitable Gift Acknowledgment

- **Chapter 8 – Special Charitable Gift Issues**

  Video: 7 Special Charitable Gift Issues

ECFA.church/TaxGuideVideos

Recent Developments

The CARES Act and new charitable contribution rules. 2020 has been a difficult year for individuals, businesses, and nonprofits as we all have navigated the various impacts of the COVID-19 pandemic. Knowing the desire of the American people to reach out and help others in time of need, lawmakers included several significant changes in the Coronavirus Aid, Relief, and Economic Security (CARES) Act that was signed into law on March 27, 2020 to encourage charitable giving.

- **Individual contributions.** Beginning in 2020, individuals who do not itemize deductions may deduct up to $300 in charitable cash contributions (the limit applies regardless of the filing status). This universal charitable deduction is an above-the-line deduction and is deducted from the taxpayer's income prior to the calculation of adjusted gross income. This deduction is in addition to the standard deduction.

  Another positive change for individual taxpayers is this: the limitation for individuals who are still able to itemize their deductions has been significantly relaxed. Prior to the CARES Act, deductions for cash contributions to qualified charitable organizations was limited to 60% of the individual's adjusted gross income. Under the CARES Act, the deduction for cash contributions to a qualified public charity in 2020 has been increased to 100% of the individual's adjusted gross income (with a 5-year carryover). It is important to note that both of these provisions, the new universal charitable contribution and the relaxed limitation on itemized deductions, apply to cash contributions to qualified public charities only. Also, these special rules do not apply to contributions made to donor-advised funds or private foundations.

- **Corporate giving.** As with individual giving, the adjusted gross income limit for cash contributions was also increased for corporate donors. For 2020, a corporation may deduct qualified contributions of up to 25% of its taxable income compared to 10% before the CARES Act (with a 5 year carryover). Once again, these new limits are applicable only to cash donations to a qualified public charity. They do not apply to contributions made to donor-advised funds or private foundations.

The "new" Form 1099-NEC. A new Form 1099-NEC (used for non-employee compensation) has been introduced by the IRS for 2020. It is actually an old form that hasn't been in use since 1982. Prior to 2020, organizations could file one Form 1099-MISC by February 28 each year to report nonemployee compensation and miscellaneous income items. In 2015, the Protecting Americans from Tax Hikes Act (PATH Act) changed the Form 1099-MISC due date to January 31 for reporting compensation. Since some data had a January 31 deadline and other data had a February 28 deadline, some organizations were filing two Form 1099-MISCs and confusion ensued.

The most common examples of payments that must be reported on Form 1099-NEC include:

- Payments to independent contractors for services including payment for parts or materials used to perform the services if they were incidental to the service

- Professional service fees paid to attorneys (including law firms established as corporations), accountants, architects, etc.

See pages 100-3 for more information.

Revised Form 1099-MISC. The new form 1099-MISC no longer has a box for nonemployee compensation because that data is now reported on Form 1099-NEC.

New Form I-9 issued. A new version of Form I-9 was issued with an effective date of January 1, 2020. All employers must complete Form I-9 to document verification of the identity and employment authorization of each new employee, both citizen and noncitizen, hired to work in the United States. Both employers and employees are responsible for completing their respective sections of Form I-9. (See pages 107-8.)

IRS issues guidance for virtual currency donations. Nonprofit organizations receiving donations of virtual currency (such as bitcoin) now have additional guidance from the IRS on donor acknowledgment and IRS reporting responsibilities.

Because virtual currency is considered property for tax purposes, this guidance on virtual currency donations follows similar principles regarding other non-cash gifts. These include issuing appropriate gift acknowledgments; filing the Form 8282 when virtual currency is sold, exchanged, or otherwise disposed within three years of the donation; and the general non-cash gift reporting requirements applicable to Form 990 filers.

Supreme Court rulings. The U.S. Supreme Court issued two rulings in 2020 significantly impacting faith-based nonprofit organizations:

- ***Espinoza vs. Montana Department of Revenue.*** It was encouraging to see the U.S. Supreme Court rule in favor of religious liberty and correctly recognize that states should not discriminate against families who choose to send their children to religious schools.

  ECFA joined the Christian Legal Society and several other ecumenical organizations in filing an amicus (friend of the court) brief to the U.S. Supreme Court in this case.

- ***Bostock v. Clayton County.*** In a 6-3 majority opinion, the Court interpreted "sex" discrimination prohibited under Title VII to also include a prohibition on sexual orientation discrimination in employment matters. Without going into detail on how its ruling would intersect with the religious liberty rights of churches and ministry employers, the Court also recognized that religious organizations may have certain defenses in such cases, including the federal Religious Freedom Restoration Act statute and the ministerial exception doctrine that courts have applied under the First Amendment. Soon after Bostock was decided, the Court released its decision in Our Lady of Guadalupe clarifying and expanding the scope of the ministerial exception (read more below).

- ***Our Lady of Guadalupe School v. Morrissey-Berru.*** In a 7-2 majority opinion, the Court reaffirmed and clarified application of the "ministerial exception" doctrine to employment disputes.

  The case involved two Catholic elementary school teachers who alleged discrimination and wrongful termination. The Ninth U.S. Circuit Court of Appeals ruled in favor of the teachers, refusing to allow the school employers to raise the ministerial exception defense in these employment-related disputes. The U.S. Supreme Court reversed the Ninth Circuit and held that the schools properly raised the ministerial exception defense in these instances.

  Importantly, the Supreme Court reaffirmed the ministerial exception that was recognized unanimously in its 2012 *Hosanna-Tabor* decision. In its latest opinion, the Court clarified that its use of a set of four factors in *Hosanna-Tabor* were not a checklist that must be met in all cases for the ministerial exception to apply.

  The majority clarified that the use of the title "minister" or other clerical titles is not necessary for the exception to apply. "What matters, at bottom, is what an employee does." All relevant factors and circumstances must be taken into account with importance given to the religious institution's explanation of the employee's role in the religion.

Court affirms churches are exempt from withholding FICA tax from ministers.
Individuals who qualify as ministers for tax purposes are never subject to FICA-type (Federal Insurance Contributions Act) Social Security. Therefore, churches (and other employers) should never withhold FICA-type Social Security from a minister's compensation. This is because qualified ministers are always subject to SECA-type (Self-Employment Contributions Act Social Security, calculated on Schedule SE).

These principles of the tax law are illustrated in a recent court decision. During a pastor's over 20-year tenure, the church classified him as an employee for income tax purposes and reported his compensation on Form W-2. The church did not withhold FICA Social Security from his compensation. The pastor did not pay SECA Social Security taxes with his annual Form 1040s. Neither did he opt out of paying SECA taxes.

Key federal tax limits, rates, and other data. The IRS makes adjustments annually for certain tax items that are required to be inflation-adjusted. The tables on these pages provide the latest inflation-adjusted amounts plus certain rates and other data that is available as we go to press.

Key Federal Tax Limits, Rates, and Other Data

	2019	2020	2021
Standard deductions, exemptions, and exclusions:			
Standard Deductions	Married-Joint Return $24,400 Head of Household 18,350 Single 12,200 Married-Separate Returns 12,200	Married-Joint Return $24,800 Head of Household 18,650 Single 12,400 Married-Separate Returns 12,400	Married-Joint Return $25,100 Head of Household 18,800 Single 12,550 Married-Separate Returns 12,550
Foreign earned income exclusion	$105,900	$107,600	$108,700
Social Security:			
SECA (OASDI & Medicare) rate	15.3% on wages up to $250,000 married-joint, $125,000 married-separate, and $200,000 all others	15.3% on wages up to $250,000 married-joint, $125,000 married-separate, and $200,000 all others	15.3% on wages up to $250,000 married-joint, $125,000 married-separate, and $200,000 all others
OASDI maximum compensation base	$132,900	$137,700	$142,800
Social Security cost of living benefit increase	2.8%	1.6%	1.3%
Medicare Part B premiums - Basic	$135.50	$144.60	$148.50
Earnings ceiling for Social Security (for employment before FRA; special formula in FRA year)	Below FRA: $17,650 Over FRA: None	Below FRA: $18,240 Over FRA: None	Below FRA: $18,960 Over FRA: None
Earnings limit in year FRA attained	$46,920	$48,600	$50,520
Benefits and contributions:			
Maximum annual contribution to defined contribution plan	$56,000	$57,000	$58,000
Maximum salary deduction for 401(k)/403(b)	$19,000	$19,500	$19,500
401(k) & 403(b) over 50 "catch up" limit	$6,000	$6,500	$6,500
Maximum income exclusion for nonqualified plans in 501(c)(3) organizations (IRC 457)	$19,000	$19,500	$19,500
RIA contribution limit – age 49 and below – age 50 and above	$6,000 $7,000	$6,000 $7,000	$6,000 $7,000
Highly compensated employee limit	$125,000	$130,000	$130,000
Maximum annual contribution to health flexible spending arrangements	$2,700	$2,750	$2,750

	2019	2020	2021
Per diem and mileage rates and other transportation:			
Standard per diem: Lowest rates in continental USA	Lodging $94 Meals & incidentals $55	Lodging $96 Meals & incidentals $55	Lodging $96 Meals & incidentals $55
Business auto mileage rate	58 cents per mile	57.5 cents per mile	56 cents per mile
Moving & medical auto mileage rate	20 cents per mile	17 cents per mile	16 cents per mile
Charitable auto mileage rate	14 cents per mile	14 cents per mile	14 cents per mile
Airplane mileage rate [1]	$1.21 per mile	$1.27 per mile	$1.27 per mile
Motorcycle mileage rate [1]	51.5 cents per mile	57.5 cents per mile	54.5 cents per mile
Maximum value of reimbursement of business expenses (other than lodging) without receipt	$75	$75	$75
Monthly limit on free parking	$265	$270	$270
Transit passes/tokens–monthly tax-free limit	$265	$270	$270
Form 990/990-T/990-N and 1099-MISC threshold:			
Threshold for filing Form 990 (if not otherwise exempt)	Gross receipts ≥ $200,000 or Total assets ≥ $500,000	Gross receipts ≥ $200,000 or Total assets ≥ $500,000	Gross receipts ≥ $200,000 or Total assets ≥ $500,000
Threshold for filing Form 990-EZ [3]	Gross receipts < $200,000 & Total assets < $500,000	Gross receipts < $200,000 & Total assets < $500,000	Gross receipts < $200,000 & Total assets < $500,000
Threshold for filing Form 990-N (Postcard) [3]	Gross receipts ≥ $50,000	Gross receipts ≥ $50,000	Gross receipts ≥ $50,000
Threshold for filing Form 990 electronically	[2]	[3]	[3]
Threshold for required filing Form 990-T [3]	$1,000 annual gross UBI	$1,000 annual gross UBI	$1,000 annual gross UBI
Threshold for required filing Form 1099-MISC/NEC	$600	$600	$600
Quid pro quo:			
Minimum contribution and maximum cost of token	Minimum gift: $55.50 Maximum cost: $11.10	Minimum gift: $56.00 Maximum cost: $11.20	Minimum gift: $56.50 Maximum cost: $11.30
Maximum value of *de minimis* benefit	2% of gift, but not more than $111	2% of gift, but not more than $112	2% of gift, but not more than $113
Other:			
Federal minimum wage per hour	$7.25	$7.25	$7.25

[1] Privately-owned vehicle mileage rates set by the U.S. General Services Administration
Note: In some instances, the rate for a particular year may apply to a tax return filed in a subsequent year.

[2] For returns covering calendar year 2019, nonprofits filing Form 990-N must do so electronically. Also, nonprofits with total assets of $10 million or more at the end of the 2019 tax year or who file at least 250 returns of any type during the calendar year 2019 must file Form 990 electronically.

[3] The Taxpayer First Act requires all nonprofits that file 990-series returns (990, 990-EZ, 900-T) must file such returns electronically. For most nonprofits, the new e-filing requirement applies to returns covering the calendar year 2020 and fiscal years that begin on or after July 2, 2019. The IRS may defer the e-filing requirement for up to two years for smaller nonprofits (those with total assets or less than $500,000 and annual revenue of less than $200,000 and for any organizations filing Form 990-T.

Upon retiring from pastoral service, the pastor learned that he did not have any Social Security coverage relating to when he served the church. The pastor sued his former employer for negligence because they did not withhold FICA from his compensation. The court dismissed the lawsuit because withholding FICA tax on ministerial compensation is not required under the tax law. See *Kuma v. Greater N.Y. Conference of Seventh-Day Adventist Church, District Court Southern District of New York*, August 28, 2020.

Author's note: While a church has no *obligation* to withhold FICA-type Social Security tax from the compensation of individuals qualifying as ministers under the tax law, neither should a church *voluntarily* withhold FICA tax from a minister's pay. To do so results in a minister underpaying income and Social Security taxes because the church's FICA match (7.65%) would be categorized as tax-free compensation when it is actually fully taxable.

For more information on the proper handling of Social Security for ministers (including the alternative of a permissible SECA tax allowance), read Chapter 3 of this guide and ECFA's eBook—*10 Essentials of Social Security for Ministers.*

Final medical expenses rules raise concerns for health care sharing ministries. The IRS has proposed expanding the definition of medical expenses to include payments to health care sharing arrangements (REG-109755-19). The intent of the IRS was to provide relief for individuals that reach or surpass the threshold for claiming medical expenses as itemized deductions on Schedule A.

The proposed regulations also raise two other important issues:

- **Employer payments.** The inclusion of payments to a health care sharing plan is important for employers. If an employer makes health care sharing payments on behalf of an employee and the payments constitute medical insurance, they could qualify for tax-free treatment under an qualified small employer health reimbursement arrangement (QSEHRA) or an individual coverage health reimbursement arrangement (ICHRA).

- **The status of health care sharing arrangements with the states.** The Alliance of Health Care Sharing Ministries objects to the treatment of healthcare sharing ministry membership contributions as payments for insurance to avoid confusion. These arrangements are generally not currently regulated under state insurance laws.

The National Association of Insurance Commissioners urged the IRS not to rely on an interpretation that classifies healthcare sharing ministries as insurance. The Association said, "They should not be permitted to at once maintain exemption from the laws that regulate insurance and at the same time derive benefits from an IRS classification that conflates them with insurance."

A hearing on the proposed rules was held on October 7, but the rules have not yet been finalized.

CHAPTER 1

Financial Integrity Foundations

In This Chapter

- Independent board
- Managing conflicts of interest
- Compensation review and approval
- Proper stewardship practices

Accountability—it's a word that engenders strong feelings. The obligation or willingness to accept the responsibility embodied in accountability is embraced by many, misunderstood by some, and feared by a few.

But how do we know whether people accept responsibility or, in other words, truly submit to accountability? Are we accountable to ourselves (self-accountability), or accountable to someone else in a verifiable way? Verifiable accountability and self-accountability differ greatly.

When someone says they are accountable to themselves, it reminds us of New Year's resolutions that are often broken within hours of the start of the new year. The landscape of Christ-centered churches and ministries is littered with examples of ministries that were accountable to themselves and now they no longer exist or operate at only a fraction of what they were at one time.

Contrast self-accountability with verifiable accountability. The latter isn't just a sound concept; it is a theme that runs through the Scriptures.

As an example of Jesus' keen interest in this topic, he tells the story about investing funds in Matthew 25:14–30. The crux of the parable is verifiable accountability.

Jesus set the verifiable accountability example when he sent out the disciples two-by-two (Mark 6), the 72 (Luke 10), and others together who were involved in the early church mission (Acts).

In 1 Corinthians 4:2, we read these words: "Now it is required that those who have been given a trust must prove faithful." Proving faithful requires verifiable accountability!

As ministry grew exponentially, there is continued attentiveness to verifiable accountability in the Apostle Paul's letters. For example, Paul instructed those he mentored to follow in his steps. He urged leaders to exhibit character that was "above reproach" and "blameless" (1 Tim. 3:1–13; Titus 1:6–11).

When Christ-centered ministries do not demonstrate verifiable accountability, they risk doing what is right in their own eyes, as the Israelites did (Judges 17:6).

In his early years, David, king of Israel, sought the counsel of wise and godly men. When his authority grew, he began to operate as the supreme ruler of Israel instead of God's servant and then his troubles mounted when he went down the road of self-accountability (2 Sam. 11).

Because people form impressions by looking at outward appearances, the pattern for accountability for Christ-centered ministries and its leaders lies in biblical accountability—in the spirit of truth and love—holding each other to high standards in our individual journeys of faith and ministry service. (See ECFA's Knowledge Center for additional Scriptural references for the biblical basis of accountability.)

"Strong patterns of verifiable accountability keep the wolves at bay," says ECFA board member Michael Batts. He continues, "Sadly, there is an element of society that revels when bad things happen in churches and ministries. This element of society looks for 'cracks in the armor' of churches and ministries to try to ruin their reputation. Maintaining appropriate accountability greatly reduces the risk of such damage. Furthermore, when a high-profile financial scandal occurs in the church and ministry realm, it increases scrutiny by government regulators and increases the likelihood of additional burdensome legislation or regulation."

How do churches and ministries measure up on the verifiable accountability index? Many are doing excellently in this arena—but in the words of Paul, we must "do so more and more" (1 Thess. 4:10). There will always be outliers, but it is necessary for all of us to begin by doing our part to earnestly model financial integrity and accountability practices for the glory of God.

Here are a few faces of verifiable accountability:

1. **Growing number of exemplar churches and ministries.** Most of the larger, Christ-centered ministries in the U.S.—more than 2,500—are accredited by ECFA and committed to ECFA's rigorous standards, and 50 of the 100 largest churches in the U.S. are ECFA members. There is a growing desire for larger churches to achieve accreditation. This is a most encouraging sign.

2. **Using the services of independent CPAs.** Large churches and most nonprofit ministries have their annual financial statements audited, reviewed, or compiled by an independent CPA.

Still, many more churches and ministries should step up and engage CPA services because the gain of increased trust far outweighs the expense. Smaller organizations that are interested in ECFA membership may save on expenses by having financial statements reviewed or compiled until a full audit is appropriate.

3. **Performing internal audits.** A few larger churches and ministries have staff dedicated to performing internal audits in addition to using external auditors. These organizations are at the top of the class.

This leaves most of the 300,000–400,000 churches in the U.S. without any internal or external audit work and tens of thousands of ministries in the same category. Internal audit work is an important step that churches and ministries can take to ensure verifiable accountability.

The foundations of financial integrity begin with board decisions made in the best interest of the ministry (often requiring a majority of independent board members), avoidance of conflicts of interest, and proper compensation-setting practices with respect to the ministry's top leader. These topics and more are discussed in this chapter.

Independent Board

The importance of an independent board cannot be overemphasized. A lack of independent board oversight can negatively impact the accountability and effectiveness of the ministry. In contrast, an independent board heightens the potential to provide fiduciary oversight, establish adequate board policies, and ensure consistent adherence to these policies.

To demonstrate board independence, a majority of the board should be other than employees or staff or those related by blood or marriage. Even when employee membership on the board is slightly less than a majority, the independence of the board may be jeopardized, especially if the majority of members in attendance at particular meetings are not independent. This is because employees often lack independence and objectivity in dealing with many board-level matters. Ministries filing Form 990 must document the number of voting board members that are independent compared to the total number of voting board members.

Does your board have robust discussions on key issues? Are the values and policies of the ministry clearly articulated? Are annual evaluations, based on predetermined goals, made of the ministry's leader? Does the board evaluate itself as rigorously as it evaluates the ministry's leader?

Boards should meet at least semiannually, and many boards meet more frequently. Each board should determine the appropriate number of meetings based on the nature of the ministry.

The actions of a ministry's board and its committees should be recorded in written minutes, signed by the secretary, on a contemporaneous basis (within a reasonable time period after the meeting is held). Ministries filing Form 990 must document whether board minutes are contemporaneously maintained. The same is true for committees with the authority to act for the board.

Key Issue

Boards should develop a cyclical pattern of self-evaluation. The purpose of self-assessment is to individually and collectively improve board performance. It can take a variety of formats, from soliciting feedback from individual board members about their contributions to the board's performance, to evaluating the effectiveness of time spent together as a board. See *ECFA Tools and Templates for Effective Board Governance* for board self-evaluation templates.

The actions of a ministry's board often include the approval and revision of policies. These policies should be reflected in the Board Policies Manual with the manual regularly updated. See *ECFA Tools and Templates for Effective Board Governance* for a Board Policies Manual template.

Managing Conflicts of Interest

The potential for a conflict of interest arises in situations in which a person is responsible for promoting one interest at the same time he or she is involved in a competing interest. Problems with conflicts of interest occur when this person exercises the competing interest over the fiduciary interest, or the simple appearance of a conflict of interest creates perception issues around the integrity of the ministry.

Related-party transactions occur between two or more parties with interlinking relationships. These transactions should be disclosed to the governing board and evaluated to ensure they are made on a sound economic basis. The organization may decide to pursue any related-party transactions that are clearly advantageous to the organization, if they are also deemed to be in the overall best interest of the organization and certain integrity safeguards are followed.

Undertake significant transactions with related parties only in the following situations:

➤ The organization's board approves the transaction as one that is in the best interest of the organization.

➤ Related parties are excluded from the discussion and approval of related-party transactions.

➤ Competitive bids or comparable valuations are considered.

➤ The audited financial statements of the organization fully disclose related-party transactions.

Caution

Integrity requires that a board member or other insider disclose a potential conflict of interest to the board. The individual should refrain from voting on the transactions involving a related issue and not be present during the discussion and voting.

Even when all of the above precautions are observed with respect to a related-party transaction, the church or nonprofit organization may be at risk to criticism from givers, the media, or other members of the public. This risk may be so significant that it overshadows all of the benefits of the transaction.

Example 1: An organization purchases insurance coverage through a firm owned by a board member. This is a related-party transaction. The transaction might be approved if the cost of the insurance is disclosed, the purchase is subject to proper approvals, the price is equal to or below the competition's, the purchase is in the best interests of the organization, and the related party is not part of the discussion and vote at the meeting when the decision is made.

Warning

Information concerning prospective and current board members may reveal potential conflicts that will disqualify the individual. If a conflict is sufficiently limited, the individual may simply need to abstain from voting on certain issues. If the conflict of interest is material, the election or reelection of the individual may be inappropriate.

Example 2: The senior pastor and several employees are members of the board. When the resolution on salary and fringe-benefit adjustments comes to the board, those affected by the resolution should not discuss and vote on the matter. The senior pastor and employees should also excuse themselves from the meeting to avoid even the appearance of a conflict of interest.

Example 3: A nonprofit board considers a significant investment through a brokerage firm in which a board member has a material ownership interest. This investment might be approved if it is in the best interest of the nonprofit organization, is consistent with its investment policies, and meets its conflicts of interest policy.

To reiterate, when considering significant transactions involving related parties, ministries should carefully follow the following four steps:

1. **Exclude.** All individuals with a conflict of interest, direct or indirect, will be excluded from the discussion and the vote related to the transaction.

2. **Compare.** Reliable comparability information will be considered, such as competitive bids, independent appraisals, or independent expert opinions.

3. **Determine.** Assess whether the transaction is in the overall best interest of the ministry, including determining whether the transaction could be misperceived by givers, constituents, or the public. *Remember, the transaction will likely be publicly disclosed.*

4. **Document.** Document Steps 1, 2, and 3 in a timely manner.

Even when a ministry takes these four essential steps, it may still be in the best interest of the ministry to avoid the related-party transaction. This is explained as three basic paths to follow when considering significant related-party transactions:

- **Path 1**—The transaction is not approved because the board determines that it is not in the best interest of the ministry. If approved, the transaction would inappropriately elevate a competing interest over the ministry's fiduciary interest.

- **Path 2**—After the board is fully informed about the nature of the related-party transaction and recusing related parties from the meeting when the matter is considered, the board determines that the transaction is advantageous to the ministry.

- **Path 3**—This is the same as Path 2 except the board decides not to approve the transaction out of an abundance of caution, discerning that the transaction could be negatively perceived by givers, the public, and more.

The following graphic illustrates the three paths:

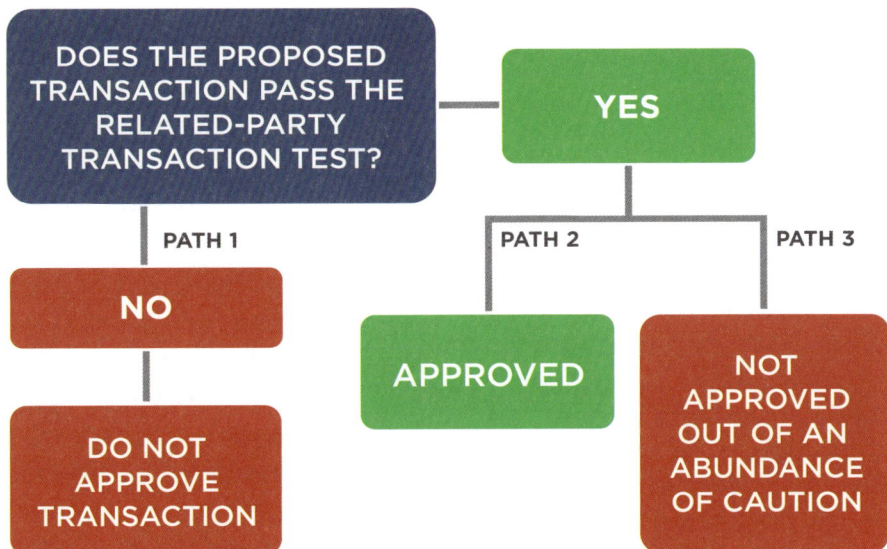

PATH 1:
DO NOT APPROVE
If the transaction is not in the best interest of the ministry, it should not be approved because it would inappropriately elevate a competing interest over the ministry's fiduciary interest.

PATH 2:
APPROVED
A significant related-party transaction could be approved after disclosing it to the ministry's governing board, who, after recusing related parties, determines the transaction is advantageous to the ministry, with a commitment to make appropriate disclosures.

PATH 3:
NOT APPROVED
The ministry could decide not to approve the related-party transaction, perhaps out of an abundance of caution, believing that the transaction could be negatively perceived by givers, the public, and more.

For more information on handling related-party transactions, see ECFA's eBooks *7 Essentials of Related-Party Transactions for Ministries* and *7 Essentials of Church Related-Party Transactions.*

Compensation Review and Approval

An annual review of a ministry leader's compensation package is essential, particularly when leadership compensation reaches more significant levels. Satisfying the following requirements creates a rebuttable presumption or "safe harbor" that the compensation for an organization's leader is reasonable:

➢ determine comparable pay for similar positions

➢ make compensation decisions in an independent setting (the individual whose compensation is being considered should be recused from the decision-making process)

➢ document gross pay and fringe benefits

Caution

Reasonable salary and fringe benefits should be carefully documented, especially for the highest paid employees of an organization. The intermediate sanction regulations provide penalties for "excess benefit transactions." Examples of such transactions include unreasonable salaries or bonuses to key employees and excessive travel expenses or other perks.

The review should focus on all elements of pay, taxable and nontaxable; an objective evaluation of responsibilities, goals reached, and available resources; and consultation with experts on nonprofit compensation. National salary surveys may provide meaningful data.

With increased scrutiny of nonprofit salaries by the media, the government, and the public, it is important that compensation amounts be accurately documented. Gross pay may include the following elements (some taxable and some tax-free or tax-deferred): cash salary, fair rental value of housing (including utilities, when provided by the ministry), cash housing or furnishings allowance, tax-deferred payments, value of the personal use of an organization-owned vehicle, value of noncash goods and services, and cash bonuses.

ECFA's Policy for Excellence in Compensation-Setting and Related-Party Transactions, a component of Standard 6, is a model for ministries to follow in reviewing and approving compensation.

Proper Stewardship Practices

Communications with givers

All statements about the use of a gift that an organization makes in its stewardship appeals must be honored. The giver's intent may be shaped by both the ministry's communication of the appeal and by any giver instructions that come with the gift. Any note or correspondence accompanying the gift or conversations between the giver and donee representatives may indicate giver intent, restricting the use of the gift for the intended purpose. If a giver responds to a specific appeal, the assumption is made that the giver's intent is that the funds will be used as outlined in the appeal.

All aspects of a proposed charitable gift should be explained fully, fairly, and accurately to givers. Any limitations on the use of the gift should be clear and complete, both on the response form and in the appeal. These items should be considered in the ministry's communications to the giver based on the circumstances and size and complexity of the gift:

➤ **The ministry's proposed use of the gift.** Realistic expectations should be communicated regarding what the gift will do within the programs of the ministry.

➤ **Representations of fact.** Any descriptions of the financial condition of the ministry or narratives about events must be current, complete, and accurate. References to past activities or events should be appropriately dated. There should be no material omissions, exaggerations of fact, use of misleading photographs, or any other communication tending to create a false impression or misunderstanding.

➤ **Valuation issues and procedures.** If an appraisal is required, the giver should fully understand the procedures and who is responsible to pay for the appraisal.

➤ **Tax consequences and reporting requirements.** While tax considerations should not be the primary focus of a gift, the giver should clearly understand the current and future income, estate, and gift tax consequences, and reporting requirements of the proposed gift. A charitable gift should never be represented as a tax shelter.

➤ **Alternative arrangements for making the gift.** The giver should understand the current and deferred gift options that are available.

➤ **Financial and family implications.** In addition to the tax consequences, the overall financial implications of the proposed gift and the potential impact on family members should be carefully explained.

Key Issue

In deciding whether to support a particular ministry or program, those who donate to Christ-centered organizations rely on the information the ministry provides. Therefore, ministries have the responsibility to represent facts truthfully when communicating with givers.

➤ **Possible conflicts of interest.** Disclose to the giver all relationships that might constitute, or appear to constitute, conflicts of interest. The disclosure should include how and by whom each party is compensated and any cost of managing the gift.

Handling restricted gifts

Properly handling giver-restricted gifts is a challenge for many ministries. This is because restricted gifts present a complex combination of accounting, tax, legal, ethical, and other issues.

A giver's written instructions accompanying a gift may provide the basis for a gift restriction. However, that is not the only way a restriction can occur. A giver's restriction may be either expressed or implied from relevant facts and circumstances. In some instances, the restrictions on donations are driven by the nature of a ministry's appeal. For example, if the appeal describes a project, then any response to the appeal is restricted. In other cases, a giver approaches a ministry desiring to make a restricted gift. Only givers can restrict a gift. In an accounting sense, gift restrictions are either temporary or permanent.

Designations of unrestricted assets or net assets by a ministry's governing board do not create restrictions. Designations may be reversed by the board when they do not result from a giver's contribution. For example, net assets without giver restrictions do not become restricted merely because a board designates a portion of them to fund future expenditures for a new building.

In certain situations, givers may exercise the power to unrestrict gifts. For example, a giver restricts a gift for a certain project. Later, the ministry asks the giver's permission to redirect the gift for another purpose (unrestricted or restricted) and the giver agrees. The gift is then reclassified from either temporarily or permanently restricted to unrestricted.

Reporting for incentives and premiums

Fundraising appeals may offer premiums or incentives in exchange for a contribution. If the value of the premiums or incentives is not insubstantial, the ministry generally must advise the giver of the fair market value of the premium or incentive and clarify that the value is not deductible for tax purposes either before or after the contribution is made (see pages 165-70 for more detailed information).

Transparency to givers and the public

Churches and other nonprofits should make appropriate disclosures about their governance, finances, programs, and activities. As a demonstration of appropriate transparency, a ministry should provide a copy of its current financial statements upon written request. Additionally, many nonprofit organizations are subject to the public disclosure rules requiring them to provide copies of annual information returns (Form 990) and certain other documents when requested to do so.

Compensation of gift planners

Payment of finders' fees, commissions, or other fees on a percentage basis by a ministry to an outside gift planner or to an organization's own employees as a condition for delivery of a gift is not appropriate under ECFA Standards. Competency-based pay is acceptable when it is paid to employees responsible for an organization's general fundraising program and includes a modest component for achieving broad fundraising goals.

Every effort must be made to maintain giver trust. Giver attitudes can be unalterably damaged in reaction to undue pressure as well as to the awareness that a direct commission will be paid to a gift planner from his or her gift, thus compromising the trust on which the ministry relies.

Acting in the interest of givers

Every effort should be made to avoid accepting a gift from, or entering into a contract with, a prospective giver when it would knowingly place a hardship on the giver or place the giver's future well-being in jeopardy.

Gift planners should recognize that it is almost impossible to properly represent the full interests of the giver and the ministry simultaneously. When dealing with persons regarding commitments on major estate assets, gift planners should seek to guide and advise givers so that they may adequately consider the broad interests of the family and the various organizations they are currently supporting before they make a final decision. Givers should be encouraged to discuss the proposed gift with competent and independent attorneys, accountants, or other professional advisors.

Peer accountability to an oversight organization

ECFA is the only peer accountability organization serving Christ-centered churches and other nonprofits. Founded in 1979, ECFA accredits over 2,500 churches and nonprofit organizations that faithfully demonstrate compliance with established standards for financial accountability, fundraising, and board governance. Members include ministries, denominations, churches, educational institutions, and other tax-exempt 501(c)(3) organizations. Annual revenue of ECFA members exceeds $30 billion.

The ECFA seal shows verifiable accountability to givers that ECFA member organizations adhere to the highest standards of financial integrity and good stewardship.

- **Setting the biblical tone for financial accountability at the top.** Biblical financial accountability starts with the ministry's board and top leadership and permeates down through the staff. In a church, the accountability tone starts with the senior pastor or equivalent leader. In a parachurch ministry, accountability starts with the president, CEO, executive director, or the person in a similar leadership position.

- **The importance of an independent board.** A majority of independent board members (*e.g.*,board members other than staff members or relatives of staff or board members) helps to ensure the board's actions are taken without partiality, undue influence, or conflict of interest.

- **Accountability to givers rises with gift restrictions.** When a giver makes an unrestricted gift, the ministry has general accountability for the funds. However, when a giver places a purpose or time restriction on a gift, the donee charity accepts the responsibility to expend the funds within the limitations of the giver's restrictions.

- **The importance of the work of an independent CPA and/or internal audits.** Churches and other nonprofit organizations of a significant size should annually utilize the services of an independent CPA. Large organizations with $3 million or more in total revenue should always have an annual audit. For smaller organizations, an annual review or compilation by an independent CPA may be sufficient. One of the most overlooked CPA services is an "agreed-upon procedures" engagement where the CPA only focuses on certain issues; e.g., bank reconciliations, payroll tax returns, expense reimbursements, or another key financial risk area for an organization.

- **Compensation-setting and related-party transactions.** Ministries should establish policies to ensure that compensation-setting and related-party transactions are handled with excellence and integrity. Appropriate policies should require board members without a conflict of interest to set compensation of top leaders and approve related-party transactions only after considering reliable comparability information and documenting the board's review and approval in writing.

CHAPTER 2 Tax Exemption

In This Chapter

- Advantages and limitations of tax exemption
- Tax exemption for churches
- Starting a church or other nonprofit organization
- Unrelated business income

- Private benefit and private inurement
- Filing federal returns
- Postal regulations
- State taxes and fees
- Political activity

Tax exemption for churches and other nonprofits is based on the federal government's recognition that many of the vital contributions to our society's common good are made outside its own agencies in the voluntary or civil society sector. Exempting these organizations from taxes (and additionally, in many instances, providing that contributions to them can be tax-deductible) is a vital governmental means of acknowledging and protecting—instead of burdening and directing—their unique identities and diverse contributions.

This same characteristic, which exists to some degree in every free society, is acknowledged in biblical theology, which regards not only persons but also a variety of institutions—families, churches, and charities—to have their own independent callings from God to serve their neighbors, beyond the government's responsibility to do good as well as to curb evildoers.

With regard to the many religious organizations that are a large part of civil society, tax-exempt status additionally reflects the government's commitment to the Establishment Clause of the constitution. By affording churches and other houses of worship automatic recognition of tax exempt status, the government refrains from illegitimate control of, and intrusion into, the sphere of religion and its institutions, and instead safeguards the free exercise of religion.

To say that government must respect religious organizations—including both churches and religious institutions whose freedom it must safeguard— is not to say that no government regulation is appropriate. Yet, to be legitimate, such regulation must as far as possible leave the institutions free to chart their own courses and practices.

How can a church or other nonprofit organization obtain federal tax exemption?

➢ **Churches.** A church is tax-exempt under Section 501(c)(3) of the Internal Revenue Code simply by functioning as a church. This includes integrated auxiliaries of churches and conventions or associations of churches. While tax law does not define a church, the IRS has developed guidelines that it applies (see pages 22-23). While there is no requirement for a church to file with the IRS for recognition of its tax-exempt status, many churches do so to formally establish this status.

➢ **Other nonprofits.** A formal filing with the IRS (using a Form 1023 or 1023-EZ) is generally required for other nonprofits to determine if the organization is tax-exempt under federal law.

Can tax-exempt status be lost? Churches rarely lose their tax-exempt status and churches are exempt from filing Form 990. For other nonprofits, failure to annually file Form 990 often triggers the loss of tax-exempt status. As discussed further in this chapter, having significant unrelated business activities may also be problematic for an organization's tax-exempt status.

Acquiring and maintaining tax-exempt status is not only vital to churches and other nonprofits but is also very important to givers who desire a charitable tax deduction for donations they make to these organizations.

Advantages and Limitations of Tax Exemption

Tax exemption is available to organizations that meet the requirements of the tax code and are approved by the IRS. This exemption provides relief from federal income tax. This income tax exemption may or may not extend to state and local income taxes. Even if an organization receives tax-exempt status, certain federal taxes may still be imposed. There may be tax due on unrelated business income, excessive compensation, certain "political" activities, and excessive legislative activities.

Tax exemption advantages

In addition to the basic exemption from federal income taxes, an organization that is recognized as a charitable organization under the Internal Revenue Code enjoys several advantages:

➢ Its givers can be offered the benefit of a tax deduction for charitable contributions.

➢ It can benefit from using special nonprofit mailing rates.

➢ It is in a favored position to seek funding from foundations and other philanthropic entities, many of which will not support organizations other than those recognized as tax-exempt organizations under 501(c)(3).

➢ It is eligible for government grants available only to entities exempt under 501(c)(3).

➢ It often qualifies for exemption not only from state and local income taxes but from property taxes (for property used directly for its exempt function) and certain sales and use taxes as well.

➢ It may qualify for exemption from the Federal Unemployment Tax Act in certain situations.

Remember

A tax-exempt organization usually means the entity is exempt, in whole or in part, from federal income taxes. The entity may still be subject to employment taxes and certain excise taxes. Tax-exempt organizations may be subject to taxes at the state level on income, franchise, sales, use, tangible property, intangible property, and real property.

➢ Its employees may participate in 403(b) tax-sheltered annuities.

➢ It may be an exclusive beneficiary of free radio and television public service announcements (PSAs) provided by local media outlets.

➢ If it is a church or a qualified church-controlled organization, it may exclude compensation to employees from the FICA Social Security base if the employee meets certain qualifications. If such is the case, the Social Security liability shifts to the employees in the form of SECA Social Security tax, in which case they may seek to exempt themselves.

Tax exemption limitations

Offsetting the advantages of tax-exempt status are some strict requirements:

➢ Organizations must comply with annual IRS reporting requirements.

➢ Organizations must be engaged "primarily" in qualified charitable, religious, educational, or other like endeavors.

➢ There are limitations on the extent to which they may engage in substantial legislative activities or other political activities.

➢ Organizations may not engage in unrelated business activities or commercial activities to an impermissible extent.

➢ There is a prohibition against private inurement or private benefit.

➢ Upon dissolution, a tax-exempt organization's assets must be distributed for one or more exempt purposes.

Tax Exemption for Churches

Tax law and IRS regulations do not define "religious," but the courts have defined "religious" broadly. In part, because of constitutional concerns, some religious organizations are subject to less intrusive reporting and auditing requirements under federal tax law.

The "religious" category includes churches, conventions of churches, associations of churches, church-run organizations (such as schools, hospitals, orphanages, nursing homes, publishing entities, broadcasting entities, and cemeteries), religious orders, apostolic groups, integrated auxiliaries of churches, missionary organizations, and Bible and tract societies. IRS regulations define religious worship as follows: "What constitutes conduct of religious worship or the ministration of sacerdotal functions depends on the interests and practices of a particular religious body constituting a church."

Although not stated in the tax law, the IRS generally applies the following 14 criteria to decide whether a religious organization can qualify as a "church":

➢ Distinct legal existence

➢ Recognized creed and form of worship

➢ Definite and distinct ecclesiastical government

➢ Formal code of doctrine and discipline

➢ Distinct religious history

➢ Membership not associated with any other church or denomination

➢ Organization of ordained ministers

➢ Established places of worship

➢ Literature of its own

➢ Ordained ministers selected after completing prescribed courses of studies

➢ Regular congregations

Remember

All churches are religious organizations, but not all religious organizations are churches. The definition of a church for IRS purposes is much broader than having a steeple. The term "church" may include religious schools, publishers, television and radio broadcasters, rescue missions, religious orders, as well as other organizations.

➤ Regular religious services

➤ Sunday schools for religious instruction of the young

➤ Schools for preparation of its ministers

Churches receive favored status in that they are not required to file either an application for recognition of exemption (Form 1023) or an annual information return (Form 990) with the IRS. A church is still subject to filing and disclosing an annual report on unrelated business income (Form 990-T) and Form 5578 for private schools as well as forms for payroll tax, sales tax, and other forms. Some particular individuals employed by churches qualify more easily for the special ministerial tax treatments, including a housing allowance.

Because of the highly restrictive requirements of the Church Audit Procedures Act, churches are subject to IRS inquiries or audits only when an appropriate high-level Treasury official makes a reasonable belief determination that a church may not qualify for tax-exempt status. These restrictive audit procedures have also been extended by the IRS to apply to tax-related employment matters.

Starting a Church or Other Nonprofit Organization

One of the first and most basic decisions when starting a church or nonprofit is to choose an organizational form. Some churches are unincorporated associations. However, many other churches incorporate for the purpose of limiting legal liability. Most other nonprofit organizations are corporations. While incorporation is usually desirable for churches and other nonprofit organizations, it is generally not mandatory.

That being said, organizations using the corporate form need articles of incorporation and bylaws. An unincorporated organization will typically have similar documents, although the articles may be in the form of a constitution.

Several planning questions should be asked. If the organization is formed for charitable purposes, is public charity status desired or is a private foundation acceptable? Are any business activities contemplated and to what degree? Will the organization be incorporated? Is an attorney competent in nonprofit matters available to help with the preparation of the legal documents? What provisions will the bylaws contain? Who will serve on the board of directors? What name will be used for the organization?

Key Issue

If a church or other nonprofit organization wishes to incorporate, it must file articles of incorporation with the appropriate state office. Some states also require the filing of trust documents.

The following materials may provide useful information when starting a church or other nonprofit organization:

irs.gov	Form 1023—Application for Recognition of Exemption with Instructions
irs.gov	Publication 557—Tax-Exempt Status for Your Organization
ECFA.org	*10 Essentials of Forming a Charitable Organization*
ECFA.church	*10 Essentials of Forming a Church*

Filing Tip

The tax-exempt status of a ministry dictates whether the organization will be recognized as tax-exempt, whether it will be eligible to receive deductible charitable contributions (and sometimes to what extent), and whether the organization will be a public charity or a private foundation.

Obtaining an employer identification number

All entities, whether exempt from tax or not, must obtain an employer identification number (EIN) by filing IRS Form SS-4. An EIN is required for a church even though churches are not required to file with the IRS for tax-exempt status. This number is not a tax-exempt number, but is simply the organization's unique identifier in the IRS's records, similar to an individual's Social Security number. An EIN will often be necessary before opening a bank account in the name of the organization.

When an organization is approved by the IRS for exemption from federal income tax (which is not required for churches), it will receive a "determination letter." This letter does *not* assign the organization a tax-exempt number.

If an organization is a "central organization" that holds a "group exemption letter," the IRS will assign that group a four-digit number, known as its group exemption number (GEN). This number must be supplied with the central organization's annual report to the IRS (updating its list of included subordinate organizations). The number is also inserted on Form 990 (if required) of the central organization and the subordinate organizations included in the group exemption.

When an organization applies for exemption from state or local income, sales, or property taxes, the state or local jurisdiction may provide a certificate or letter of exemption, which, in some jurisdictions, includes a serial number. This number is often called a "tax-exempt number." This number should not be confused with an EIN.

Form **SS-4** (Rev. December 2019) Department of the Treasury Internal Revenue Service	**Application for Employer Identification Number** (For use by employers, corporations, partnerships, trusts, estates, churches, government agencies, Indian tribal entities, certain individuals, and others.) ▶ Go to *www.irs.gov/FormSS4* for instructions and the latest information. ▶ See separate instructions for each line. ▶ Keep a copy for your records.	OMB No. 1545-0003 EIN

<table>
<tr><td rowspan="13" style="writing-mode: vertical-rl">Type or print clearly.</td><td colspan="4">1   Legal name of entity (or individual) for whom the EIN is being requested
     Lynn Haven Church</td></tr>
<tr><td colspan="2">2   Trade name of business (if different from name on line 1)</td><td colspan="2">3   Executor, administrator, trustee, "care of" name</td></tr>
<tr><td colspan="2">4a   Mailing address (room, apt., suite no. and street, or P.O. box)
      PO Box 4382</td><td colspan="2">5a   Street address (if different) (Don't enter a P.O. box.)
      3801 North Florida Avenue</td></tr>
<tr><td colspan="2">4b   City, state, and ZIP code (if foreign, see instructions)
      Miami, FL 33014</td><td colspan="2">5b   City, state, and ZIP code (if foreign, see instructions)
      Miami, FL 33133</td></tr>
<tr><td colspan="4">6   County and state where principal business is located
     Dade County, FL</td></tr>
<tr><td colspan="2">7a   Name of responsible party
      Mark Smith, Treasurer</td><td colspan="2">7b   SSN, ITIN, or EIN
      123-45-6789</td></tr>
</table>

8a	Is this application for a limited liability company (LLC) (or a foreign equivalent)? . . . . ☐ Yes ☒ No	8b	If 8a is "Yes," enter the number of LLC members . . . . . . ▶

8c	If 8a is "Yes," was the LLC organized in the United States? . . . . ☐ Yes ☐ No

9a	**Type of entity** (check only one box). **Caution:** If 8a is "Yes," see the instructions for the correct box to check.

☐ Sole proprietor (SSN) _____   ☐ Estate (SSN of decedent) _____
☐ Partnership   ☐ Plan administrator (TIN) _____
☐ Corporation (enter form number to be filed) ▶ _____   ☐ Trust (TIN of grantor) _____
☐ Personal service corporation   ☐ Military/National Guard   ☐ State/local government
☒ Church or church-controlled organization   ☐ Farmers' cooperative   ☐ Federal government
☐ Other nonprofit organization (specify) ▶ _____   ☐ REMIC   ☐ Indian tribal governments/enterprises
☐ Other (specify) ▶ _____   Group Exemption Number (GEN) if any ▶ _____

9b	If a corporation, name the state or foreign country (if applicable) where incorporated	State	Foreign country

10	**Reason for applying** (check only one box) ☒ Started new business (specify type) ▶ _____ Church ☐ Hired employees (Check the box and see line 13.) ☐ Compliance with IRS withholding regulations ☐ Other (specify) ▶	☐ Banking purpose (specify purpose) ▶ _____ ☐ Changed type of organization (specify new type) ▶ _____ ☐ Purchased going business ☐ Created a trust (specify type) ▶ _____ ☐ Created a pension plan (specify type) ▶ _____

11	Date business started or acquired (month, day, year). See instructions. 2/01/20	12	Closing month of accounting year
13	Highest number of employees expected in the next 12 months (enter -0- if none). If no employees expected, skip line 14.	14	If you expect your employment tax liability to be $1,000 or less in a full calendar year **and** want to file Form 944 annually instead of Forms 941 quarterly, check here. (Your employment tax liability generally will be $1,000 or less if you expect to pay $5,000 or less in total wages.) If you don't check this box, you must file Form 941 for every quarter. ☐

	Agricultural	Household	Other
			3

15	First date wages or annuities were paid (month, day, year). **Note:** If applicant is a withholding agent, enter date income will first be paid to nonresident alien (month, day, year) . . . . ▶

16	Check **one** box that best describes the principal activity of your business. ☐ Health care & social assistance ☐ Wholesale-agent/broker ☐ Construction ☐ Rental & leasing ☐ Transportation & warehousing ☐ Accommodation & food service ☐ Wholesale-other ☐ Retail ☐ Real estate ☐ Manufacturing ☐ Finance & insurance ☒ Other (specify) ▶ Religious Organization

17	Indicate principal line of merchandise sold, specific construction work done, products produced, or services provided.

18	Has the applicant entity shown on line 1 ever applied for and received an EIN? ☐ Yes ☒ No If "Yes," write previous EIN here ▶

Third Party Designee	Complete this section **only** if you want to authorize the named individual to receive the entity's EIN and answer questions about the completion of this form.	
	Designee's name	Designee's telephone number (include area code)
	Address and ZIP code	Designee's fax number (include area code)

Under penalties of perjury, I declare that I have examined this application, and to the best of my knowledge and belief, it is true, correct, and complete. | Applicant's telephone number (include area code)
Name and title (type or print clearly) ▶

Signature ▶ *Mark Smith*   Date ▶ 2/28/20 | Applicant's fax number (include area code)

For Privacy Act and Paperwork Reduction Act Notice, see separate instructions.	Cat. No. 16055N	Form **SS-4** (Rev. 12-2019)

25

Application for recognition of tax-exempt status

Although a church is not required to apply to the IRS for tax-exempt status under Section 501(c)(3) of the Internal Revenue Code—and is exempt from filing Form 990—it may be appropriate, nevertheless, in some situations to apply for recognition:

> ➢ A denomination typically files for group exemption to cover all local churches. A copy of the body's IRS determination letter may be used by the local group to provide evidence of tax-exempt status.

> ➢ Independent local churches that are not a part of a denominational body often file for tax-exempt status to obtain evidence of their status.

> ➢ If a local congregation ordains, licenses, or commissions ministers, it may be helpful to apply for tax-exempt status. Ministers that are ordained by a local church may be required to provide evidence that the church is tax-exempt. This could be particularly true if the minister files Form 4361, applying for exemption from self-employment tax.

Organizations desiring recognition of tax-exempt status must submit Form 1023 or Form 1023-EZ (see pages 22-23 for churches filing for tax-exempt status). The streamlined Form 1023-EZ may generally be used by most ministries with annual gross receipts of $50,000 or less and total assets with a fair market value of $250,000 or less.

Key Issue

Approval of tax-exempt status by the IRS is usually effective as of the date of formation of an organization. Importantly, the effective date determines when contributions to the organization are deductible by givers. If an organization is required to alter its activities or substantially amend its charter to qualify, the effective date for tax-exempt purposes will be the date specified in the ruling or determination letter.

The IRS must be notified that the organization is applying for recognition of exemption within 27 months from the end of the month in which it was organized. Applications made after this deadline will not be effective before the date the application is filed. In other words, a later application won't be retroactive to the organization's date of formation. If approved, the IRS will provide a determination letter recognizing that the organizational and operational plans of the nonprofit entitle it to be classified as tax-exempt. The exempt status is usually effective as of the date of formation of the organization, if filing deadlines are met.

Organizations that have applied and been approved for tax-exempt status are reflected on the IRS website in the "Tax-Exempt Organization Search" database.

Determination letter request

A user fee of $600 must accompany Form 1023 applications for recognition of tax-exempt status. There is also a $275 user fee for organizations using the Form 1023-EZ. Use *www.Pay.gov* to pay the appropriate fee for a determination letter request.

Group exemption

An affiliated group of organizations under the common control of a central organization can obtain a group exemption letter. Churches that are part of a denomination are not required to file a separate application for exemption if they are covered by the group letter. Group exemption letter fees are $3,000.

The central organization is required to report annually its exempt subordinate organizations to the IRS. (The IRS does not provide a particular form for this reporting.) The central organization is responsible to evaluate the tax status of its subordinate groups.

Unrelated Business Income

Most churches and nonprofits are supported primarily from either contributions or revenue from activities directly related to their exempt purposes. Sales of religious books, tuition at schools, and campers' fees are examples of exempt purpose revenue. On the other hand, income from activities not directly related to fulfilling an organization's exempt purposes may be subject to the tax on unrelated business income (UBI).

All income of tax-exempt organizations is presumed to be exempt from federal income tax *unless* the income is generated by an activity that meets *all* of the following:

➢ not substantially related to the organization's exempt purpose or function,

➢ a trade or business, and

➢ regularly conducted.

UBI is permitted for tax-exempt organizations. However, these organizations may have |to pay tax on income derived from activities unrelated to their exempt purpose. Furthermore, UBI must not comprise a substantial part of the organization's operation. There is no specific percentage limitation on how much UBI is "substantial." However, organizations with 50% or more of their activities classified as unrelated have faced revocation of their tax-exempt status.

Form 990-T must be completed annually to report the source(s) of UBI and related expenses and to compute any tax. UBI amounts are also reportable on Form 990 (if the filing of Form 990 is required). Organizations required to file a Form 990-T will generally also be required to make a state filing related to the UBI. The Form 990-T is subject to the public disclosure rules, as well (see pages 38-39).

Although exempt from filing Form 990, churches must file Form 990-T if they have $1,000 or more of gross UBI in a year. There is a specific deduction of $1,000 in computing unrelated business taxable income. This specific deduction applies to a religious order or a convention or association of churches with respect to each individual church, district, or other local unit.

Filing Tip

Although churches are exempt from filing Form 990 with the IRS, they are still subject to tax on their unrelated business income and may need to file Form 990-T. Tax law allows churches and other nonprofit organizations to conduct profit-making activities, but that profit is taxed if the income is from an unrelated business activity and none of the exceptions to the tax apply.

Unrelated business income consequences

Some church and nonprofit leaders are paranoid about UBI to the point that they feel it must be avoided altogether. Some people equate UBI with the automatic loss of exempt status. A more balanced view is to understand the purpose of UBI and to minimize the UBI tax through proper planning.

The most common adverse result of having UBI is that all or part of it may be taxed. A less frequent, but still possible, result is that the organization will lose its tax exemption. It is possible that the IRS will deny or revoke the tax-exempt status of an organization when it regularly derives over one-half of its annual revenue from unrelated activities.

Congress has recognized that some nonprofits may need to engage in unrelated business activities to survive. For example, a nonprofit with unused office space might rent the space to another organization. Also, nonprofits are expected to invest surplus funds to supplement the primary sources of the organization's income.

A trade or business regularly conducted

A trade or business means any activity regularly conducted which produces income from the sale of goods or services and where there is a reasonable expectation of a profit. To decide whether a trade or business is regularly conducted, the IRS considers whether taxable organizations would carry on a business with the same frequency and continuity. Intermittent activities may escape the "regularly conducted" definition.

> *Example 1:* If a church sells sandwiches at a local community event for only two weeks, the IRS likely would not treat this as the regular conduct of a trade or business.

Sample Unrelated Business Income Checklist

To determine whether an activity produces unrelated business taxable income, answer these questions:

➤ *Is the activity regularly conducted?*

A specific business activity is regularly carried on if it is conducted with a frequency, continuity, and manner of pursuit comparable to the conduct of the same or similar activity by a taxable organization. An activity is regularly carried on if it is conducted:

- intermittently year round, or
- during a significant portion of the season for a seasonal type of business

However, an activity is not regularly carried on if it is conducted:

- on a very infrequent basis (once or twice a year)
- for only a short period of the year, or
- without competitive or promotional efforts

➤ *Is the activity substantially related to the exempt purposes of the nonprofit?*

To be substantially related (and not considered UBI), the business activity must contribute importantly to the accomplishment of a purpose for which the nonprofit was granted tax exemption, other than the mere production of income to support such purpose.

➤ *Is the activity conducted with volunteer services?*

Any business activity in which substantially all (85% or more) of the work is performed by volunteers is specifically exempted from unrelated business income tax.

➤ *Is the activity primarily for the convenience of clients, patients, faculty, staff, students, or visitors?*

So-called "convenience" activities are exempt regardless of their nature. Examples are parking lots, food service, bookstores, laundry, telephone service, and vending machines.

➤ *Is the income from the rental of real property?*

Rental income is generally tax-exempt if it does not relate to debt-financed property. But if significant services such as setup, cleaning, and laundry service are also provided, then the income is usually taxable.

➤ *Is the income derived from debt-financed property?*

Examples of income from debt-financed property (considered UBI) are dividends, interest, rents, etc., earned from stocks, bonds, and rental property that have been purchased with borrowed money.

Example 2: A one-time sale of property is not an activity that is regularly conducted and therefore does not generate unrelated business income unless the property was used in an unrelated business activity or was debt-financed.

Example 3: A church is located in the downtown section of a city. Each Saturday, the church parking lot is operated commercially to accommodate shoppers. Even though the business activity is carried on for only one day each week on a year-round basis, this constitutes the regular conduct of a trade or business. It is subject to the unrelated business income tax.

Substantially related

According to the IRS regulations, a trade or business must "contribute importantly to the accomplishment of the exempt purposes of an organization" if it is to be considered "substantially related." Even if all the profits from a business go to support the work of the nonprofit, the profits may still be taxed.

Example: If a church operates a restaurant and devotes all the proceeds to mission work, the church still will not escape taxation on the restaurant's income.

Examples of types of income that may be "related" because they contribute importantly to accomplishing the organization's exempt purposes are:

➢ the sale of products made by handicapped individuals as a part of their rehabilitation

➢ the sale of homes constructed by students enrolled in a vocational training course

➢ a retail grocery store operated to provide emotional therapy for disturbed adolescents

Tours conducted by nonprofits usually create UBI. Tours may be exempt from UBI only if they are strongly educationally oriented, with reports, daily lectures, and so on. Tours with substantial recreational or social purposes are not exempt.

The definition of "unrelated trade or business" does not include:

➢ activities in which unpaid volunteers do most of the work for an organization

➢ activities provided primarily for the convenience of the organization's members

➢ activities involving the sale of merchandise mostly donated to the organization

Form **990-T**	**Exempt Organization Business Income Tax Return**	OMB No. 1545-0047
	(and proxy tax under section 6033(e))	**2020**

Department of the Treasury
Internal Revenue Service

For calendar year 2020 or other tax year beginning _____, 2020, and ending _____, 20 _____

▶ Go to *www.irs.gov/Form990T* for instructions and the latest information.
▶ Do not enter SSN numbers on this form as it may be made public if your organization is a 501(c)(3).

Open to Public Inspection for 501(c)(3) Organizations Only

A ☐ Check box if address changed.

Print or Type

Name of organization (☐ Check box if name changed and see instructions.)
Family Bible Church

D Employer identification number
35-4427081

B Exempt under section
☒ 501(**C**)(**3**)
☐ 408(e) ☐ 220(e)
☐ 408A ☐ 530(a)
☐ 529(a) ☐ 529A

Number, street, and room or suite no. If a P.O. box, see instructions.
400 North Sunset Avenue

City or town, state or province, country, and ZIP or foreign postal code
Lemon Grove, CA 92045

C Book value of all assets at end of year . . . . ▶ 2,342,700

E Group exemption number
(see instructions)
532000

F ☐ Check box if an amended return.

G Check organization type ▶ ☒ 501(c) corporation ☐ 501(c) trust ☐ 401(a) trust ☐ Other trust ☐ Applicable reinsurance entity

H Check if filing only to ▶ ☐ Claim credit from Form 8941 ☐ Claim a refund shown on Form 2439

I Check if a 501(c)(3) organization filing a consolidated return with a 501(c)(2) titleholding corporation . . . . ▶ ☐

J Enter the number of attached Schedules A (Form 990-T) . . . . ▶ 1

K During the tax year, was the corporation a subsidiary in an affiliated group or a parent-subsidiary controlled group? ▶ ☐ Yes ☒ No
If "Yes," enter the name and identifying number of the parent corporation ▶

L The books are in care of ▶ **Tom Jones** Telephone number ▶ **506-321-145**

Part I	**Total Unrelated Business Taxable Income**		
1	Total of unrelated business taxable income computed from all unrelated trades or businesses (see instructions)	1	27,439
2	Reserved	2	
3	Add lines 1 and 2	3	27,439
4	Charitable contributions (see instructions for limitation rules)	4	
5	Total unrelated business taxable income before net operating losses. Subtract line 4 from line 3 . .	5	
6	Deduction for net operating loss. See instructions	6	
7	Total of unrelated business taxable income before specific deduction and section 199A deduction. Subtract line 6 from line 5	7	27,439
8	Specific deduction (generally $1,000, but see instructions for exceptions)	8	1,000
9	**Trusts.** Section 199A deduction. See instructions	9	
10	**Total deductions.** Add lines 8 and 9	10	1,000
11	**Unrelated business taxable income.** Subtract line 10 from line 7. If line 10 is greater than line 7, enter zero	11	26,439

Part II	**Tax Computation**		
1	**Organizations taxable as corporations.** Multiply Part I, line 11 by 21% (0.21) . . . . . . ▶	1	5,552
2	**Trusts taxable at trust rates.** See instructions for tax computation. Income tax on the amount on Part I, line 11 from: ☐ Tax rate schedule or ☐ Schedule D (Form 1041) . . . . ▶	2	
3	**Proxy tax.** See instructions . . . . ▶	3	
4	Other tax amounts. See instructions	4	
5	Alternative minimum tax (trusts only)	5	
6	**Tax on noncompliant facility income.** See instructions	6	
7	**Total.** Add lines 3 through 6 to line 1 or 2, whichever applies	7	5,552

For Paperwork Reduction Act Notice, see instructions. Cat. No. 11291J Form **990-T** (2020)

The Form 990-T has more pages. Only page 1 is shown here.

Rental income

Nonprofits often rent facilities, equipment, and other assets for a fee, with the following UBI implications:

Remember

Nonprofits are normally not taxed on income they receive from renting or leasing real estate, even if the rental activity has nothing to do with their exempt purpose. If the property is financed by debt, however, a portion of the otherwise nontaxable income is typically taxed as debt-financed income.

➢ Renting to another nonprofit may be termed "related" if the rental expressly serves the landlord's exempt purposes.

➢ Rental of real estate is excluded from UBI unless the excludable property is acquired or improved with original indebtedness. Rental income from the property becomes UBI to the extent of the ratio of the "average acquisition indebtedness" during the year to the total purchase price. The nonprofit may deduct the same portion of the expenses directly connected with the production of the rental income. Depreciation is allowable using only the straight-line method.

Debt-financed income

To discourage exempt organizations from borrowing money to purchase passive income (usually not UBI) items, Congress imposed a tax on debt-financed income. Any property held to produce income is debt-financed property if at any time during the tax year there was "acquisition indebtedness" outstanding for the property.

Acquisition indebtedness is the outstanding amount of principal debt incurred by the organization:

➢ when acquiring or improving the property,

➢ before the property was acquired or improved, if the debt was incurred because of the acquisition or improvement of the property, or

➢ after the property was acquired or improved, if the debt was incurred because of the acquisition or improvement, and the organization could reasonably foresee the need to incur the debt at the time the property was acquired or improved.

There are exceptions to the debt-financed income rules, including:

➢ use of substantially all (85% or more) of any property for an organization's exempt purposes

➤ use of property by a related exempt organization to further its exempt purposes

➤ life income contracts, if the remainder interest is payable to an exempt charitable organization

➤ neighborhood land rule, if an organization acquires real property in its "neighborhood" (the neighborhood restriction does not apply to churches) mainly to use it for exempt purposes within 10 years (15 years for churches)

Activities that are not taxed

Income from the following sources is generally not considered UBI:

➤ **Passive income.** Income earned from most passive investment activities is not UBI, unless the underlying property is subject to debt. Types of passive income include:

□ dividends, interest, and annuities

□ capital gains or losses from the sale, exchange, or other disposition of property

□ rents from real property (some rent is UBI if the rental property was purchased or improved subject to a mortgage)

□ royalties (however, oil and gas working interest income generally constitutes UBI)

Idea

The use of volunteers to conduct an activity is one of the best ways to avoid tax on what would otherwise be a taxable activity. Intermittent activities may also avoid the tax. To decide whether a trade or business is regularly carried on, the IRS considers whether taxable organizations would carry on a business with the same frequency and continuity.

➤ **Volunteers.** Any business where volunteers perform most of the work without compensation does not qualify as UBI. To the IRS, "substantially" means at least 85% of total work performed.

Example: A used-clothing store operated by a nonprofit orphanage where volunteers do all the work in the store would likely be exempt.

➤ **Convenience.** A cafeteria, bookstore, or residence operated for the convenience of patients, visitors, employees, or students is not a business. Stores, parking lots, and other facilities may be dually used (part related and part unrelated).

➤ **Donated goods.** The sale of merchandise, mostly received as gifts or contributions, does not qualify as UBI. A justification for this exemption is that contributions of property are merely being converted into cash.

> ➤ **Low-cost items.** Items (costing less than $11.20—2020 adjusted amount) distributed incidental to the solicitation of charitable contributions are not subject to UBI. The amounts received are not considered an exchange for the low-cost articles, and therefore they do not create UBI.

> ➤ **Mailing lists.** Mailing lists exchanged with or rented to another exempt organization are excluded from UBI, although the commercial sale of the lists will generally create UBI. The structuring of the agreement as a royalty arrangement may make the income exempt from UBI treatment.

Calculating the unrelated business income tax

Income tax rules applicable to businesses, such as depreciation method limitations and rates, apply to the UBI computation. Direct and indirect costs, after proration between related and unrelated activities, may be used to offset income. The first $1,000 of annual net unrelated income is exempt from taxation.

Unrelated business income summary

> ➤ Organizations should be aware of the types of activities that may create UBI.

> ➤ Maintain careful records of income and related expenses (both direct and indirect, including depreciation) for any activities that might be considered unrelated to the organization's exempt purpose. These records should include allocations of salaries and fringe benefits based on time records or, at a minimum, time estimates.

> ➤ It may be wise to keep a separate set of records on potential unrelated activities. This separate set of records would need to be submitted to the IRS only upon audit.

> ➤ Be sure that board minutes, contracts, and other documents reflect the organization's view of relatedness of various activities to the exempt purpose of the entity.

> ➤ If the organization has over $1,000 of gross UBI in a given fiscal (tax) year, file Form 990-T.

Private Benefit and Private Inurement

Tax laws and regulations impose prohibitions on nonprofit organizations concerning private benefit and private inurement. Excise taxes are imposed on "excess benefit transactions" between "disqualified persons" and nonprofits. An excess benefit transaction occurs when an economic benefit is provided by an organization, directly or indirectly, to or for the use of a disqualified person, and the value of the economic benefit provided by the organization exceeds the value of the consideration received by the organization in return for providing the benefit. A disqualified person is any person in a position to exercise substantial influence over the affairs of the organization (often referred to as an "insider").

Private benefit

Nonprofit organizations must serve public, and not private, interests. The private benefit prohibition applies to anyone outside the intended charitable class. The law does allow some private benefit if it is incidental to the public benefits involved. It is acceptable if the benefit to the public cannot be achieved without necessarily benefiting private individuals.

> *Example:* The IRS revoked the exemption of a charity as having served the commercial purposes and private interests of a professional fundraiser when the fundraiser distributed only 3% of the amount collected to the nonprofit organization.

Private inurement

Private inurement is a subset of private benefit. This is a prohibition that generally applies to a distinct class of private interests. These "insiders" may be founders, trustees or directors, officers, managers, or significant givers to the organization. Transactions involving these individuals are not necessarily prohibited, but they must be subject to reasonableness, documentation, and applicable reporting to the IRS.

Technically, private inurement is a transfer of resources from a tax-exempt organization to an individual insider that creates a financial benefit for the individual, solely because of that individual's close relationship with the organization and without regard to accomplishing the organization's exempt purposes. In other words, when an individual insider receives something from a nonprofit organization for nothing or even for less than what it is worth, private inurement may have occurred. Excessive, and therefore unreasonable, compensation can also result in prohibited inurement. The IRS may ask the following questions to determine if private inurement exists:

> ➤ Did the expenditure further an exempt purpose, and if so, how?

> ➤ Was the payment at fair market value or represent reasonable compensation for goods and services?

> ➤ Does a low-interest or no-interest loan to an employee or director fall within a reasonable compensation package?

Compensation-Setting Check List

1. Name: _____Frank Basinger, CEO_____

2. Effective date of compensation: _____January 1, 2021_____

3. Effective period (one year, two years, etc.): _____one year_____

4. Types of appropriate comparable data relied upon in approving compensation package (check applicable boxes):

    X   Compensation paid by similarly situated organizations (taxable and tax-exempt)

    X   Availability of similar services in the geographical area

    X   Independent compensation surveys

5. Explain how comparable data relied upon was obtained: _____From nationally published compensation surveys._____

6. Range of total compensation from comparability data: _____$120,000 –140,000_____

7. Annual compensation summary:

	Approved Compensation
Cash	
• Salary	$ 95,000
• Bonus or contingent payment (estimate)	5,000
Noncash	
• Deferred compensation	10,000
• Premiums paid on insurance coverage (life, health, disability, liability, etc.)	18,000
• Automobile (value of personal use)	2,000
• Foregone interest on below market loan(s)	
• Other (excluding nontaxable benefits under IRC Sec. 132)	1,000
Total compensation	$131,000

8. Members of authorized body present during discussion of compensation package and vote cast:

Present	In Favor	Opposed
7	7	0

9. Members of authorized body having a conflict of interest with respect to the compensation arrangement and how the conflict was handled (e.g., left room during discussions and votes):

Member	Action re: Conflict
William McIlvain	Absent from board meeting for discussion and vote
Hugh Temple	Absent from board meeting for discussion and vote

10. Date compensation package approved: _____November 10, 2020_____

➤ On an overseas trip for the nonprofit, did the employee (and perhaps a spouse) stay an additional week for a personal vacation and charge the expenses to the organization?

Remember

The most common example of private inurement is excessive compensation. However, the following transactions between a charity and a private individual are other examples of possible private inurement: (1) sale, exchange, or leasing of property; (2) lending of money or other extension of credit; or (3) furnishing of goods, services, or facilities.

Example 1: An organization lost its exemption when it engaged in numerous transactions with an insider, including the purchase of a boat for the personal use of the insider. The insider also benefited from several real estate transactions, including donations and sales of real property to the organization that were never reflected on its books.

Example 2: A church lost its tax exemption after it operated commercial businesses and paid substantial private expenses of its founders, including expenses for jewelry and clothing in excess of $30,000 per year. The church also purchased five luxury cars for the founders' personal use. None of these benefits were reported as personal income to the founders.

Example 3: A tax-exempt organization transfers an auto to an employee for $1,000. The transfer was not approved by the board and does not constitute a portion of a reasonable pay package. The fair market value of the auto is $10,000. The net difference of $9,000 is not reported to the IRS as compensation. Private inurement has occurred.

Example 4: Same facts as Example 3, except the transfer was approved by the board and properly constituted a portion of the reasonable pay package, and the $9,000 was added to the employee's Form W-2 as compensation. There is no private inurement.

A two-tiered system of penalty taxes is imposed on insiders who improperly benefit from excess benefit transactions and on organization managers who are involved in illegal transactions. Sanctions cannot be imposed on the organizations themselves.

A first-tier penalty tax equal to 25% of the amount of the excess benefit is followed by a tax of 200% if there is no correction of the excess benefit within a certain time period. Additionally, there is a 10% penalty on an organization's managers if they knowingly approve an excess benefit transaction.

Filing Federal Returns

Many nonprofit organizations must file an annual return with the IRS. Churches, organizations with convention or association of churches status, religious orders, and certain foreign missionary organizations are exempt from filing Form 990. The basic filing requirements are as follows:

Form to Be Filed	Conditions
Form 990-N	Gross annual receipts normally $50,000 or less
Form 990-EZ	Gross annual receipts less than $200,000 and total assets of less than $500,000
Form 990	Gross annual receipts over $200,000 or total assets over $500,000
Form 990-T	Any organization exempt under Sec. 501(a) with $1,000 or more gross income from a regularly conducted unrelated trade or business
Form 1120	Any nonprofit corporation that is not tax-exempt
Form 5500	Pension, profit-sharing, medical benefit, cafeteria, and certain other plans must annually be filed on one of several series 5500 Forms

Remember

Form 990 should generally use the same accounting method as the organization uses to keep its books. If the accrual method is used for the books or the audit, use the accrual method on Form 990.

Public inspection of information returns

IRS regulations require the public disclosure of certain documents:

➢ **Materials made available for public inspection.** Nonprofits, other than private foundations, must provide public access to the application for tax exemption (Form 1023 or Form 1023-EZ) and any supporting documents filed by the organization. These also include any letter or other documents issued by the IRS in connection with the application.

Remember

The law requires certain disclosures of financial information. Further, a general attitude of transparency serves to deter improper diversions of funds and other misdeeds. It also provides a defense to critics and a witness to both believers and nonbelievers.

Nonprofits must also provide access to their three most recent information returns. This generally includes Forms 990, 990-T, and schedules and attachments filed with the IRS. There is not a requirement to disclose parts of the information returns that identify names and addresses of contributors to the organization.

➤ **Places and times for public inspection.** Specified documents must be made available without charge at the nonprofit's principal, regional, and district offices during normal business hours. An office is considered a regional or district office only if the aggregate hours per week worked by its paid part-time employees are 120 or more, or it has three or more full-time employees.

➤ **Responding to requests.** If someone requests copies in person, the request generally must be fulfilled on the day of the request. In unusual circumstances, an organization will be permitted to furnish the copies on the next business day. When the request is made in writing, the organization must provide the requested copies within 30 days. If the organization requires advance payment for reasonable copying and mailing fees, it can provide copies within 30 days of the date it is paid, instead of the date of the request.

Filing Tip

As with all tax returns, nonprofits are required by law to provide complete and accurate information on these annual returns.

➤ **Fees for providing copies.** Reasonable fees may be charged by nonprofits for copying and mailing documents. The fees cannot exceed the amounts charged by the IRS (based on fees listed in the Freedom of Information Act). Organizations are also allowed to charge actual postage costs incurred in providing the copies.

➤ **Documents widely available.** A nonprofit organization does not have to comply with requests for copies if it has made the appropriate materials widely available. This requirement is satisfied if the document is posted on the organization's web page on the internet or in another database of similar materials.

Reporting substantial organizational changes

An organization's tax-exempt status remains in effect if there are no material changes in the organization's character, purposes, or methods of operation. Significant changes should be reported by letter to the IRS soon after the changes occur and reported on Form 990 if appropriate. Visit *www.irs.gov* for more information and reporting instructions.

Example: An organization received tax-exempt status for the operation of a religious radio ministry. Several years later, the organization decided to add a facility for homeless children. This change would likely be considered to be material and should be reported to the IRS.

Change in accounting methods

For its financial records, a nonprofit organization may adopt any reasonable method of accounting that clearly reflects income. These methods include the cash receipts and disbursements method; the accrual method; or any other method (including a combination of methods) that clearly reflects income.

An organization that wishes to change from one method of accounting to another generally must secure the consent of the IRS to make that change. Consent must be obtained both for a general change of method and for any change of method with respect to one or more particular items. Thus, a nonprofit organization that generally uses the cash method, but uses the accrual method with respect to publications for which it maintains inventories, may change its method of accounting by adopting the accrual method for all purposes. But the organization must secure the IRS's consent to do so.

To obtain the consent of the IRS to change an accounting method, the organization should file IRS Form 3115, Application for Change in Accounting Method.

Change of fiscal years

Generally, an exempt organization may change its fiscal year simply by timely filing Form 990 with the appropriate Internal Revenue Service Center for the "short year." The return for the short year should indicate at the top of page 1 that a change of accounting period is being made. It should be filed no later than the 15th day of the fifth month following the close of the short year.

If neither Form 990 nor Form 990-T must be filed, the ministry is not required to notify the IRS of a change in the fiscal year, with one exception. The exception applies to exempt organizations that have changed their fiscal years within the previous ten calendar years. For this exception, Form 1128 must be filed with the IRS.

Other IRS forms commonly used

➢ **Form 5578.** Form 5578 (see pages 104-6) must be completed and furnished to the IRS to provide information regarding racial nondiscrimination policies of private schools, but only for those organizations not already required to file and report this information on Form 990, Schedule E. Form 5578 must be filed for schools operated by a church, including preschools.

Form **990**		**Return of Organization Exempt From Income Tax**		OMB No. 1545-0047
		Under section 501(c), 527, or 4947(a)(1) of the Internal Revenue Code (except private foundations)		**2020**
Department of the Treasury Internal Revenue Service		▶ Do not enter social security numbers on this form as it may be made public. ▶ Go to *www.irs.gov/Form990* for instructions and the latest information.		**Open to Public Inspection**

A For the 2020 calendar year, or tax year beginning _____ , 2020, and ending _____ , 20 ____

B Check if applicable:	**C** Name of organization **Lifetime Ministries**		**D** Employer identification number
☐ Address change	Doing business as		35 - 7438041
☐ Name change	Number and street (or P.O. box if mail is not delivered to street address) **1212 South Palo Verde**	Room/suite	**E** Telephone number **480-344-8174**
☐ Initial return			
☐ Final return/terminated	City or town, state or province, country, and ZIP or foreign postal code **Phoenix, AZ 85035**		
☐ Amended return			**G** Gross receipts $
☐ Application pending	**F** Name and address of principal officer:		**H(a)** Is this a group return for subordinates? ☐ Yes ☒ No

H(b) Are all subordinates included? ☐ Yes ☐ No
If "No," attach a list. See instructions

I   Tax-exempt status: ☒ 501(c)(3)   ☐ 501(c) (___) ◀ (insert no.)   ☐ 4947(a)(1) or   ☐ 527

H(c) Group exemption number ▶

J   Website: ▶

K Form of organization: ☒ Corporation ☐ Trust ☐ Association ☐ Other ▶   **L** Year of formation: **1994**   **M** State of legal domicile: **AZ**

Part I   Summary

1	Briefly describe the organization's mission or most significant activities: **Lifetime Ministries is an international child sponsorship program. It provides food, education, health care, and spiritual nurture to children in need in 22 countries.**		
2	Check this box ▶ ☐ if the organization discontinued its operations or disposed of more than 25% of its net assets.		
3	Number of voting members of the governing body (Part VI, line 1a)	**3**	11
4	Number of independent voting members of the governing body (Part VI, line 1b) . . .	**4**	4
5	Total number of individuals employed in calendar year 2020 (Part V, line 2a)	**5**	12
6	Total number of volunteers (estimate if necessary)	**6**	30
7a	Total unrelated business revenue from Part VIII, column (C), line 12	**7a**	4,100
b	Net unrelated business taxable income from Form 990-T, Part I, line 11	**7b**	(1,875)

		Prior Year	Current Year
8	Contributions and grants (Part VIII, line 1h)	976,624	1,063,877
9	Program service revenue (Part VIII, line 2g)	433,801	489,863
10	Investment income (Part VIII, column (A), lines 3, 4, and 7d)	1,012	608
11	Other revenue (Part VIII, column (A), lines 5, 6d, 8c, 9c, 10c, and 11e) . . .	9,480	10,343
12	Total revenue—add lines 8 through 11 (must equal Part VIII, column (A), line 12)	1,420,917	1,573,691
13	Grants and similar amounts paid (Part IX, column (A), lines 1–3)	10,000	15,000
14	Benefits paid to or for members (Part IX, column (A), line 4)		
15	Salaries, other compensation, employee benefits (Part IX, column (A), lines 5–10)	431,002	452,900
16a	Professional fundraising fees (Part IX, column (A), line 11e)		
b	Total fundraising expenses (Part IX, column (D), line 25) ▶ _____		
17	Other expenses (Part IX, column (A), lines 11a–11d, 11f–24e)	984,903	930,087
18	Total expenses. Add lines 13–17 (must equal Part IX, column (A), line 25) .	1,425,905	1,397,987
19	Revenue less expenses. Subtract line 18 from line 12	5,012	175,704

		Beginning of Current Year	End of Year
20	Total assets (Part X, line 16)	1,625,043	2,043,015
21	Total liabilities (Part X, line 26)	1,610,412	1,852,680
22	Net assets or fund balances. Subtract line 21 from line 20	14,631	190,335

Part II   Signature Block

Under penalties of perjury, I declare that I have examined this return, including accompanying schedules and statements, and to the best of my knowledge and belief, it is true, correct, and complete. Declaration of preparer (other than officer) is based on all information of which preparer has any knowledge.

Sign Here	▶ Signature of officer		Date **5/15/21**
	▶ **Harold T. Baldwin, President**		
	Type or print name and title		

Paid Preparer Use Only	Print/Type preparer's name	Preparer's signature	Date	Check ☐ if self-employed	PTIN
	Firm's name ▶			Firm's EIN ▶	
	Firm's address ▶			Phone no.	

May the IRS discuss this return with the preparer shown above? See instructions . . . . ☐ Yes ☒ No

For Paperwork Reduction Act Notice, see the separate instructions.   Cat. No. 11282Y   Form **990** (2020)

The Form 990 has many pages. Only page 1 is shown here.

➢ **Forms 8717 and 8718.** Nonprofits desiring IRS private letter rulings on employee plans or on exempt organization information must include Form 8717 or 8718, respectively, with the appropriate fees.

➢ **Form 8282.** If a nonprofit donee sells or otherwise disposes of gift property for which an appraisal summary is required on Form 8283 within three years after receipt of the property, it generally must file Form 8282 with the IRS. See Chapter 8 for more information on these reporting rules.

➢ **Employee and nonemployee payments.** As an employer, a nonprofit organization must file federal and state forms concerning payment of compensation and the withholding of payroll taxes. Payments to nonemployees may require the filing of information returns. See Chapters 4 and 5 for more coverage of these requirements.

Postal Regulations

Churches and other nonprofits may qualify to mail at special standard nonprofit mail rates (formerly called bulk third-class). The application (Form 3624) is available at the post office where you wish to deposit the mail. The following information must be provided (some items apply only if the organization is incorporated):

➢ description of the organization's primary purpose, which may be found in the articles of incorporation or bylaws

➢ evidence that the organization is nonprofit, such as a federal (and state) tax exemption determination letter

➢ materials showing how the organization actually operated in the previous 6 to 12 months, such as program literature, newsletters, bulletins, and any other promotional materials

The U.S. Postal Service offers rate incentives to nonprofit mailers that provide automation-compatible mail. Automated mail must be readable by an Optical Character Reader (OCR). Oralizations should contact their local post office for more information.

State Taxes and Fees

Separate filings are often necessary to obtain exemption from state income tax. The requirements vary from state to state. In some states, it is also possible to obtain exemption from licensing fees and sales, use, franchise, and property taxes.

A nonprofit organization may be required to report to one or more states regarding its exemption from—or compliance with—state income, sales, use, or property taxation. Many states accept a copy of Form 990 as adequate annual reporting for tax-exempt status purposes. Annual reporting to the state in which the organization is incorporated is normally required even if there is no requirement to file Form 990 with the IRS. Check with the offices of the secretary of state and attorney general to determine the required filings.

Caution

Do not send a list of major contributors to the state unless it is specifically required. While this list is not open to public inspection with respect to the federal filing, it may not be confidential for state purposes.

Property taxes

Church property is generally exempt from property tax. Whether real estate of a nonprofit organization is exempt from property tax or not usually depends on its use and ownership and varies based on local law. Many states restrict the exemption of church property to property used for worship. It is also important to note that not all religious organizations are churches. Contact the office of the county tax assessor or collector to determine what property tax exemptions might be available.

Church-owned parsonages may be exempt from real estate tax in certain jurisdictions. This is true even though there may be several ministers on the staff of one church and therefore multiple parsonages. If the pastor owns the property instead of the church, the property *is* usually subject to property tax.

Church parking lots are usually exempt if properly recorded, and it may be possible to obtain an exemption for other church land. Property tax exemption of church camps and recreation facilities often comes under attack because of income that may be generated through their use. Property partially used for church use and partially leased to a third-party for-profit entity generally results in the proration of the tax exemption.

Caution

An initial (and perhaps annual) registration of the property with the proper state authorities is generally necessary to record exempt property. The initial purchase of real estate with notification of state authorities is usually not sufficient to exempt property from tax.

Sales taxes

There are presently five states (Alaska, Delaware, Montana, New Hampshire, and Oregon) without a state-wide sales tax law (some localities may have sales taxes).

In some states, a nonprofit organization is exempt from sales tax as a purchaser of goods used in ministry. It is generally necessary to obtain recognition of sales tax exemption from the state revenue department. Some states will accept a federal tax exemption as sufficient for a state sales tax exemption.

Even if an organization is exempt from paying sales tax, purchases used for the private benefit of the organization's members or employees are not eligible for exemption.

When a nonprofit organization sells goods to others, a sales tax may or may not be applicable. There are some indications that states may begin a stricter enforcement of laws on the books that allow them to impose sales tax on sales by nonprofit organizations. Occasional dinners and sales of goods at local community events are typically exempt from sales tax.

Sales by a nonprofit within the state where the nonprofit is located are sometimes taxable. Sales to customers located outside of the state, or interstate sales, may not be subject to sales tax. A 2018 Supreme Court decision cleared the way for states to require organizations to collect state sales taxes on out-of-state online purchases. This is a developing area of the law and organizations should review their potential sales tax liabilities.

When a nonprofit organization operates a conference or convention outside of its home state, it is often possible to obtain sales tax exemption for purchases made within the state where the meeting is held. Sales of products at the convention would generally be covered under sales tax laws without an approved exemption.

Political Activity

Churches and other organizations exempt from federal income tax under section 501(c)(3) of the Internal Revenue Code are prohibited from participating or intervening, directly or indirectly, in any political campaign on behalf of or in opposition to any candidate for public office. Even certain activities that encourage people to vote for or against a particular candidate on the basis of nonpartisan criteria violate the political campaign prohibition law.

To avoid violating the political campaign provisions of the law:

➢ Do not use a rating program to evaluate candidates.

➢ Do not endorse a candidate, or a slate of candidates, directly or indirectly through a sermon, speech, newsletter, or sample ballot.

➢ Do not publish a candidate's statement.

➤ Do not publish the names of candidates who agree to adhere to certain practices.

➤ Do not publish candidate responses to a questionnaire that evidences a bias on certain issues. Classifying particular candidates as too conservative or too liberal is an improper rating system.

➤ Do not publish responses to an unbiased questionnaire focused on a narrow range of issues.

➤ Do not raise funds for a candidate or provide support to a political party.

Warning

If a church or nonprofit organization (under Section 501(c)(3)) participates in even one political campaign activity (no matter how small the occasion), it can potentially lose its tax-exempt status. The organization must not be involved or participate in the campaign of the individual seeking public office.

➤ Do not provide volunteers, mailing lists, publicity, or free use of facilities unless all parties and candidates in the community receive the same services.

➤ Do not pay campaign expenses for a candidate.

➤ Do not publish or distribute printed or oral statements about candidates.

➤ Do not display campaign literature on the organization's premises.

If the IRS finds that an organization has engaged in these activities, the organization could lose its exempt status. Also, the IRS may assess an excise tax on the amount of the funds spent on the activity.

Forums or debates at which all candidates are treated equally may be conducted to educate voters, or a mailing list may be rented to candidates on the same basis as it is made available to others. Organizations may engage in voter registration or get-out-the-vote activities. However, it is wise to avoid defining a target group by political or ideological criteria (e.g., encouraging individuals to vote who are "registered Republicans" or "registered Democrats").

- **The church audit potential.** Very few churches are audited each year. The number of churches audited is low because approval of an appropriate high-level IRS official is required to open a church tax inquiry. This is the protection provided in the tax law in recognition of the legitimate separation of church and state.

  The danger is for churches that conduct their financial operations beyond the bounds of the law believing they will never be audited. Integrity requires compliance with the law even if the IRS never calls!

- **The danger of "excess benefit transactions."** Excess benefit transactions (as defined on pages 34-35, 37) are often overlooked by churches and other ministries. The "insider" involved in the transaction can be subjected to a penalty of up to 225%.

  An excess benefit transaction can be as simple as providing a taxable fringe benefit and not reflecting it as taxable income to a senior pastor, executive director, president, CEO, or other insider. It could be as easy as transferring equipment from a nonprofit organization to an insider at less than fair market value and failing to treat the amount as taxable income to the recipient.

- **The challenge of the Form 990.** Most charities other than churches must annually file Form 990.

  The staff of very few ministries have the ability to accurately file the Form 990. At a minimum, a charity should have the Form 990 reviewed by their external CPA or attorney. Better yet is to have the Form 990 prepared by an external professional. After the Form 990 is filed with the IRS, it is soon posted (minus Schedule B) on the internet. So, an improperly prepared Form 990 soon becomes available for anyone in the world to see. A poorly prepared Form 990 reflects negatively on the nonprofit and its mission.

Compensating Employees

In This Chapter

- Reasonable compensation
- Housing and the housing exclusion
- Deferred compensation
- Maximizing fringe benefits
- Workers' compensation

- Overtime and minimum pay
- Internships
- Paying employee expenses
- Reimbursing medical expenses
- Nondiscrimination rules

The three primary challenges for churches and nonprofits in the area of compensating employees are:

➤ **Determining the appropriate level of compensation.** Compensating employees too little can create issues for employees covered by the Fair Labor Standards Act. On the other hand, in a few situations, compensating employees excessively may jeopardize a ministry's tax-exempt status. While no absolute limits have been placed on compensation amounts to ministry leaders, appropriate total compensation should be determined, taking into consideration reliable comparability data, as well as the employee's skills, talents, education, experience, performance, and knowledge.

➤ **Documenting and reporting compensation.** The approval of the compensation, including fringe benefits, of the ministry's top leader should be contemporaneously documented. The taxable portions of compensation and fringe benefits should be reported to the appropriate taxing authorities.

➤ **Maximizing the tax advantages of certain fringe benefits.** Compensation may be maximized by effectively structuring fringe benefits. The tax-free or tax-deferred features of certain fringe benefits can significantly increase an employee's take-home pay without expending additional ministry funds.

Reasonable Compensation

Ministry employees may receive reasonable compensation for their services. However, excessive compensation can result in private inurement and may jeopardize the tax-exempt status of the organization. Reasonable compensation is based on what would ordinarily be paid for like services by a like organization under similar circumstances, according to the IRS.

The intermediate sanctions regulations impose penalties when excessive compensation or benefits are received by certain key employees and other individuals. These penalties may be avoided if the compensation arrangement was approved by an independent body that: (1) was composed entirely of individuals unrelated to and not subject to the control of the employee involved in the arrangement, (2) obtained and relied upon appropriate data as to comparability, and (3) adequately documented the basis for its determination.

Excellence in Compensation Tips

- Prepare a compensation philosophy statement. This should take into account the present situation as well as long-term goals and objectives. Broad categories may include (1) attraction, (2) retention, and (3) motivation and reward.

- Be certain that pastoral or executive compensation is determined by the board or a board-appointed committee, completely independent of the individual.

- Notify the board of any family members of the top leader receiving compensation. For appropriate transparency with the board, the board should be notified at least annually of all family member compensation.

- Determine comparable compensation. Consider what other organizations pay for similar roles.

- Consider all compensation, not just wages. Fringe benefits should be considered as part of compensation and may include (1) taxable, (2) non-taxable, and (3) tax-deferred elements. Compensation may also include forgiveness of debt, bonuses, deferred compensation arrangements, or other non-wage related amounts.

- Adopt an accountable expense reimbursement plan.

- Maximize the minister's housing exclusion, when appropriate.

- Ensure compensation is fair and reasonable.

- Review compensation periodically to determine if changes to the structure or benefits are needed based on changes in the organization or from outside influences.

Compensation-setting practices should not cause a diminished Christian witness and should comply with ECFA's Policy for Excellence in Compensation-Setting and Related-Party Transactions in ECFA Standard 6.

The general framework of the Policy for Excellence must be followed by all members, and the following two aspects of the policy, plus others, must be followed when the ECFA member's top leader receives annual compensation of $150,000 or more:

1. The board, or an authorized independent committee of the board, must make the decision regarding total compensation, and those participating in the decision-making process may not have conflicts of interest in the decision, whether direct or indirect.

2. The board or committee must obtain reliable comparability data at least every five years.

For more information, see ECFA's eBooks—*8 Essentials of Compensating Ministry Leaders* and *8 Essentials of Compensating Ministers*.

Housing and the Housing Exclusion

Housing for nonministers

Housing provided to nonminister employees by a church or nonprofit organization for its convenience, as a condition of employment, and on its premises:

➤ is exempt from income tax and FICA tax withholding by the church or nonprofit organization, and

➤ is excluded from wages reported by the church and employee

If these criteria are not met, the fair rental value should be reported as compensation on Form W-2 and is subject to withholding and FICA taxation.

Housing for ministers

The 2021 edition of the *Minister's Tax & Financial Guide* includes a thorough discussion of the availability of the housing allowance for ministers serving local churches. Ordained, commissioned, or licensed ministers not serving local churches may qualify as "ministers" for federal tax purposes in the following situations:

➤ **Denominational service.** This category encompasses the administration of religious denominations and their integral agencies, including teaching or administration in parochial schools, colleges, or universities that are under the authority of a church or denomination.

The IRS uses the following criteria to determine if an institution is an integral agency of a church:

- ☐ Did the church incorporate the institution?

- ☐ Does the corporate name of the institution suggest a church relationship?

- ☐ Does the church continuously control, manage, and maintain the institution?

- ☐ If the institution were to dissolve, would the assets be turned over to the church?

- ☐ Are the trustees or directors of the institution appointed by, or must they be approved by, the church, and may they be removed by the church?

- ☐ Are annual reports of finances and general operations required to be made to the church?

- ☐ Does the church contribute to the support of the institution?

➢ **Assignment by a church.** Services performed by a minister for a parachurch organization based upon a substantive assignment or designation by a church may provide the basis for ministerial tax treatment. The housing allowance should be designated by the employing organization, not the assigning church.

The following characteristics must be present for an effective assignment:

- ☐ There must be a sufficient relationship between the minister and the assigning church to justify the assignment of the minister.

- ☐ There must be an adequate relationship between the assigning church and the parachurch organization to which the minister is assigned to justify the assignment.

To substantiate the relationship between the minister and the church, the church must determine "if there is sufficient authority, power, or legitimacy for the church to assign this particular minister." Such matters as being the ordaining church; providing ongoing supervision; having denominational affiliation; contributing significant financial support; or being the long-term "home church" would all appear to support this relationship.

In addressing the relationship between the church and the parachurch organization, the church must answer the question of "why should the church assign a minister to this particular ministry?" Essentially, the assignment of the minister must accomplish the church's ministry purposes.

In considering an assignment, it is important to distinguish between the process of assigning and the documentation of the assignment. The *process of assigning* may include the church's theology, philosophy, and policy of operation—its way of doing ministry. The *documentation of the assignment* provides evidence that the church is doing ministry through the particular individual assigned. The following are keys to a proper assignment:

☐ A written policy describing the specific requirements for the relationship of the church both to the minister being assigned and to the parachurch organization to which the minister is assigned. This would include the church's theological and policy goals for the assignment.

☐ A formal review to confirm that the minister and the proposed ministry with a parachurch organization qualify.

☐ A written assignment coupled with guidelines for supervision of, and reporting by, the minister and the parachurch organization to the church.

☐ A periodic (at least annual) formal review of the minister's activities to confirm that the assignment continues to comply with the policy.

Caution

Often, a denomination lists a minister as being assigned to a parachurch ministry, for example, in an annual directory, and the minister believes he or she has been assigned for tax purposes. But effective assignments are rare because of the substantive relationship and ongoing documentation of the assignment that are needed.

➤ **Other service.** If a minister is not engaged in service performed in the exercise of ministry of a local church or an integral agency of a church, or a church does not assign a minister's services, the definition of a qualifying minister becomes much narrower. Tax law and regulations provide little guidance for ministers in this category. However, Tax Court cases and IRS rulings suggest that an individual will qualify for the special tax treatments of a minister only if the individual's services for the employer substantially involve conducting religious worship or performing sacerdotal functions. This definition includes conducting Bible studies and spiritual counseling.

How much time constitutes substantial involvement in conducting worship or administering the sacraments? This is difficult to say. However, in two IRS letter rulings, the IRS determined that 5% of the minister's working hours was not sufficient to qualify for tax treatment as a minister.

Based on IRS rulings, it is clear that ministers serving as chaplains in government-owned-and-operated hospitals or in state prisons fall in a special category. They are employees for Social Security (FICA) purposes but do qualify for the housing allowance.

An individual does *not* qualify as a "minister" for federal income tax purposes in the following circumstances:

- a theological student who does not otherwise qualify as a minister

- an unordained, uncommissioned, or unlicensed individual not performing sacerdotal functions or conducting religious worship

- an ordained, commissioned, or licensed minister working as an administrator or on the faculty of a nonchurch-related college or seminary

- an ordained, commissioned, or licensed minister working as an executive of a nonreligious, nonchurch-related organization

- a civilian chaplain at a Veteran's Administration hospital (the tax treatment of ministers who are chaplains in the armed forces is the same as for other members of the armed forces)

- an ordained, licensed, or commissioned minister employed by a parachurch organization but does not perform sacerdotal functions or conduct religious worship

Caution

Many ministers are serving organizations other than local churches or integral agencies of churches and do not have an effective assignment by a church. The employer may be a rescue mission, a youth ministry, a Christian radio or TV station, or a missionary-sending organization. Qualifying for ministerial status is often based on the degree to which the individual is performing sacerdotal functions or conducting religious worship.

Applying the minister's housing allowance

Qualified ministers receive preferred treatment for their housing. If a minister has a home provided as part of compensation, the minister pays no income tax on the rental value of the home. If a home is not provided but the minister receives a rental or housing allowance designated in the minister's salary, the minister pays no income tax on the allowance *if* it is used for housing expenses subject to certain limitations.

Every minister should have a portion of salary designated as a housing allowance. For a minister living in ministry-owned housing, the housing allowance may be only a modest amount to cover incidental expenses such as maintenance, furnishings, and utilities. But a properly designated housing allowance may be worth thousands of dollars in tax savings for ministers living in their own homes or rented quarters.

The excludable housing allowance for ministers, which is part of a total compensation package that is determined to be reasonable pay for services performed, is the *lowest* of these factors:

Filing Tip

The designation of a housing allowance for a minister living in church-provided housing is often overlooked. While the largest housing allowance benefits go to ministers with mortgage payments on their own homes, a housing allowance is often also beneficial to a pastor living in church-provided housing.

➤ **Amount prospectively and officially designated by the employer.** The allowance must be officially designated *before* payment by the organization. The designation should be evidenced in writing, preferably by resolution of the appropriate governing body, in an employment contract, or, at a minimum, in the budget and payroll records.

If the only reference to the housing allowance is in the ministry's budget, the budget should be formally approved by the top governing body. However, it is highly preferable for the governing board to use a specific resolution to authorize housing allowance designations.

➤ **Amount used from current ministerial income to provide the home.** Only actual housing-related expenses can be excluded from income.

➤ **The fair rental value of the home including utilities and furnishings.** The IRS has not provided any guidance to assist ministers in determining the fair rental value of the home. The value should be based on comparable rental values of other similar residences in the immediate community, comparably furnished.

For more information on the housing exclusion, see ECFA's eBook, *10 Essentials of the Minister's Housing Exclusion.*

Deferred Compensation

In addition to 403(b) and 401(k) plans, churches and nonprofit organizations have available all the qualified retirement plan options that are available to any for-profit organization. These must be operated according to their terms and are generally subject to the same nondiscrimination and coverage rules as plans in for-profit organizations.

Churches and nonprofit organizations may defer the compensation of executives, but the amount of the deferral is limited for nonprofit organizations by Internal Revenue Code Section 457. For the year 2020, the annual limitation was $19,500, with a catch-up contribution of $6,500 allowed for participants who are 50 years or older. Unlike in a 401(k) or 403(b), any employer match counts toward the annual limit.

Sample Housing Allowance Resolutions

Parsonage Owned by or Rented by a Church

Whereas, The Internal Revenue Code permits a minister of the gospel to exclude from gross income "the rental value of a home furnished as part of compensation" or a church-designated allowance paid as a part of compensation to the extent that actual expenses are paid from the allowance to maintain a parsonage owned or rented by the church;

Whereas, Nelson Street Church compensates the senior minister for services in the exercise of ministry; and

Whereas, Nelson Street Church provides the senior minister with the rent-free use of a parsonage owned by (rented by) the church as a portion of the compensation for services rendered to the church in the exercise of ministry;

Resolved, That the compensation of the senior minister is $3,500 per month, of which $600 per month is a designated housing allowance; and

Resolved, That the designation of $600 per month as a housing allowance shall apply until otherwise provided.

Home Owned or Rented by a Minister

Whereas, The Internal Revenue Code permits a minister of the gospel to exclude from gross income a church-designated allowance paid as part of compensation to the extent used for actual expenses in owning or renting a home; and

Whereas, Nelson Street Church compensates the senior minister for services in the exercise of ministry;

Resolved, That the compensation of the senior minister is $5,500 per month, of which $2,250 per month is a designated housing allowance; and

Resolved, That the designation of $2,250 per month as a housing allowance shall apply until otherwise provided.

Special Speakers

Whereas, The Internal Revenue Code permits a minister of the gospel to exclude from gross income a church-designated allowance paid as part of compensation to the extent used in owning or renting a permanent home; and

Whereas, Nelson Street Church compensated a special speaker for services in the exercise of ministry as a special speaker;

Resolved, That the honorarium paid to the special speaker shall be $1,512, consisting of $312 in travel expenses (with documentation provided to the church), a $500 housing allowance, and a $700 honorarium.

Under Section 457(f) there is the ability to set aside deferred compensation without limit if it is not "vested." The requirement is that it be subject to "significant risk of forfeiture." This is often established by requiring future years of service for it to vest. When vested, it becomes taxable income at that date.

Setting up the deferred compensation as a 457(f) arrangement requires a written agreement that meets the requirements. The agreement between the employee and employer to defer the income must be made *before it is earned*. Once it has been earned, it is too late for the employee to request its deferral.

Idea

Occasionally, churches and nonprofit organizations will set up a reserve to pay bonuses to employees at a later date. Such a reserve cannot be "designated" or "subject to an understanding" that it will be used for a specific employee. It avoids current taxation because the organization has not allocated it to specific employees nor paid it over.

Amounts that are deferred are often put into a "Rabbi Trust." A Rabbi Trust is established with an independent trustee who invests the amounts that have been deferred. The assets may still be used to pay creditors of the organization (in a bankruptcy, for instance), but cannot be reclaimed by the corporation for its operations. Essentially, a Rabbi Trust protects the executive from the board's changing its mind and using the money somewhere else.

403(b) plans

Employees of churches and other nonprofit organizations may have a Section 403(b) salary reduction arrangement based on a written plan. These plans are also called tax-sheltered annuities (TSAs).

Both nonelective and elective employer contributions to a TSA for a minister are excludable for income and Social Security tax (SECA) purposes. Elective contributions for nonministers are subject to FICA. Some individuals choose to contribute additional amounts to their plans utilizing after-tax or "Roth" contributions. This is permissible but must be included in the organization's plan document.

See the 2021 edition of the *Minister's Tax & Financial Guide* for additional information on TSA contribution limitations.

Typically, there is very little cost to establish and maintain a 403(b) plan. It is an important planning option to defer taxes and encourage individuals in a ministry to save for retirement. Employer contributions are not required and could be evaluated annually if the plan is written accordingly. This would allow flexibility from a budget perspective while not eliminating the benefit entirely.

401(k) plans

A church or nonprofit organization may offer a 401(k) plan to its employees. Under a 401(k) plan, an employee can elect to have the employer make tax-deferred contributions to the plan (up to $19,500 for 2020), of amounts that had been withheld from employee pay.

Maximizing Fringe Benefits

A "fringe benefit" is a form of pay (including property, services, cash, or cash equivalent) in addition to base salary, for the performance of services by an employee to the ministry. Additionally, the personal use of property by a ministry employee is a form of a fringe benefit.

All fringe benefits are taxable and must be included in the recipient's pay, except for those the law specifically excludes. Therefore, it is beneficial to employees when a ministry provides qualified fringe benefits which are tax-free for income and Social Security tax purposes.

A few key benefits for ministry and church staff are covered in this section. For more information on fringe benefits, see ECFA's eBooks *9 Essentials of Fringe Benefits for Ministries* and *9 Essentials of Church Fringe Benefits*. Also, see IRS Publication 15-B.

Employer-provided cell phones

If an employer provides a cell phone to an employee primarily for noncompensatory business reasons, it is treated as a tax-free fringe benefit. Additionally, an employee's personal use will be treated as a *de minimis* fringe benefit. The net effect is that employer-provided cell phones are not taxable income to employees as long as the phone is provided primarily for noncompensatory purposes.

While the IRS has not identified all business purposes, if cell phones are provided to promote the morale or goodwill of an employee, this is not a sufficient business purpose, and the value would be treated as taxable compensation.

To assist in demonstrating the business purpose for employer-provided cell phones, employers may want to consider adding the business reason as part of an employee's job description, in a written cell phone policy, or as part of the employment handbook. Employers should generally avoid considering a cell phone as some type of employment perk or as recruitment incentive, as this may give the appearance of compensatory purposes.

Employers should also consider any security risks that may be caused with the loss of a mobile device such as a cell phone. Some phone systems offer additional location and remote data erasing features that can mitigate the risks associated with losing one of these devices. The accidental release of sensitive ministry information could pose serious risks to an organization or its employees.

Employer reimbursement for employee-owned cell phones

Internal guidance from the IRS to its field staff addresses situations where employers provide a reimbursement for employee-owned cell phones. In this guidance, the IRS indicates that a similar analysis should be used for reimbursements as if the employer had actually provided a cell phone to an employee. Thus, where employers have substantial business reasons other than providing compensation to employees, then this may not result in taxable income to the employee.

Tip

Employers should avoid considering a cell phone as a type of employment perk. To be tax-free, cell phones must be provided for noncompensatory purposes.

In order to be eligible for the nontaxable treatment, the reimbursement:

➤ must be for business reasons other than providing compensation to employees

➤ must not exceed actual expenses in maintaining the cell phone, and

➤ must not substitute a portion of an employee's wages

Examples of substantial noncompensatory business reasons for requiring employees to maintain personal cell phones and reimbursing them for their use include, but are not limited to the following:

➤ employer needing to contact the employee at all times for work-related emergencies

➤ employer requiring that the employee be available at times outside of an employee's normal work schedule

It is not considered reasonable to reimburse an employee for international or satellite phone usage if all the employer's necessary contacts are in the local geographic area where the employee works or where reimbursements deviate significantly from normal use in the employer's work.

Employer-owned laptops or reimbursements

The treatment of employer-owned laptops or reimbursements now follow similar rules for cell phones as discussed above. As long as an employer has provided computer equipment (or reimbursements for the equipment) primarily for noncompensatory business reasons, it is treated as a tax-free fringe benefit.

Personal use of employer-provided vehicles

Vehicles provided by ministries to employees for business use are often also used for personal purposes. The IRS (see IRS Publication 535) treats most types of personal use of an employer-provided vehicle as a noncash fringe benefit and generally requires the fair market value of such use be included in the employee's gross income (to the extent that the value is not reimbursed to the employer).

If the employee reimburses the employer for the full dollar value of the personal use, it will cost the employee more than if the employer includes the personal-use value in the taxable income of the employee.

> *Example:* The personal use value of an automobile provided to a lay employee is determined to be $100; if fully reimbursed, the employee would pay $100 to the employer. If there is no reimbursement, the employer includes the $100 in the employee's income, and the employee will be subject to payroll taxes on $100 of income. Assuming a federal income tax rate of 28% and a FICA rate of 7.65%, the total would be $35.65 compared with the $100 cash out-of-pocket chargeback.

> *Note:* If the employee had been a minister, in this example, instead of a key employee, the difference would have been even greater because the Social Security tax of 15.3% would be paid by the minister instead of the 7.65% FICA rate that applies to other lay employees.

➤ **Valuation of personal vehicle use.** There are three special valuation rules, in addition to a set of general valuation principles, which may be used under specific circumstances for valuing the personal use of an employer-provided vehicle. This value must be included in the employee's compensation if it is not reimbursed by the employee.

Under the general valuation rule, the value is based on what the cost would be to a person leasing from a third party the same or comparable vehicle on the same or comparable terms in the same geographic area. The two most commonly used special valuation rules, which are used by most employers, are these:

☐ **Cents-per-mile valuation rule.** Generally, this rule may be used if the employer reasonably expects that the vehicle will be regularly used in the employer's trade or business, and if the vehicle is driven at least 10,000 miles a year and is primarily used by employees. This valuation rule is available only if the fair market value of the vehicle—as of the date the vehicle was first made available for personal use by employees—does not exceed a specified value set by the IRS. For 2020, this value is $54,000.

The value of the personal use of the vehicle is computed by multiplying the number of miles driven for personal purposes by the current IRS standard mileage rate (56 cents per mile for 2021). For this valuation rule, personal use is "any use of the vehicle other than use in your trade or business."

☐ **Annual lease valuation rule.** Under the annual lease valuation rule, the fair market value of a vehicle is determined by referring to an annual lease value table published by the IRS (see below). The annual lease value corresponding to this fair market value, multiplied by the personal use percentage, is the amount to be added to the employee's gross income. If the ministry provides the fuel, 5.5 cents per mile must be added to the annual lease value. Amounts reimbursed by the employee are offset.

Idea

Start with a policy that requires a contemporaneous log, with the date and personal miles recorded for all ministry vehicles. The log is the basis for determining the personal vs. business use of the vehicle. Then the employer chooses a valuation rule to determine the value of the personal use for Form W-2 reporting. Simply paying for the gas during personal use does not satisfy these rules.

The fair market value of a vehicle owned by an employer is generally the employer's cost of purchasing the vehicle (including taxes and fees). The fair market value of a vehicle leased by an employer is generally either the manufacturer's suggested retail price less 8%, the manufacturer's invoice plus 4%, or the retail value as reported in a nationally recognized publication that regularly reports automobile retail values.

Lease Value Table

Fair Market Value of Car			Annual Lease Value	Fair Market Value of Car			Annual Lease Value
$0	–	$999	$600	21,000	–	21,999	5,850
1,000	–	1,999	850	22,000	–	22,999	6,100
2,000	–	2,999	1,100	23,000	–	23,999	6,350
3,000	–	3,999	1,350	24,000	–	24,999	6,600
4,000	–	4,999	1,600	25,000	–	25,999	6,850
5,000	–	5,999	1,850	26,000	–	27,999	7,250
6,000	–	6,999	2,100	28,000	–	29,999	7,750
7,000	–	7,999	2,350	30,000	–	31,999	8,250
8,000	–	8,999	2,600	32,000	–	33,999	8,750
9,000	–	9,999	2,850	34,000	–	35,999	9,250
10,000	–	10,999	3,100	36,000	–	37,999	9,750
11,000	–	11,999	3,350	38,000	–	39,999	10,250
12,000	–	12,999	3,600	40,000	–	41,999	10,750
13,000	–	13,999	3,850	42,000	–	43,999	11,250
14,000	–	14,999	4,100	44,000	–	45,999	11,750
15,000	–	15,999	4,350	46,000	–	47,999	12,250
16,000	–	16,999	4,600	48,000	–	49,999	12,750
17,000	–	17,999	4,850	50,000	–	51,999	13,250
18,000	–	18,999	5,100	52,000	–	53,999	13,750
19,000	–	19,999	5,350	54,000	–	55,999	14,250
20,000	–	20,999	5,600	56,000	–	57,999	14,750
				58,000	–	59,999	15,250

Note: The annual lease value (calculated using the above table) is based on four-year terms. In other words, employers should refigure the annual lease value every four years that the vehicle is in service, based on the vehicle's fair market value at the beginning of each four-year cycle.

☐ **Commuting valuation rule.** Under this rule, the church must require the employee to commute to and/or/ from work in the vehicle for bona fide noncompensatory business reasons. This rule is rarely applicable to churches or ministries.

Employer-provided dependent care assistance plan

A ministry can provide employees with child care or disabled dependent care services to allow employees to work. The amount excludable from tax is limited to the smallest of the employee's earned income, the spouse's earned income, or $5,000 ($2,500 if married filing separately). The dependent care assistance must be provided under a separate written plan that does not favor highly compensated employees and that meets other qualifications.

Dependent care assistance payments are excluded from income if the payments cover expenses that would be deductible by the employee as child and dependent care expenses on Form 2441 if the expenses were not reimbursed. It may be necessary to file Form 2441, even though the dependent care assistance payments are excluded from income, to document the appropriateness of the payments.

Medical, dental, and vision insurance

Insurance may be provided or made available for purchase by employees for group medical, dental, and vision coverage. Premiums paid by the employer for the employee, including dependents, are excluded from income for income tax purposes as well as Social Security and Medicare.

Ministries may reimburse employees tax-free for their medical expenses, including individual health insurance premiums under either a qualified small employer health reimbursement arrangement (QSEHRA) or an individual coverage health reimbursement arrangement (ICHRA).

The similarities of the two arrangements are these:

- **Employees purchase health care.** Employees buy health insurance, products and services they want. Any expense listed in IRS Publication 502 can be reimbursed.

- **Employees submit reimbursement requests.** Employees submit expense documentation to the ministry.

- **Ministries review and reimburse.** Ministries review the documentation submitted, and if approved, reimburses employees tax-free.

Now, for the differences between the arrangements:

- **Number of employees.** To offer a QSEHRA, a ministry must have fewer than 50 full-time employees, and it cannot offer a group insurance policy. However, ministries of all sizes can offer an ICHRA. Ministries can offer a group health insurance policy to one class of employees and an ICHRA to another class of employees, provided they meet minimum class size standards.

- **Employee eligibility.** With a QSEHRA, all full-time employees and their families are eligible for the benefit, and the ministry can choose to extend eligibility to part-time employees. With an ICHRA, ministries can structure their eligibility requirements based on a given set of employee classes.

- **Allowance caps.** With a QSEHRA, ministries cannot offer allowance amounts that exceed annual caps set by the IRS. For 2020, those caps are $5,250 for single employees and $10,600 for employees with a family. Balances in the QSEHRA can roll over month to month and year to year, though total reimbursements cannot exceed the year's IRS cap. With the ICHRA, there are no annual contribution caps, and allowance amounts can roll over month to month and year-to-year without restriction.

When establishing either a QSEHRA or ICHRA arrangement, ministries will often benefit by obtaining counsel from an employee benefits specialist.

Disability insurance

Disability insurance may be provided for church and nonprofit organization employees. Coverage is usually limited to 60% to 75% of the annual salary of each individual. Social Security and pension benefits are often offset against disability insurance benefits. Disability insurance premiums may be paid through a flexible benefit plan (FSA) to obtain income tax and FICA savings.

If the organization pays the disability insurance premiums, the premiums are excluded from the employee's income. If the organization pays the premiums (and the employee is the beneficiary) as part of the compensation package, any disability

Idea

The probability of disability greatly exceeds the probability of death during an individual's working years. Individual or group disability policies may be purchased. These plans may include a probationary period, which excludes preexisting sickness from immediate coverage, and an elimination period, which specifies the time after the start of a disability when benefits are not payable.

policy proceeds are fully taxable to the employee. This is based on who paid the premiums for the policy covering the year when the disability started. If the premiums are shared between the employer and the employee, then the benefits are taxable in the same proportion as the payment of the premiums.

Compensation-related loans

Some ministries make loans to employees. The loans are often restricted to the purchase of land or a residence or the construction of a residence. Before a loan is made, the ministry should determine if the transaction is legal under state law. Such loans are prohibited in many states.

If an organization receives interest of $600 or more in a year relating to a loan secured by real estate, a Form 1098 must be provided to the payer. For the interest to be deductible as an itemized deduction, an employee loan must be secured by the residence and properly recorded.

If an organization makes loans to employees at below-market rates, the organization may be required to report additional compensation to the employee. If the loan is below $10,000, there is no additional compensation to the borrower. For loans over $10,000, additional compensation is calculated equal to the foregone interest that would have been charged if the loan had been made at a market rate of interest. The market rate of interest is the "applicable federal rate" for loans of similar duration. The IRS publishes these rates monthly. The additional compensation must be reported on Form W-2, Box 1.

Social Security tax reimbursement

Ministries often reimburse ministers for a portion or all of their self-employment tax (SECA) liability. Reimbursement also may be made to lay employees for all or a portion of the FICA tax that has been withheld from their pay. Any Social Security reimbursement must be reported as taxable income for both income and Social Security tax purposes. Any FICA reimbursement to a lay employee is also subject to income tax and FICA withholding.

Because of the deductibility of the self-employment tax in both the income tax and self-employment tax computations, a full reimbursement is effectively less than the gross 15.3% rate:

Marginal Tax Rate	Effective SECA Rate
0%	14.13%
12	13.28
22	12.58
24	12.43

For missionaries who are not eligible for the income tax deduction of one-half of the self-employment tax due to the foreign earned-income exclusion, the full reimbursement rate is effectively 14.13%.

Sabbaticals

Some ministries choose to provide their leaders a sabbatical either to focus on a project such as writing a book, or as a respite for a certain number of years of service. A leader typically receives full or part pay during the sabbatical. If sabbatical payments qualify as a nonqualified deferred compensation plan, then plan requirements, such as documentation, elections, funding, distributions, withholding, and reporting must be considered. Otherwise, sabbatical pay generally represents taxable pay reportable on Form W-2.

A ministry sometimes reimburses travel expenses (for example, transportation, meals, and lodging) for the leader during the sabbatical. These expenses generally do not qualify for reimbursement under an accountable expense reimbursement plan as ordinary and necessary business expenses and should be added to compensation for Form W-2 reporting.

Property transfers

➤ **Unrestricted.** If an employer transfers property (for example, a car, residence, equipment, or other property) to an employee at no charge or below the fair market value, this constitutes taxable income to the employee. The amount of income is generally the fair market value of the property transferred.

➤ **Restricted.** To recognize and reward good work, some churches or nonprofits transfer property to an employee subject to certain restrictions. The ultimate transfer may occur only if the employee lives up to the terms of the agreement. Once the terms are met, the property is transferred free and clear. Property that is subject to substantial risk of forfeiture and is nontransferable is not vested. No tax liability will occur until title to the property is vested with the employee. This is a deferral of income and Social Security tax.

Caution

Don't forget to evaluate intellectual property transfers. These may also result in taxable income to the minister. See *6 Essentials of Copyright Law for Churches* eBook at *www.ECFA.church/eBooks*.

When restricted property becomes substantially vested, the employee must report the transfer as taxable income. The amount reported must be equal to the excess of the fair market value of the property at the time it becomes substantially vested, over the amount the employee pays for the property.

> *Example:* A church transfers a house to the pastor subject to the completion of 20 years of service for the church. The pastor does not report any taxable income from the transfer until the 20th year. This situation will generally require advance tax planning since the pastor could have a substantial tax liability in the year of the transfer.

➤ **Property purchased from employer.** If the employer allows an employee to buy property at a price below its fair market value, the employer must include as extra wages in income the difference between the property's fair market value and the amount paid and liabilities assumed by the employee.

Moving expenses

Moving expenses paid by an employer on behalf of an employee or reimbursed by the employer are taxable as compensation on the employee's Form W-2.

Gifts

The value of a turkey, ham, or other nominally valued item distributed to an employee on holidays need not be reported as income. However, a distribution of cash, a gift certificate, or a similar item of value readily convertible to cash must be included in the employee's income. Gifts to certain nonemployees up to $25 per year may be tax-free. Certain gifts of an advertising nature that cost $4 or less given for use on the ministry's premises are excluded from the $25 annual limit.

Workers' Compensation

Workers' compensation insurance coverage compensates workers for losses caused by work-related injuries. It also limits the potential liability of the organization for injury to the employee related to his or her job.

Workers' compensation benefits are required by law in all states to be provided by the employer. This may be done by insurance, or many states allow for self-funded or group-funded plans within specific guidelines. A few states exempt churches from workers' compensation coverage, and several states exempt all nonprofit employers. Most states also consider ministers to be employees regardless of the

Key Issue

Even if a church or nonprofit organization is exempt from workers' compensation, the voluntary purchase of the coverage or the securing of additional general liability coverage may be prudent. This is because other types of insurance typically exclude work-related accidents: health, accident, disability, auto, and general liability insurance policies are some examples.

income tax filing method used by the minister, and therefore they must be covered under the workers' compensation policy. Ministries should contact their state department of labor to find out how their state applies workers' compensation rules to churches and nonprofits.

Workers' compensation premiums are based on the payroll of the ministry with a minimum premium charge to issue the policy. An audit is done later to determine the actual charge for the policy.

Most workers' compensation insurance is purchased through private insurance carriers. A few states provide the coverage and charge the covered organizations.

Overtime and Minimum Pay

The Fair Labor Standards Act (FLSA) provides protection for employees engaged in interstate commerce concerning minimum wages, equal pay, overtime pay, record-keeping, and child labor (some states even have more restrictive versions of the FLSA).

The current FLSA minimum wage is $7.25 per hour. (Caution: Several states have established minimum wages that exceed the federal rate.)

Overtime pay is generally required regardless of whether an employee is paid on an hourly or salary basis. For employees in 2020 to be exempt from the overtime and minimum wage requirements, they must meet the $684 per week threshold and be paid on a salary basis with a minimum salary threshold of $35,568 per year. In other words, employees paid on an hourly basis do not meet the exemption requirements.

Any employee paid over $684 per week must meet the duties test in order to be classified as an exempt employee. The duties test is divided into employee type categories. These categories are executive, administrative, and professional employees. For specific information on these exemptions, go to *www.dol.gov/whd/overtime/fs17a_overview.pdf*.

Tip

See ECFA's eBook *Answering Your Overtime Questions* at *www.ECFA.church* for answers to some of the most frequently asked questions regarding overtime pay rules.

The employees of ministries involved in commerce or in the production of goods for commerce are generally considered covered by the provisions of the FLSA. Commerce is defined by the FLSA as "trade, commerce, transportation, transmission, or communication among several states or between any state and any place outside thereof." Conversely, nonprofits that are not engaged in commerce or fall below the $500,000 annual gross sales volume requirement are generally exempt from the Act.

Are ministers exempt from the Fair Labor Standards Act? Generally, yes under the ministerial exception. This common law doctrine received prominent exposure by the U.S. Supreme Court in its unanimous decision in the 2012 *Hosanna Tabor* case and subsequently in the 2020 *Our Lady of Guadalupe School* case. This doctrine may apply more broadly than the tax determination of who qualifies as a minister. Organizations should consult with their legal counsel in analyzing this potential exemption.

Warning

There is significant confusion over "compensatory time," or giving time off in lieu of paying overtime. If an employee is covered under the Fair Labor Standards Act, providing compensatory time is not an option. Payment for the overtime must be made in cash.

The FLSA applies to schools regardless of whether they are nonprofit entities operated by religious organizations. However, there are special rules for teachers. Church-operated day care centers and elementary and secondary schools are generally considered subject to the FLSA.

Many local churches and small nonprofits do not meet the $500,000 threshold (see above). However, individual employees are generally covered under the FLSA if they send or receive just a few emails each year across state lines. Therefore, most churches and nonprofits should follow the FLSA regulations as a precaution against possible action by the Department of Labor. Ministers are generally exempt under the professional provisions of this exemption.

Internships

There are many factors for churches and nonprofits to consider when offering an internship. If the individual receives no compensation and is treated as a volunteer, there are few regulations that must be followed. However, any compensation will likely result in the individual being treated as an employee and subject to regulations such as minimum wage and overtime requirements as well as various state compliance issues.

The Department of Labor has published a list of criteria in which an intern is receiving the benefit of the internship and the organization is not, and therefore a stipend may be paid that does not meet the requirements above. That information is found in *Fact Sheet #71: Internship Programs Under the Fair Labor Standards Act* on the Department of Labor website (*dol.gov*).

Paying Employee Expenses

An accountable plan is a reimbursement or expense allowance arrangement that requires (1) a business purpose for the expenses, (2) employees to substantiate the expenses, and

(3) the return of any excess reimbursements. This plan is required for reimbursement of expenses to be excluded from taxable income for employees.

The substantiation of expenses and return of excess reimbursements must be handled within a reasonable time. The following methods meet the "reasonable time" definition:

➤ The **fixed date method** applies if (1) an advance is made 30 days before an expense is paid or incurred, (2) an expense is substantiated to the employer within 60 days after the expense is paid or incurred, and (3) any excess amount is returned to the employer within 120 days after the expense is paid or incurred.

➤ The **periodic statement method** applies if (1) the employer provides employees with a periodic statement that identifies the amount paid under the arrangement in excess of the substantiated expense, (2) statements are provided at least quarterly, and (3) the employer requests that the employee provide substantiation for any additional expenses that have not yet been substantiated and/or return any amounts remaining unsubstantiated within 120 days of the statement.

If employees substantiate expenses and return any unused excess payments to the church or nonprofit organization on a timely basis, payments to the employee for business expenses have no impact on tax reporting. They are not included on Form W-2.

The timing of documenting expenses for reimbursement is of utmost importance. Under the fixed date method (see above), the IRS provides a safe harbor of 60 days after the expense is paid or incurred. In other words, the IRS may contest a reimbursement, based on timeliness of submitting the documentation, if the documentation is not provided to the employer. Does this mean that the IRS will disallow expenses reimbursed on the 61st day? Not necessarily. It simply means 60 days is a safe harbor as a "reasonable time."

Example: A church approves $50,000 of compensation for the pastor and tells her to let the church know at the end of the year how much she has spent on business expenses, and they will show the net amount on Form W-2. Is this valid? No. The salary must be established separately from expense reimbursements. Further, even if an accountable expense reimbursement plan is used, the annual submission of expense documentation would fail the timeliness safe harbor for expenses incurred in all but the last portion of the year.

For more information on expense reimbursements, see ECFA's eBooks—*5 Essentials of Reimbursing Expenses for Ministries* and *5 Essentials of Reimbursing Church Expenses*.

Per diem allowance

Ministries that help their employees cover business travel expenses have two basic options: (1) The employer can pay employees the precise amount of their expenses, or (2) the employer can opt for convenience and pay a set "per diem" allowance for each day of business travel.

The standard per diem rates for travel within the continental United States (CONUS) are $96 for lodging and $55 for meals and entertainment (based on October 1, 2020, to September 30, 2021).

Given the efficiency and administrative advantages of the per diem approach, some ministries choose to make per diem payments to volunteers within the IRS limits based on location. However, unlike in the case of employees, volunteers must include in income any part of per diem allowances that exceed deductible travel expenses.

Tip

With a per diem, the organization doesn't need receipts for each meal; the documents showing the organization paid the per diem are proof of expense, if it is at the federal rate.

Reimbursing Medical Expenses

Medical expenses that are not eligible for reimbursement under a health insurance plan are deductible on Schedule A as itemized deductions. However, many employees may take a standard deduction and not itemize, and those that do itemize and complete the Schedule A generally have their medical expenses subject to a limitation of only amounts over 10% of adjusted gross income for 2020 and future years. There are multiple options employers may use to assist in the reimbursement of medical expenses including:

➢ **Health Savings Account (HSA).** These are individual portable, tax-free, interest-bearing accounts through which individuals with high-deductible health insurance can save for medical expenses. The purpose of an HSA is to pay what basic coverage would ordinarily pay. Within limits, HSA contributions made by employers are excludable from income tax and Social Security wages, or contributions may be funded through a salary reduction agreement. The 2020 annual deductible contribution limits to an HSA are $3,550 for an individual and $7,100 for a family. The limits apply to combined employer and employee contributions. Earnings on amounts in an HSA are not taxable, and HSA distributions used to pay for medical expenses are not taxable. Distributions from HSAs which are not used for qualified medical expenses are subject to an additional tax of 20% on the amount includible in gross income.

➢ **Flexible Spending Account (FSA).** An FSA may be established with or without any other cafeteria plan options. It allows an employee to pre-fund medical and dental expenses in pre-tax dollars using a salary reduction election. If an FSA only covers medical expenses, it is commonly referred to as a health care FSA. These plans cannot reimburse for over-the-counter drugs except for insulin. Salary reductions for FSAs were limited to $2,750 in 2020.

Some employers provide a grace period for an FSA. If so, the grace period begins the day following the end of the plan year and lasts for two and a half months. It is designed to allow employees the opportunity to take full advantage of their non-taxable contributions when expenses fall short of what was originally projected. If a grace period is offered, a rollover (see "Tip" above) of $500 from one plan year to the next may not be provided and vice versa.

Tip

Up to $500 in unused funds can roll over into the following plan year. While the employer can elect to allow less than $500 to be rolled over, the same rollover limit must apply to all plan participants.

➤ **Health Reimbursement Arrangement (HRA).** Under an HRA, an employer may reimburse medical expenses up to a maximum dollar amount for the coverage period. The employer decides how much will be available for each employee, and this amount is generally the same for all eligible employees because nondiscrimination rules apply. Funding by a salary reduction election is not permitted. Typical expenses covered by such a plan are deductible, coinsurance, and noncovered amounts paid by the individual. Account balances can be carried forward to a future year with no tax implications to the individual. The balance is forfeited at retirement or other separation of employment.

Nondiscrimination Rules

To qualify for exclusion from income, many fringe benefits must be nondiscriminatory. This is particularly true for many types of benefits for certain key employees. Failure to comply with the nondiscrimination rules does not disqualify a fringe benefit plan entirely. The benefit is simply fully taxable for the highly compensated or key employees.

The nondiscrimination rules apply to the following types of fringe benefit plans: qualified tuition and fee discounts, eating facilities on or near the employer's premises, educational assistance benefits, dependent care assistance plans, tax-sheltered annuities (TSAs), 401(k) plans and other deferred compensation plans, group-term life insurance benefits, certain group medical insurance plans, health savings accounts (including health reimbursement arrangements), and cafeteria plans (including a flexible spending account dependent care plan and a health care flexible spending account).

Fringe benefit plans that limit benefits only to officers or highly compensated employees are clearly discriminatory. An officer is an employee who is appointed, confirmed, or elected by the board of the employer. A highly compensated employee for 2020 is someone who was paid more than $130,000, or if the employer elects, was in the top 20% of paid employees for compensation for the previous year.

- **Qualifying for the housing allowance.** Determining which individuals qualify for ministerial status (and, therefore, qualify for a housing allowance designation) can be a challenging issue for the employing church or other nonprofit organization—it's always the employer's decision, not the employee's. It's fairly simple to make this determination for a local church and for religious denominations. However, it does require understanding of the processes for ordaining, licensing, or commissioning of ministers by churches and the question of whether these practices are valid.

  Moving beyond local churches and denominations, ministerial status is more murky. It requires an understanding of assignment of ministers and perhaps what constitutes performing significant sacerdotal functions.

- **Fringe benefits, stewardship, and compliance.** The decision of which fringe benefits to offer staff is often indicative of a ministry's stewardship. It isn't just how much an employee is paid; it's also *how* compensation is paid. Are tax-free and tax-deferred opportunities maximized? And then there is the proper reporting of taxable fringe benefits which reflects a ministry's willingness to comply with tax law. For example, providing a vehicle to a key employee is an excellent fringe benefit from the employee's compensation view, but there are compliance issues to be followed with respect to personal miles.

- **Fair Labor Standards Act (FLSA) issues.** The overtime and minimum wage rules included in the FLSA are sometimes overlooked and abused by churches and other charities. Many churches and most other ministries are subject to the FLSA. With the Department of Labor's generous interpretation of "interstate commerce," just a few emails sent across state lines each year by an employee will often qualify that employee for FLSA coverage even if the ministry is not covered. Another common FLSA abuse is "paying" overtime by giving employees "compensatory" time off. While Congress has periodically considered compensatory time off with respect to the FLSA, it has not passed.

CHAPTER 4

Employer Reporting

In This Chapter

- Classification of workers
- Reporting compensation
- Payroll tax withholding

- Depositing withheld payroll taxes
- Filing quarterly payroll tax forms
- Filing annual payroll tax forms

The tax withholding and reporting requirements that employers must comply with are complicated. The special tax treatment of qualified ministers simply adds another level of complexity.

Churches and nonprofit organizations are generally required to withhold federal (and state and local, as applicable) income taxes and Social Security taxes and to pay employer Social Security tax on all wages paid to all full-time or part-time employees—except qualified ministers.

Classification of Workers

Whether an individual is classified as an employee or independent contractor has far-reaching consequences. This decision determines an organization's responsibility under the Federal Insurance Contributions Act (FICA), income tax withholding responsibilities, potential coverage under the Fair Labor Standards Act (FLSA) (see pages 65-66), and coverage under an employer's benefit plans. Misclassification can lead to significant penalties.

Questions frequently arise about the classification of certain nonprofit workers. Seasonal workers and those working less than full-time such as secretaries, custodians, nursery workers, and musicians require special attention for classification purposes. If a worker receives pay at an hourly rate, it will be difficult to justify independent contractor status. This conclusion holds true even if the workers are part-time.

Since 1935, the IRS has relied on certain common law rules (see below through page 74) to determine whether workers are employees or independent contractors.

Employees

If a worker is a nonministerial employee, the employer must withhold federal income tax (and state income tax, if applicable) and Federal Insurance Contributions Act (FICA) taxes, match the employee's share of FICA taxes, and unless exempted, pay unemployment taxes on the employee's wages. In addition, the employer may incur obligations for employee benefit plans such as vacation, sick pay, health insurance, and retirement plan contributions.

"Control" is the primary factor in determining whether an individual is an employee or an independent contractor. The higher degree of control that an organization has over a worker, the more likely it is that the worker should be classified as an employee. Among other criteria, *employees* comply with instructions, have a continuous relationship, perform work personally, work full-time or part-time, are subject to dismissal, can quit without incurring liability, are often reimbursed for expenses, and must submit reports.

Independent contractors

If the worker is classified as an independent contractor, quarterly estimated income taxes and Social Security taxes under the Self-Employment Contributions Act (SECA) are paid by the worker. For the organization, there is no unemployment tax liability or income or Social Security tax withholding requirement for independent contractors.

Key Issue

The employee vs. independent contractor decision is one of the most fundamental issues facing an employer making payments to workers. If a worker is truly an employee but is treated as an independent contractor, this can result in not withholding the appropriate income and FICA-type Social Security tax amounts.

Independent contractors normally set the order and sequence of work, set their hours of work, work for others at the same time, are paid by the job, offer their services to the public, have an opportunity for profit or loss, furnish their own tools, may do work on another's premises, and there is often substantial investment by the worker.

Common law rules

Defining a worker as an employee or as an independent contractor depends on the employer's degree of control over the worker to establish an employer-employee relationship. The IRS identifies three general ways a ministry may exercise such control:

Independent Contractor Status Myths

- *Myth:* A written contract will characterize a person as an independent contractor.

  Fact: It is the substance of the relationship that governs.

- *Myth:* Casual labor or seasonal workers are independent contractors, or their classification is a matter of choice.

  Fact: There is never a choice. The classification is determined by the facts and circumstances.

- *Myth:* If a person qualifies as an independent contractor for federal payroll tax purposes, he or she is automatically exempt for workers' compensation and state unemployment tax purposes.

  Fact: State workers' compensation and unemployment tax laws are often broader, and an individual may actually be covered under these laws even though qualifying as an independent contractor for federal payroll tax purposes.

---

behavioral control, financial control, and through the ministry-worker relationship. As a ministry analyzes these factors, it is safest to start from the assumption that a worker is an employee unless the factors clearly indicate independent contractor status. No single factor is determinative, but rather all forms of control must be analyzed.

➤ **Behavioral control.** These are factors regarding behavioral control:

1. **Types of instructions** – An employee is generally subject to the employer's instructions about the when, where, and how work is to be performed.

2. **Degree of instructions** – An employee is generally subject to more detailed instructions than an independent contractor.

3. **Evaluation systems** – A system that evaluates how a worker performs a job is indicative of an employment relationship, whereas a contractor relationship will generally just focus on the result.

4. **Training** – Generally an employer does not provide training to a contractor.

Key Issue

The amount of control and direction the employer has over a worker's services is the most important issue in deciding whether a worker is an employee or an independent contractor.

➤ **Financial control.** These are factors regarding financial control:

1. **Significant investment** – An employer will usually provide all equipment and resources to an employee, but contractors will provide their own.

2. **Unreimbursed expenses** – Contractors are more likely to have unreimbursed expenses than an employee.

3. **Opportunity for profit or loss** – A contractor generally has an opportunity for loss as well as an opportunity for profit.

4. **Services available to the public** – An employee tends to only work for one organization, whereas a contractor tends to work for a number of different organizations, sometimes simultaneously.

5. **Method of payment** – A contractor is generally contracted for a flat fee for a job. However, there are some professions where contractors are also paid on an hourly basis.

➤ **Relationship of the parties.** These are factors regarding relationship of the parties:

1. **Written contract** – While there can be contracts between an employee and an employer, a contract generally tends to indicate the type of independent contractor relationship.

2. **Employee benefits** – Does the worker receive benefits that would be more typical of an employment relationship?

3. **Permanency of the relationship** – A contractor is typically hired with a set time frame in mind, whereas an employee relationship is more likely open-ended.

4. **Services provided as a key activity of the organization** – The more central a worker's actions are to the core activities of the organization, the more likely the organization will exercise a higher degree of control over their operations, indicative of an employment relationship.

Once an organization has analyzed these factors to determine the nature of the relationship between the worker and the organization, it's time to review the overall level of behavioral control and financial control along with nature of the relationship to determine if it is an employment or independent contractor situation. Organizations should remember to be conservative and start from the assumption that there is an employment relationship.

The classification of ministers

It is important that the organization decide whether the services of ministers employed by the organization qualify for special tax treatment as ministerial services.

Most ordained, commissioned, or licensed ministers serving local churches are eligible for six special tax provisions with respect to services performed in the exercise of ministry. The IRS and courts apply certain tests to ministers serving local churches, including whether the minister administers the sacraments, conducts worship services, is considered a spiritual leader by the church, and performs management services in the "control, conduct, or maintenance of a religious organization." It may not be necessary for a minister to meet all of these factors to qualify for the special tax treatment. For a complete discussion of this topic, see the 2021 edition of the *Minister's Tax & Financial Guide*.

An individual ordained, commissioned, or licensed *not* serving a local church (or an organization with convention or association of churches status) may qualify as a minister for federal tax purposes without meeting additional tests if the individual's duties include the following (see also pages 49-52):

➤ Administration of church denominations and their integral agencies, including teaching or administration in parochial schools, colleges, or universities that are under the authority of a church or denomination

➤ Performing services for an institution which itself is not an integral agency of a church pursuant to an assignment or designation by ecclesiastical superiors, but only if those services relate to the assigning church's purposes

If a church does not assign the minister's services, they will be qualified services only if they substantially involve performing sacerdotal functions or conducting religious worship (including preaching, leading Bible studies, spiritual counseling, etc.).

Special Tax Provisions for Ministers

1. Exclusion for income tax purposes of the housing allowance or the fair rental value of ministry-owned housing provided rent-free to ministers.

2. Exemption of ministers from self-employment tax under very limited circumstances.

3. Treatment of ministers (who do not elect Social Security exemption) as self-employed for Social Security tax purposes for income from ministerial services.

4. Exemption of ministerial compensation from mandatory income tax withholding.

5. Eligibility for a voluntary income tax withholding arrangement between the minister-employee and the employer.

6. Potential double benefit of mortgage interest and real estate taxes as itemized deductions and as housing expenses for housing allowance purposes.

Reporting Compensation

➤ **Minister-employees**

Forms W-2 are annually provided to minister-employees. There is no requirement to withhold income taxes, but they may be withheld under a voluntary agreement. Social Security taxes should not be withheld.

➤ **Nonminister employees**

If an employee does not qualify as a minister for tax purposes, the organization must withhold and pay FICA and income taxes. Certain FICA tax exceptions are discussed on page 77.

➤ **Nonemployees**

Self-employed recipients of compensation or contractors should receive Form 1099-NEC instead of Form W-2 (if the person has received compensation of at least $600 for the year).

Payroll Tax Withholding

FICA Social Security

Most churches and nonprofit organizations must withhold FICA taxes from their employees' wages and pay them to the IRS along with the employer's share of the tax. Minister-employees are an exception to this rule.

FICA includes both a Social Security and Medicare tax component. In 2020, employers and employees each pay Social Security tax at a rate of 6.2% (12.4% total) on the Social Security wage base of up to $137,700.

The employer and employee also must each pay a 1.45% Medicare tax rate (2.9% total) on all employee wages (unlike Social Security, there is no wage base limit for Medicare tax). Additionally, employers are responsible for withholding an additional 0.9% Medicare tax on all employee wages in excess of $200,000.

Warning

FICA-type Social Security taxes should never be withheld from the compensation of a qualified minister. Ministers are self-employed for Social Security purposes, even when performing ministerial duties for a parachurch organization. They must file Schedule SE to compute self-employment Social Security tax, unless they have opted out of Social Security.

There are a few exceptions to the imposition of FICA. Generally, wages of less than $100 paid to an employee in a calendar year are not subject to FICA. Services excluded from FICA include:

➤ services performed by a minister of a church in the exercise of ministry or by a member of a religious order in the exercise of duties required by the order

➤ services performed in the employ of a church or church-controlled organization that opposes for religious reasons the payment of Social Security taxes (see later discussion of filing Form 8274)

➤ services performed by a student in the employ of a school, college, or university

Churches and church-controlled organizations opposed to Social Security taxes

Very few churches and church-controlled organizations are exempt from payment of FICA taxes. An organization must certify opposition for religious reasons to the payment of employer Social Security taxes.

Organizations in existence on September 30, 1984, were required to file Form 8274 by October 30, 1984, to request exemption from payment of FICA taxes. Any organization created after September 30, 1984, must file before the first date on which a quarterly or annual employment tax return is due from the organization (whichever comes first).

Organizations desiring to revoke their exemption made earlier by filing Form 8274 should file Form 941 with full payment of Social Security taxes for that quarter.

Caution

FICA-type Social Security taxes should *never* be withheld from the salary of a minister-employee. But under a voluntary withholding agreement for ministers' federal income taxes, additional federal income tax may be withheld sufficient to cover the minister's self-employment tax liability. This withholding must be identified as "federal income tax withheld" (not as FICA Social Security taxes withheld).

Federal income tax

Most nonprofit organizations are exempt from the payment of federal income tax on the organization's income (see pages 27-34 for the tax on unrelated business income). But they must withhold and pay federal, state, and local income taxes on the wages paid to each employee. Minister-employees are an exception to this rule.

A minister-employee may have a voluntary withholding agreement with a ministry relating to the minister's income taxes (or he or she may file Form 1040-ES), or both. An agreement to withhold income taxes from wages must be in writing. There is no required form for the agreement. A minister may request voluntary withholding by submitting Form W-4 (Employee's Withholding Allowance Certificate) to the employer, indicating the amount to be withheld, or the written request may be in another format.

Federal income taxes for all employees (except ministers) are calculated based on the chart and tables shown in IRS Publication 15. State and local income taxes are usually required to be withheld according to state withholding tables.

➢ **Form W-4.** All employees, part-time or full-time, must complete a W-4 form (see page 79). (Ministers are an exception to this requirement, unless a voluntary withholding arrangement is used.) Instead of claiming allowances on the new Form W-4 for 2020, employees use the form to provide their employer with the information needed to determine the amount of income tax to withhold.

To get the most accurate withholding, employees should use the IRS's Tax Withholding Estimator when completing Form W-4. Although the withholding system is designed to produce the most accurate withholding possible (*i.e.*, low tax payment or refund when a return is filed), the W-4 form can be tweaked to generate a refund (or larger refund) by adding an additional amount on Line 4c for extra withholding. If an existing employee desires to adjust the amount of tax being withheld, a new W-4 form must be completed.

If an employee qualifies for an exemption, it can be claimed by writing "Exempt" in the space below Line 4c. An exemption is only good for one year, so it must be reclaimed each year by filing a new Form W-4.

Employers are only required to file Forms W-4 with the IRS if directed to do so in a written notice from the IRS.

➢ **Form W-7.** Certain individuals who are not eligible for a Social Security number (SSN) may obtain an individual taxpayer identification number (see page 80). The following individuals may file Form W-7: (1) nonresident aliens who are required to file a U.S. tax return, (2) nonresident aliens who are filing a U.S. tax return only to claim a refund, (3) individuals being claimed as dependents on U.S. tax returns and who are not eligible to obtain a Social Security number, (4) individuals being claimed as husbands or wives for exemptions on U.S. tax returns and who are not eligible to obtain an SSN, and (5) U.S. residents who must file a U.S. tax return but are not eligible for an SSN.

Form **W-4**	**Employee's Withholding Certificate**	OMB No. 1545-0074
Department of the Treasury Internal Revenue Service	▶ Complete Form W-4 so that your employer can withhold the correct federal income tax from your pay. ▶ Give Form W-4 to your employer. ▶ Your withholding is subject to review by the IRS.	2020

Step 1:
Enter Personal Information

(a) First name and middle initial	Last name	(b) Social security number
Walter R.	Knight	511-02-7943

Address
601 Oakridge Boulevard

City or town, state, and ZIP code
Vinton, VA 24179

▶ **Does your name match the name on your social security card?** If not, to ensure you get credit for your earnings, contact SSA at 800-772-1213 or go to www.ssa.gov.

(c) ☐ Single or Married filing separately
   ☒ Married filing jointly (or Qualifying widow(er))
   ☐ Head of household (Check only if you're unmarried and pay more than half the costs of keeping up a home for yourself and a qualifying individual.)

Complete Steps 2–4 ONLY if they apply to you; otherwise, skip to Step 5. See page 2 for more information on each step, who can claim exemption from withholding, when to use the online estimator, and privacy.

Step 2:
Multiple Jobs or Spouse Works

Complete this step if you (1) hold more than one job at a time, or (2) are married filing jointly and your spouse also works. The correct amount of withholding depends on income earned from all of these jobs.

Do **only one** of the following.

(a) Use the estimator at *www.irs.gov/W4App* for most accurate withholding for this step (and Steps 3–4); **or**

(b) Use the Multiple Jobs Worksheet on page 3 and enter the result in Step 4(c) below for roughly accurate withholding; **or**

(c) If there are only two jobs total, you may check this box. Do the same on Form W-4 for the other job. This option is accurate for jobs with similar pay; otherwise, more tax than necessary may be withheld . . . . . ▶ ☐

TIP: To be accurate, submit a 2020 Form W-4 for all other jobs. If you (or your spouse) have self-employment income, including as an independent contractor, use the estimator.

Complete Steps 3–4(b) on Form W-4 for only ONE of these jobs. Leave those steps blank for the other jobs. (Your withholding will be most accurate if you complete Steps 3–4(b) on the Form W-4 for the highest paying job.)

Step 3:
Claim Dependents

If your income will be $200,000 or less ($400,000 or less if married filing jointly):

Multiply the number of qualifying children under age 17 by $2,000 ▶ $ 4000

Multiply the number of other dependents by $500 . . . . ▶ $ 1000

Add the amounts above and enter the total here . . . . **3** $ 5000

Step 4 (optional):
Other Adjustments

(a) **Other income (not from jobs).** If you want tax withheld for other income you expect this year that won't have withholding, enter the amount of other income here. This may include interest, dividends, and retirement income . . . . **4(a)** $

(b) **Deductions.** If you expect to claim deductions other than the standard deduction and want to reduce your withholding, use the Deductions Worksheet on page 3 and enter the result here . . . . **4(b)** $

(c) **Extra withholding.** Enter any additional tax you want withheld each **pay period** . **4(c)** $

Step 5:
Sign Here

Under penalties of perjury, I declare that this certificate, to the best of my knowledge and belief, is true, correct, and complete.

▶ *Walter R. Knight*   ▶ 1/01/20
Employee's signature (This form is not valid unless you sign it.)   Date

Employers Only

Employer's name and address	First date of employment	Employer identification number (EIN)

For Privacy Act and Paperwork Reduction Act Notice, see page 3.   Cat. No. 10220Q   Form **W-4** (2020)

This form must be completed by all lay employees, full- or part-time. The withholding certificate for 2021 expires February 17, 2022. If a minister completes this form, it can be the basis to determine income tax withholding under a voluntary agreement.

79

Form **W-7** (Rev. August 2019) Department of the Treasury Internal Revenue Service	**Application for IRS Individual Taxpayer Identification Number** ▶ For use by individuals who are not U.S. citizens or permanent residents. ▶ See separate instructions.	OMB No. 1545-0074

An IRS individual taxpayer identification number (ITIN) is for U.S. federal tax purposes only.

Before you begin:	Application type (check one box):
• **Don't submit** this form if you have, or are eligible to get, a U.S. social security number (SSN).	☐ Apply for a new ITIN ☒ Renew an existing ITIN

Reason you're submitting Form W-7. Read the instructions for the box you check. **Caution:** If you check box **b, c, d, e, f,** or **g,** you must file a U.S. federal tax return with Form W-7 unless you meet one of the exceptions (see instructions).

a ☐ Nonresident alien required to get an ITIN to claim tax treaty benefit

b ☐ Nonresident alien filing a U.S. federal tax return

c ☒ U.S. resident alien **(based on days present in the United States)** filing a U.S. federal tax return

d ☐ Dependent of U.S. citizen/resident alien ⎤ If **d,** enter relationship to U.S. citizen/resident alien (see instructions) ▶ _____

e ☐ Spouse of U.S. citizen/resident alien ⎦ If **d** or **e,** enter name and SSN/ITIN of U.S. citizen/resident alien (see instructions) ▶ _____

f ☐ Nonresident alien student, professor, or researcher filing a U.S. federal tax return or claiming an exception

g ☐ Dependent/spouse of a nonresident alien holding a U.S. visa

h ☐ Other (see instructions) ▶ _____

Additional information for **a** and **f:** Enter treaty country ▶ _____ and treaty article number ▶ _____

Name (see instructions)	**1a** First name Liam	Middle name Ethan	Last name Martin
Name at birth if different . . ▶	**1b** First name	Middle name	Last name

Applicant's Mailing Address

2 Street address, apartment number, or rural route number. **If you have a P.O. box, see separate instructions.**
1200 Palm Street

City or town, state or province, and country. Include ZIP code or postal code where appropriate.
Sarasota, FL 34234

Foreign (non-U.S.) Address (see instructions)

3 Street address, apartment number, or rural route number. **Don't use a P.O. box number.**
121 Maple Run

City or town, state or province, and country. Include ZIP code or postal code where appropriate.
Toronto, ON M5A 2N4

Birth Information	**4** Date of birth (month / day / year) 06 / 20 / 1975	Country of birth Canada	City and state or province (optional) Toronto, ON	**5** ☒ Male ☐ Female

Other Information	**6a** Country(ies) of citizenship Canada	**6b** Foreign tax I.D. number (if any)	**6c** Type of U.S. visa (if any), number, and expiration date Religious Workers

6d Identification document(s) submitted (see instructions) ☒ Passport ☐ Driver's license/State I.D.

☐ USCIS documentation ☐ Other _____

Issued by: Canada No.: 12345678 Exp. date: 6 / 1 / 2023 Date of entry into the United States (MM/DD/YYYY): 5 / 1 / 2020

6e Have you previously received an ITIN or an Internal Revenue Service Number (IRSN)?

☒ **No/Don't know.** Skip line 6f.

☐ **Yes.** Complete line 6f. If more than one, list on a sheet and attach to this form (see instructions).

6f Enter ITIN and/or IRSN ▶ ITIN ☐☐☐ – ☐☐ – ☐☐☐☐ IRSN ☐☐☐ – ☐☐ – ☐☐☐☐ and name under which it was issued ▶ _____

First name	Middle name	Last name

6g Name of college/university or company (see instructions) ▶ First Baptist Church

City and state ▶ Sarasota, FL Length of stay ▶ 6 months

Sign Here

Under penalties of perjury, I (applicant/delegate/acceptance agent) declare that I have examined this application, including accompanying documentation and statements, and to the best of my knowledge and belief, it is true, correct, and complete. I authorize the IRS to share information with my acceptance agent in order to perfect this Form W-7, Application for IRS Individual Taxpayer Identification Number.

Keep a copy for your records.

Signature of applicant (if delegate, see instructions) *Liam Ethan Martin*	Date (month / day / year) 5 / 1 / 20	Phone number 914-123-1234
Name of delegate, if applicable (type or print)	Delegate's relationship to applicant	☐ Parent ☐ Court-appointed guardian ☐ Power of attorney

Acceptance Agent's Use ONLY

Signature	Date (month / day / year) / /	Phone Fax
Name and title (type or print)	Name of company	EIN Office code	PTIN

For Paperwork Reduction Act Notice, see separate instructions.   Cat. No. 10229L   Form **W-7** (Rev. 8-2019)

Personal liability for payroll taxes

Ministry officers and employees may be personally liable if payroll taxes are not withheld and paid to the IRS. If the organization has willfully failed to withhold and pay the taxes, the IRS has the authority to assess a 100% penalty of withheld income and Social Security taxes.

This penalty may be assessed against the individual responsible for withholding and paying the taxes, even if the person is an unpaid volunteer such as a church treasurer. The penalty assessed against that person could be the total that should have been withheld for *all* paid employees.

Remember

A new organization (or one filing payroll tax returns for the first time) will be required to file monthly until a "look-back period" is established. A look-back period begins on July 1 and ends on June 30 of the preceding calendar year.

Depositing Withheld Payroll Taxes

The basic rules for depositing withheld payroll taxes are as follows:

➢ If your total accumulated and unpaid employment tax (income tax withheld, FICA tax withheld and matched by the organization) is less than $2,500 in a calendar quarter, taxes can be paid directly to the IRS when the organization files Form 941. These forms are due one month after the end of each calendar quarter.

➢ If payroll taxes are over $2,500 for a quarter, payroll tax deposits must be made monthly or before the 15th day of each month for the payroll paid during the preceding month. Large organizations with total employment taxes of over $50,000 per year are subject to more frequent deposits.

Only very small organizations are exempted from depositing electronically—employers with $2,500 or less in quarterly employment taxes can pay their liability by check when filing their form 941 returns. All other coupon users must switch to making deposits by wire using the Treasury's Electronic Federal Tax Payment System (EFTPS): *www.eftps.gov* or call 800-555-3453.

Filing Quarterly Payroll Tax Forms

Employers must report covered wages paid to their employees by filing Form 941, Employer's Quarterly Federal Tax Return, with the IRS.

Form 941

Church and other nonprofit employers that withhold income tax and both Social Security and medicare taxes must file Form 941 quarterly (see page 83). There is no requirement to file Form 941 for organizations if they have not been required to withhold payroll taxes even if they have one or more minister-employees. However, if the *only* employee is a minister and voluntary federal income tax has been withheld, Form 941 must be filed.

Most common errors made on Form 941

The IRS has outlined the most common errors discovered during the processing of Form 941 and the best ways to avoid making these mistakes.

There is a checklist for avoiding common errors:

> ➤ Do not include titles or abbreviations, such as Dr., Mr., or Mrs.

> ➤ On Line 2, do not include amounts designated as housing allowance for qualified ministers.

> ➤ Make sure that taxable Social Security wages and the Social Security tax on Line 5a and

Idea

Do not file more than one Form 941 per quarter even if you deposit payroll taxes monthly. If you have multiple locations or divisions, you still must file only one Form 941 per quarter. Filing more than one return may result in processing delays and require correspondence with the IRS.

the taxable Medicare wages and the Medicare tax on Line 5c are reported separately. Most employers will need to complete both Lines 5a and 5c.

> ➤ The preprinted form sent by the IRS should be used. If the return is prepared by a third-party preparer, make certain that the preparer uses exactly the name that appears on the preprinted form that was sent.

> ➤ Check the math for Lines 5e, 10, and 12.

> ➤ Make sure the Social Security tax on Line 5a is calculated correctly (Social Security wages x 12.4%).

> ➤ Make sure the Medicare tax on Line 5c is calculated correctly (Medicare wages x 2.9%).

> ➤ Be sure to use the most recent Form 941 sent by the IRS. The IRS enters the date the quarter ended after the employer identification number. If the form is used for a later quarter, the IRS will have to contact the employer.

> ➤ Make sure there is never an entry on both Lines 14 and 15. There cannot be a balance due and a refund.

Page 1 (left)

950117

Form **941 for 2020:** Employer's QUARTERLY Federal Tax Return
(Rev. January 2020) — Department of the Treasury — Internal Revenue Service
OMB No. 1545-0029

Employer identification number (EIN) 3 5 – 2 0 1 7 8 8 3

Name (not your trade name) Barnett Ridge Church

Trade name (if any)

Address PO Box 517
Number   Street   Suite or room number
Selma   AL   36704
City   State   ZIP code

Foreign country name   Foreign province/county   Foreign postal code

Report for this Quarter of 2020
(Check one.)
☒ 1: January, February, March
☐ 2: April, May, June
☐ 3: July, August, September
☐ 4: October, November, December
Go to www.irs.gov/Form941 for instructions and the latest information.

Read the separate instructions before you complete Form 941. Type or print within the boxes.

Part 1: Answer these questions for this quarter.

1 Number of employees who received wages, tips, or other compensation for the pay period including: Mar. 12 (Quarter 1), June 12 (Quarter 2), Sept. 12 (Quarter 3), or Dec. 12 (Quarter 4) ... **1** 1

2 Wages, tips, and other compensation ... **2** 24,811 .

3 Federal income tax withheld from wages, tips, and other compensation ... **3** 4,642 .

4 If no wages, tips, and other compensation are subject to social security or Medicare tax ☐ Check and go to line 6.

	Column 1		Column 2
5a Taxable social security wages .	16,340 .	× 0.124 =	2,026 .
5b Taxable social security tips .	.	× 0.124 =	.
5c Taxable Medicare wages & tips .	16,340 .	× 0.029 =	474 .
5d Taxable wages & tips subject to Additional Medicare Tax withholding	.	× 0.009 =	.

5e Add Column 2 from lines 5a, 5b, 5c, and 5d ... **5e** 2,500 .

5f Section 3121(q) Notice and Demand—Tax due on unreported tips (see instructions) ... **5f**

6 Total taxes before adjustments. Add lines 3, 5e, and 5f ... **6** 7,142 .

7 Current quarter's adjustment for fractions of cents ... **7** .

8 Current quarter's adjustment for sick pay ... **8** .

9 Current quarter's adjustments for tips and group-term life insurance ... **9** .

10 Total taxes after adjustments. Combine lines 6 through 9 ... **10** 7,142 .

11 Qualified small business payroll tax credit for increasing research activities. Attach Form 8974 ... **11** .

12 Total taxes after adjustments and credits. Subtract line 11 from line 10 ... **12** 7,142 .

13 Total deposits for this quarter, including overpayment applied from a prior quarter and overpayments applied from Form 941-X, 941-X (PR), 944-X, or 944-X (SP) filed in the current quarter ... **13** 7,142 .

14 Balance due. If line 12 is more than line 13, enter the difference and see instructions ... **14** 0 .

15 Overpayment. If line 13 is more than line 12, enter the difference . Check one: ☐ Apply to next return. ☐ Send a refund.

► You MUST complete both pages of Form 941 and SIGN it.   Next ►

For Privacy Act and Paperwork Reduction Act Notice, see the back of the Payment Voucher.   Cat. No. 17001Z   Form **941** (Rev. 1-2020)

Page 2 (right)

950217

Name (not your trade name) Barnett Ridge Church   Employer identification number (EIN) 35 - 2017883

Part 2: Tell us about your deposit schedule and tax liability for this quarter.

If you are unsure about whether you are a monthly schedule depositor or a semiweekly schedule depositor, see section 11 of Pub. 15.

16 Check one:
☐ Line 12 on this return is less than $2,500 or line 12 on the return for the prior quarter was less than $2,500, and you didn't incur a $100,000 next-day deposit obligation during the current quarter. If line 12 for the prior quarter was less than $2,500 but line 12 on this return is $100,000 or more, you must provide a record of your federal tax liability. If you are a monthly schedule depositor, complete the deposit schedule below; if you are a semiweekly schedule depositor, attach Schedule B (Form 941). Go to Part 3.

☒ You were a monthly schedule depositor for the entire quarter. Enter your tax liability for each month and total liability for the quarter, then go to Part 3.

Tax liability: Month 1 2,201 .
               Month 2 2,493 .
               Month 3 2,448 .

Total liability for quarter 7,142 . Total must equal line 12.

☐ You were a semiweekly schedule depositor for any part of this quarter. Complete Schedule B (Form 941), Report of Tax Liability for Semiweekly Schedule Depositors, and attach it to Form 941.

Part 3: Tell us about your business. If a question does NOT apply to your business, leave it blank.

17 If your business has closed or you stopped paying wages ... ☐ Check here, and
enter the final date you paid wages

18 If you are a seasonal employer and you don't have to file a return for every quarter of the year ... ☐ Check here.

Part 4: May we speak with your third-party designee?

Do you want to allow an employee, a paid tax preparer, or another person to discuss this return with the IRS? See the instructions for details.

☐ Yes. Designee's name and phone number

Select a 5-digit Personal Identification Number (PIN) to use when talking to the IRS.

☐ No.

Part 5: Sign here. You MUST complete both pages of Form 941 and SIGN it.

Under penalties of perjury, I declare that I have examined this return, including accompanying schedules and statements, and to the best of my knowledge and belief, it is true, correct, and complete. Declaration of preparer (other than taxpayer) is based on all information of which preparer has any knowledge.

Sign your name here [signature: David Baker]

Print your name here David Baker
Print your title here Office Manager

Date 4 /15/ 20   Best daytime phone 334-873-1754

Paid Preparer Use Only   Check if you are self-employed ☐

Preparer's name   PTIN
Preparer's signature   Date / /
Firm's name (or yours if self-employed) EIN
Address   Phone
City   State ZIP code

Page 2   Form **941** (Rev. 1-2019)

File this form to report Social Security (FICA) and Medicare taxes and federal income tax withheld.

```
Form 941-X:    Adjusted Employer's QUARTERLY Federal Tax Return or Claim for Refund
(Rev. October 2020)           Department of the Treasury — Internal Revenue Service          OMB No. 1545-0029

Employer identification number    3  5  –  6  3  0  9  2  9  4
(EIN)

Name (not your trade name)    Little Valley Church

Trade name (if any)

Address    4865 Douglas Road
           Number    Street                              Suite or room number

           Springfield                         OH     45504
           City                                State     ZIP code

           Foreign country name          Foreign province/county     Foreign postal code
```

Return You're Correcting...
Check the type of return you're correcting.
- [X] 941
- [ ] 941-SS

Check the ONE quarter you're correcting.
- [X] 1: January, February, March
- [ ] 2: April, May, June
- [ ] 3: July, August, September
- [ ] 4: October, November, December

Enter the calendar year of the quarter you're correcting.
2020 (YYYY)

Enter the date you discovered errors.
05 / 10 / 2020
(MM / DD / YYYY)

Read the separate instructions before completing this form. Use this form to correct errors you made on Form 941 or 941-SS. Use a separate Form 941-X for each quarter that needs correction. Type or print within the boxes. You MUST complete all four pages. Don't attach this form to Form 941 or 941-SS unless you're reclassifying workers; see the instructions for line 36.

Part 1:   Select ONLY one process. See page 5 for additional guidance.

[X] 1.   **Adjusted employment tax return.** Check this box if you underreported amounts. Also check this box if you overreported amounts and you would like to use the adjustment process to correct the errors. You must check this box if you're correcting both underreported and overreported amounts on this form. The amount shown on line 27, if less than zero, may only be applied as a credit to your Form 941, Form 941-SS, or Form 944 for the tax period in which you're filing this form.

Use this form to correct income, Social Security (FICA), and Medicare tax information reported on Form 941. It may be necessary to issue Form W-2c to employees relating to prior year data. The Form 941-X has three pages.

Filing Annual Payroll Tax Forms

Form W-2

By January 31, each employee must be given a Form W-2 (see page 87). Be sure to reconcile the data reflected on Forms W-2, W-3, and 941 before distributing Forms W-2 to employees. If these forms do not reconcile, the IRS generally sends a letter to the employer requesting additional information.

Make all entries without a dollar sign or comma but with a decimal point and cents (do not use whole dollars).

Void. Put an X in this box when an error has been made on this W-2.

Box 1 – Wages, tips, other compensation. Items to include in Box 1 (before any payroll deductions) are:

➢   total wages paid during the year (including love offerings paid by the church or nonprofit organization to a minister or other employee)

➢   the value of any noncash payments

➤ business expense payments under a *nonaccountable* plan

➤ payments of per diems or mileage rates paid for business expense purposes that exceed the IRS-specified rates

➤ payments made by a ministry to an employee's Individual Retirement Account

➤ payments of or for moving expenses

➤ all other compensation, including taxable fringe benefits ("other compensation" represents amounts a ministry pays to an employee from which federal income tax is not withheld. If you prefer, you may show other compensation on a separate Form W-2.)

➤ the cash housing allowance or the fair market rental value of housing and utilities for lay employees (non-ministerial employees), unless lodging is furnished on the employer's premises and the employee is required to accept the lodging as a condition of employment

Exclude the following:

➤ the fair rental value of a church-provided parsonage or a properly designated housing allowance for ministers

➤ business expense reimbursements paid through an *accountable* expense plan

Remember

One of an employer's primary challenges is to determine if all of an employee's compensation is reported on Form W-2. Taxable compensation that is often erroneously omitted includes life insurance premiums paid for the employee (only group-term life up to $50,000 is tax-free) and nonaccountable expense allowances (only expenses reimbursed under an accountable plan are tax-free).

➤ contributions to 403(b) tax-sheltered annuities or 401(k) plans (Roth contributions not excluded)

Box 2 – Federal income tax withheld. Enter the total federal income tax withheld according to the chart and tables in IRS Publication 15.

A minister-employee may enter into a voluntary withholding arrangement with the ministry. Based on Form W-4 or other written withholding request, federal income tax withholding may be calculated from the chart and tables in Publication 15, excluding any housing allowance amount.

The minister may request that an additional amount of income tax be withheld to cover self-employment tax. The additional amount withheld is reported as income tax withheld on the quarterly Form 941 and in Box 2 of Form W-2.

A ministry that provides additional compensation to the minister-employee to cover part or all of the self-employment tax liability:

➤ may pay the additional compensation directly to the IRS and enter that amount on the ministry's Form 941 and in Boxes 1 and 2 of Form W-2, or

➤ may pay the additional compensation to the minister, with the minister being responsible for remitting the amounts to the IRS with a Form 1040-ES. If this procedure is followed, the ministry reports this amount only as additional compensation on Form 941 and only in Box 1 of Form W-2.

Box 3 – Social Security wages. Show the total wages paid (before payroll deductions) subject to employee Social Security tax (FICA). This amount must not exceed $137,700 in 2020 (the maximum Social Security tax wage base). Include nonaccountable employee business expenses reported in Box 1. Generally, all cash and noncash payments reported in Box 1 must also be shown in Box 3. Section 403(b) voluntary salary reduction contributions for nonminister employees are included in Box 3, as are Roth contributions.

Checklist for Completing Box 1 of Form W-2

Minister Only	Both	Nonminister Only	
			Data Included for
yes			Salary
no		yes	Housing/furnishings allowance (designated in advance)
no		yes	Parsonage rental value
no		yes	Parsonage utilities paid by church or nonprofit
	yes		Social Security/Medicare "allowance" or reimbursement
	no		Transportation/travel and other business and professional expense reimbursements only if paid under a board-adopted accountable reimbursement plan
	yes		Expense reimbursements if *not* paid under an accountable reimbursement plan
	yes		Love offerings or cash gifts in excess of $25 total
	no		Contributions to a tax-sheltered annuity plan
	no		Group qualified health/dental/long-term care insurance premiums paid directly by the employer
	no		Group-term life insurance premiums (for up to $50,000 coverage) paid directly by the employer
	yes		Moving expenses paid for or reimbursed to an employee
	yes		Value of personal/nonbusiness use of organization's vehicle

Box 3 should be blank for a qualified minister (an individual who meets the ministerial factors of the IRS).

Box 4 – Social Security tax withheld. Show the total FICA Social Security tax (not including the ministry's share) withheld (or paid by the ministry) for the employee. The amount shown must equal 6.2% of the amount in Box 3 and must not exceed $8,537.40 for 2020. Do not include the employer portion of FICA tax (6.2%).

Some ministries pay the employee's share of FICA tax for some or all nonminister employees instead of deducting it from the employee's wages. These amounts paid by the organization must be included in Boxes 1, 3, and 5.

Box 4 should be blank for qualified ministers. Any amount of withholding to meet the minister's SECA tax liability must be reported in Box 2, not in Box 4 or Box 6.

Box 5 – Medicare wages. The wages subject to Medicare tax are the same as those subject to Social Security tax (Box 3), except there is no wage limit for the Medicare tax.

Example: In 2020, a *nonminister employee* is paid wages of $140,000. The amount shown in Box 3 (Social Security wages) should be $137,700, but the amount

22222 VOID □	**a** Employee's social security number 517-38-6451	For Official Use Only ▶ OMB No. 1545-0008	
b Employer identification number (EIN) 35-2948039		**1** Wages, tips, other compensation 93800.00	**2** Federal income tax withheld 7000.00
c Employer's name, address, and ZIP code		**3** Social security wages 95000.00	**4** Social security tax withheld 5890.00
ABC Charity 2870 North Hull Road Traverse City, MI 49615		**5** Medicare wages and tips 95000.00	**6** Medicare tax withheld 1377.50
		7 Social security tips	**8** Allocated tips
d Control number		**9**	**10** Dependent care benefits
e Employee's first name and initial Michael A Last name Black Suff.		**11** Nonqualified plans	**12a** See instructions for box 12 E 1200.00
15550 Cleveland Avenue Traverse City, MI 49615		**13** Statutory employee □ Retirement plan □ Third-party sick pay □	**12b**
		14 Other	**12c**
			12d
f Employee's address and ZIP code			
15 State Employer's state ID number MI 6309294	**16** State wages, tips, etc. 93800.00	**17** State income tax 700.00	**18** Local wages, tips, etc. **19** Local income tax **20** Locality name

Form **W-2** Wage and Tax Statement   **2020**   Department of the Treasury—Internal Revenue Service

Copy A—For Social Security Administration. Send this entire page with Form W-3 to the Social Security Administration; photocopies are **not** acceptable.

For Privacy Act and Paperwork Reduction Act Notice, see the separate instructions.

Cat. No. 10134D

Do Not Cut, Fold, or Staple Forms on This Page

Form W-2 must be filed for each employee who received taxable compensation or for whom income tax or FICA-type Social Security tax was withheld. The example shown above is for a lay employee.

shown in Box 5 (Medicare wages) should be $140,000. If the wages are less than $137,700, the amounts entered in Boxes 3 and 5 will be the same.

Box 5 should be blank for qualified ministers. Nonaccountable business expense reimbursements for lay employees are included in Box 5. Section 403(b) salary reduction contributions for nonminister employees are included in Box 5, as are Roth contributions.

Box 6 – Medicare tax withheld. Enter the total employee Medicare tax (not the ministry's share) withheld or paid by the ministry for the employee. The amount shown must equal 1.45% of the amount in Box 5. Box 6 should be blank for qualified ministers.

Box 9 – Advance EIC payment. Show the total paid to the employee as advance earned income credit payments.

Box 10 – Dependent care benefits. Show the total amount of dependent care benefits under Section 129 paid or incurred by the organization for the employee, including any amount over the $5,000 exclusion. Also include in Box 1, Box 3, and Box 5 any amount over the $5,000 exclusion.

Box 11 – Nonqualified plans. Enter the total amount of distributions to the employee from a nonqualified deferred compensation plan. Nonqualified plans do not include a tax-sheltered annuity or a "Rabbi Trust." Include an amount in Box 11 only if it is also includible in Box 1 or Boxes 3 and 5.

Box 12 – Additional entries. The following items are most frequently inserted in Box 12 by churches and other nonprofit organizations:

C – If the organization provided the employee more than $50,000 of group-term life insurance, show the cost of the premiums for coverage over $50,000. Also include the amount in Box 1 (also in Boxes 3 and 5 if a lay employee).

DD – Cost of employer-provided health coverage. This data is required for employers issuing Form W-2 to 250 or more employees.

E – Section 403(b) voluntary salary deferrals are shown in Box 12 with code E for pre-tax amounts and code BB for Roth amounts. This amount would not be included in Box 1 for either ministers or lay employees. This amount *would* be included in Boxes 3 and 5 for a lay employee.

L – Generally, payments made under an accountable plan are excluded from the employee's gross income and are not required to be reported on Form W-2. But if the organization pays a per diem or mileage rate, and the amount paid exceeds any amount substantiated under IRS rules, wages must be reported on Form W-2, (the amount in excess of the amount substantiated). Report the amount substantiated (the nontaxable portion) in Box 12. In Box 1, show the portion of the reimbursement that is more than the amount treated as substantiated. For lay employees the excess amount is subject to income tax withholding, Social Security tax, Medicare tax, and possibly federal unemployment tax.

> *Example 1:* An employee is paid for business mileage at the rate of 57.5 cents per mile for 2020 and substantiates the business miles driven to the organization. The mileage reimbursement is not reported on Form W-2.

> *Example 2:* An employee receives a mileage allowance of $2,000 per year and does not substantiate the business miles driven. The $2,000 allowance is includible in Box 1 as compensation for a minister, and Boxes 1, 3, and 5 for a lay employee.

Payments made to *nonminister employees* under a nonaccountable plan are reportable as wages on Form W-2 and are subject to income tax withholding, Social Security tax, Medicare tax, and possibly federal unemployment tax.

Payments made to *minister-employees* under a nonaccountable plan are reportable as wages on Form W-2 and may be subject to income tax withholding under a voluntary agreement, but they are not subject to mandatory withholding or Social Security (FICA) or Medicare tax.

R – Employer contributions to an Archer medical savings account.

S – Salary reductions to a savings incentive match plan for employees with a SIMPLE retirement account.

T – Employer payments under an adoption assistance plan.

Y – Deferrals under a section 409A nonqualified deferred compensation plan.

Z – Income under a section 409A nonqualified deferred compensation plan.

Box 13 – Check the appropriate boxes. The box that may apply to employees of ministries is the retirement plan box. Mark this check box if the employee was an active participant (for any part of the year) in any of the following: (1) a qualified pension plan described in section 401(a), including a 401(k) plan; (2) an annuity plan described in section 403(a); (3) an annuity contract or custodial account described in section 403(b); or (4) a simplified employee pension (SEP) plan described in section 408(k).

Filing Tip

The minister's housing allowance could be included in Box 14 with the words "Housing Allowance." However, some employers prefer to provide the minister with a separate statement reflecting the housing allowance amount.

Box 14 – Other. You may use this box for any other information the employer wishes to provide to an employee. Label each item and include information such as health insurance premiums deducted or educational assistance payments.

If a ministry owns or leases a vehicle for an employee's use, the value of the personal use of the vehicle is taxable income. The value of the use of the vehicle is established by using one of the methods described on pages 58-60. The amount of the personal use must be included in Box 1 (and in Boxes 3 and 5 if a lay employee) or on a separate statement to the employee. The employee is required to maintain a mileage log or similar records to substantiate business and personal use of the vehicle and submit this to the employer. If its use is not substantiated, the employer must report 100% of the use of the vehicle as taxable income.

Caution

Do not include any per diem or mileage allowance or other reimbursements for employee business expenses under an accountable plan in Boxes 1 or 14 if the total reimbursement is less than or equal to the amount substantiated.

If the employee fully reimburses the employer for the value of the personal use of the vehicle, then no value would be reported in either Box 1 or in Box 14. Reimbursement of the amount spent for gas on personal trips does not constitute a reimbursement of the full value of the personal use of the vehicle.

Form W-3

A Form W-3 (see page 91) is submitted to the IRS as a transmittal form with Forms W-2. Form W-3 and all attached W-2s must be submitted to the Social Security Administration Center by January 31. No money is sent with Form W-3.

Forms W-2c and W-3c

Use Form W-2c (see page 91) to correct errors on a previously filed Form W-2. Use Form W-3c to transmit *corrected* W-2c forms to the Social Security Administration. If you are correcting only an employee's name or Social Security number, you do not have to file Form W-3c with Form W-2c. File Forms W-2c and W-3c as soon as possible after you discover an error. Also provide Form W-2c to employees as soon as possible.

Wages paid in error in a prior year remain taxable to the employee for that year. This is because the employee received and had use of those funds during that year. The employee is not entitled to file an amended return (Form 1040X) to recover the income tax on these wages. Instead, the employee is entitled to a deduction for the repaid wages on his or her Form 1040 for the year of repayment.

DO NOT STAPLE

33333	a Control number	For Official Use Only ▶ OMB No. 1545-0008	

b Kind of Payer (Check one): 941 [X] Military [ ] 943 [ ] 944 [ ] CT-1 [ ] Hshld. emp. [ ] Medicare govt. emp. [ ]

Kind of Employer (Check one): None apply [ ] 501c non-govt. [X] State/local non-501c [ ] State/local 501c [ ] Federal govt. [ ]

Third-party sick pay (Check if applicable) [ ]

c Total number of Forms W-2 **20**	d Establishment number	1 Wages, tips, other compensation **243987.00**
		2 Federal income tax withheld **39142.00**
e Employer identification number (EIN) **35-2948039**		3 Social security wages **236431.00**
		4 Social security tax withheld **14659.00**
f Employer's name **ABC Charity**		5 Medicare wages and tips **243987.00**
		6 Medicare tax withheld **3538.00**

**2870 North Hull Road
Traverse City, MI 49615**

7 Social security tips	8 Allocated tips
9	10 Dependent care benefits
11 Nonqualified plans	12a Deferred compensation

g Employer's address and ZIP code

h Other EIN used this year	13 For third-party sick pay use only	12b

15 State **MI** Employer's state ID number **6309294**	14 Income tax withheld by payer of third-party sick pay
16 State wages, tips, etc. **243987.00** 17 State income tax **4387.00**	18 Local wages, tips, etc. 19 Local income tax

Employer's contact person **Daniel L. Lewis**	Employer's telephone number **231-435-2201**	For Official Use Only
Employer's fax number **231-435-2205**	Employer's email address **dlewis@gmail.com**	

Under penalties of perjury, I declare that I have examined this return and accompanying documents, and, to the best of my knowledge and belief, they are true, correct, and complete.

Signature ▶ *Daniel L. Lewis*   Title ▶ **Treasurer**   Date ▶ **1/31/21**

Form **W-3** Transmittal of Wage and Tax Statements   **2020**   Department of the Treasury Internal Revenue Service

Form W-3 is the "cover sheet" or transmittal form for all Forms W-2.

DO NOT CUT, FOLD, OR STAPLE THIS FORM

44444	For Official Use Only ▶ OMB No. 1545-0008

a Employer's name, address, and ZIP code	c Tax year/Form corrected **2020 / W-2** d Employee's correct SSN **404-82-1034**

**Little Valley Church
4865 Douglas Road
Springfield, OH 45504**

e Corrected SSN and/or name (Check this box and complete boxes f and/or g if incorrect on form previously filed.) [ ]

Complete boxes f and/or g only if incorrect on form **previously filed** ▶

f Employee's **previously reported** SSN

b Employer's Federal EIN **35-6309294**

g Employee's **previously reported** name

h Employee's first name and initial **Norman R.**   Last name **Tice**   Suff.

**418 Trenton Street
Springfield, OH 45504**

i Employee's address and ZIP code

Note. Only complete money fields that are being corrected (exception: for corrections involving MQGE, see the General Instructions for Forms W-2 and W-3, under Specific Instructions for Form W-2c, boxes 5 and 6).

Previously reported	Correct information	Previously reported	Correct information
1 Wages, tips, other compensation **10000.00**	1 Wages, tips, other compensation **12500.00**	2 Federal income tax withheld **4800.00**	2 Federal income tax withheld **2000.00**
3 Social security wages **10000.00**	3 Social security wages **12500.00**	4 Social security tax withheld **820.00**	4 Social security tax withheld **775.00**
5 Medicare wages and tips **10000.00**	5 Medicare wages and tips **12500.00**	6 Medicare tax withheld **145.00**	6 Medicare tax withheld **181.25**
7 Social security tips	7 Social security tips	8 Allocated tips	8 Allocated tips
9	9	10 Dependent care benefits	10 Dependent care benefits
11 Nonqualified plans	11 Nonqualified plans	12a See instructions for box 12	12a See instructions for box 12
13 Statutory employee Retirement plan Third-party sick pay	13 Statutory employee Retirement plan Third-party sick pay	12b	12b

Form W-2c is used to submit changes to data previously filed on Form W-2.

Unemployment taxes

The federal and state unemployment systems provide temporary unemployment compensation to workers who have lost their jobs. Employers provide the revenue for this program by paying federal unemployment taxes, under the Federal Unemployment Tax Act (FUTA), as well as state unemployment taxes. These are strictly employer taxes, and no deductions are taken from employees' wages.

Ministries are generally not required to pay federal unemployment tax (FUTA). The instructions for Form 940, the form used to report and pay FUTA tax, states: "Religious, educational, scientific, charitable, and other organizations described in section 501(a) are not subject to FUTA tax and do not have to file Form 940." *Note:* Ministries that operate a for-profit school or day care may be required by state law to pay unemployment taxes or provide unemployment benefits in some states.

A few states require religious nonprofit organizations to pay state unemployment taxes, but most states provide an exemption for churches. However, the current federal unemployment tax law exempts from coverage (based on a 1970 amendment):

➢ services performed "in the employment of a church, a convention, or an association of churches, or an organization that is operated primarily for religious purposes or that is operated, supervised, or controlled or principally supported by a church or convention or association of churches"

➢ services performed by an "ordained, commissioned, or licensed minister of a church in the exercise of ministry, or by a member of a religious order in the exercise of duties required by such order." (*Note:* The exemption is not limited to employees performing strictly religious duties.)

➢ services are generally exempt when performed in the employment of an unincorporated elementary or secondary school controlled by a church

➢ services performed in the employment of an incorporated religious elementary or secondary school if it is operated primarily for religious purposes and is operated, supervised, controlled, or principally supported by a church, a convention, or an association of churches

➢ services performed in the employment of an elementary or secondary school that is operated primarily for religious purposes and *is not* operated, supervised, controlled, or principally supported by a church, a convention, or an association of churches

In many states, exemption is also provided for:

➤ services performed in the employment of a separately incorporated church school if the school is operated primarily for religious purposes and is operated, supervised, controlled, or principally supported by a church, a convention, or an association of churches

While it may be possible for an otherwise exempt church, convention, or association of churches to voluntarily pay state unemployment taxes, this rarely occurs.

Unemployment reporting requirements

Organizations that are liable for FUTA taxes (generally, those other than 501(c)(3) organizations) are required to file Form 940, or 940-EZ Employer's Annual Federal Unemployment Tax Return, due on January 31, if *either* one of the following tests apply.

➤ The organization paid wages of $1,500 or more in any calendar quarter in the current or prior year.

➤ The organization had one or more employees for at least some part of a day in any 20 or more different weeks in the current or prior year.

Although Form 940 covers a calendar year, the organization may have to make deposits of the tax before filing the return. Generally, deposit FUTA tax quarterly if the FUTA tax exceeds $500.

The taxable wage base under FUTA is $7,000 for 2020. (The state wage base may be different.) The tax applies to the first $7,000 paid to each employee as wages during the year. For example, if there was only one employee for the year and the salary was $20,000, only $7,000 is subject to FUTA. The gross FUTA tax rate is 6.0% for 2020.

Generally, organizations can take a credit against the FUTA tax for amounts paid into the state unemployment funds. This credit cannot be more than 5.4% of taxable wages. Moreover, the credit is reduced for organizations that have not repaid loans from the federal jobless fund.

Use Form 940 or 940-EZ to report this tax. The organization may be able to use Form 940-EZ instead of Form 940 if (1) unemployment taxes ("contributions") were paid to only one state, (2) state unemployment taxes were paid by the due date of Form 940 or 940-EZ, and (3) all wages that were taxable for FUTA tax purposes were also taxable for the state's unemployment tax.

- **Worker classification issues.** Classifying workers correctly is very important in the minds of two important federal government agencies: the Department of Labor (DOL) and the IRS. The DOL's interest relates to being sure workers who are employees are classified as such because of the implications for the Fair Labor Standards Act (minimum wage and overtime), workers' compensation, and other fringe benefit purposes. The IRS wants to see federal income tax and FICA-type Social Security tax (for lay employees) withheld for all workers who qualify as employees.

  Too often ministries make a decision on employee versus independent contractor based on what the FICA Social Security cost (and perhaps other paperwork costs) will be for the organization. Actually, the Social Security cost factor has no relationship to an appropriate employee versus independent contractor decision. Integrity requires proper evaluation of worker classification to ensure workers receive the benefits to which they are entitled.

  Many states have also taken a more strict approach to worker classification, making it more difficult for ministries to legitimately classify workers as independent contractors.

- **Ministers and Social Security.** One of the most common mistakes made by ministries is to withhold FICA-type Social Security tax from a qualified minister. The employing organization may inappropriately give a minister a choice (of FICA withholding or paying their own Social Security). A minister may also inappropriately request that FICA tax be withheld because it was done this way by a previous employer. Unfortunately, there is no choice on this issue.

  Qualified ministers must pay their own Social Security by completing Schedule SE, filed with their Form 1040. If an employer withholds and matches FICA-type Social Security tax from the pay of a minister, then it has not correctly reported the minister's taxable compensation, because the matched portion of the FICA tax escapes income tax when it is fully taxable for a minister. Ministries must apply these rules with integrity, sometimes in spite of pressure from employees to do otherwise.

Information Reporting

Beyond the employer-reporting issues discussed in detail in the previous chapter, there are other information reporting requirements to the IRS that apply for almost all churches and other nonprofit organizations.

These are three key issues to consider for information reporting:

➤ **Classifying payments to workers.** An organization generally makes many payments to individuals providing services to the organization. Some of the recipient individuals are employees (discussed in Chapter 4) and others are independent contractors. The organization must first determine which workers are independent contractors before reporting information with respect to these workers. Payments of $600 or more in a calendar year to an independent contractor triggers filing Form 1099-NEC.

➤ **Information filing for other payments.** Certain payments other than to independent contractors also trigger information reporting such as payments of interest or royalties and payments to annuitants and nonresident aliens.

➤ **Information filing for receipt of funds.** The receipt of certain funds may trigger information reporting such as the receipt of interest on mortgages.

General Filing Requirements

Information returns (Forms 1098 and 1099) must be provided to the payees/recipients on or before January 31 following the calendar year that the funds were paid or received.

Form **W-9**
(Rev. October 2018)
Department of the Treasury
Internal Revenue Service

**Request for Taxpayer
Identification Number and Certification**

► Go to *www.irs.gov/FormW9* for instructions and the latest information.

Give Form to the requester. Do not send to the IRS.

1 Name (as shown on your income tax return). Name is required on this line; do not leave this line blank.
Richard K. Bennett

2 Business name/disregarded entity name, if different from above

3 Check appropriate box for federal tax classification of the person whose name is entered on line 1. Check only **one** of the following seven boxes.

[X] Individual/sole proprietor or single-member LLC   [ ] C Corporation   [ ] S Corporation   [ ] Partnership   [ ] Trust/estate

[ ] Limited liability company. Enter the tax classification (C=C corporation, S=S corporation, P=Partnership) ►

Note: Check the appropriate box in the line above for the tax classification of the single-member owner. Do not check LLC if the LLC is classified as a single-member LLC that is disregarded from the owner unless the owner of the LLC is another LLC that is **not** disregarded from the owner for U.S. federal tax purposes. Otherwise, a single-member LLC that is disregarded from the owner should check the appropriate box for the tax classification of its owner.

[ ] Other (see instructions) ►

4 Exemptions (codes apply only to certain entities, not individuals; see instructions on page 3):

Exempt payee code (if any) _____

Exemption from FATCA reporting code (if any) _____

(Applies to accounts maintained outside the U.S.)

5 Address (number, street, and apt. or suite no.) See instructions.
829 Garner Street

6 City, state, and ZIP code
Thomasville, SC 27360

7 List account number(s) here (optional)

Requester's name and address (optional)

Part I   Taxpayer Identification Number (TIN)

Enter your TIN in the appropriate box. The TIN provided must match the name given on line 1 to avoid backup withholding. For individuals, this is generally your social security number (SSN). However, for a resident alien, sole proprietor, or disregarded entity, see the instructions for Part I, later. For other entities, it is your employer identification number (EIN). If you do not have a number, see *How to get a TIN*, later.

Note: If the account is in more than one name, see the instructions for line 1. Also see *What Name and Number To Give the Requester* for guidelines on whose number to enter.

Social security number
4 0 3 — 9 9 — 1 2 9 7

or

Employer identification number

Part II   Certification

Under penalties of perjury, I certify that:

1. The number shown on this form is my correct taxpayer identification number (or I am waiting for a number to be issued to me); and
2. I am not subject to backup withholding because: (a) I am exempt from backup withholding, or (b) I have not been notified by the Internal Revenue Service (IRS) that I am subject to backup withholding as a result of a failure to report all interest or dividends, or (c) the IRS has notified me that I am no longer subject to backup withholding; and
3. I am a U.S. citizen or other U.S. person (defined below); and
4. The FATCA code(s) entered on this form (if any) indicating that I am exempt from FATCA reporting is correct.

Certification instructions. You must cross out item 2 above if you have been notified by the IRS that you are currently subject to backup withholding because you have failed to report all interest and dividends on your tax return. For real estate transactions, item 2 does not apply. For mortgage interest paid, acquisition or abandonment of secured property, cancellation of debt, contributions to an individual retirement arrangement (IRA), and generally, payments other than interest and dividends, you are not required to sign the certification, but you must provide your correct TIN. See the instructions for Part II, later.

Sign Here   Signature of U.S. person ► *Richard K. Bennett*   Date ► 1/2/21

Use Form W-9 to obtain the taxpayer identification number in non-employee situations.

Do Not Staple   6969

Form **1096**

Department of the Treasury
Internal Revenue Service

**Annual Summary and Transmittal of
U.S. Information Returns**

OMB No. 1545-0108

20**20**

FILER'S name
ABC Charity

Street address (including room or suite number)
2870 North Hull Street

City or town, state or province, country, and ZIP or foreign postal code
Traverse City, MI 49615

Name of person to contact
Marianne Smith

Telephone number
231-435-2201

Email address
marsmith@msn.com

Fax number
231-435-2205

For Official Use Only

1 Employer identification number	2 Social security number	3 Total number of forms	4 Federal income tax withheld	5 Total amount reported with this Form 1096
35-2946039		10	$	$ 9843.00

6 Enter an "X" in only one box below to indicate the type of form being filed.

W-2G 32	1097-BTC 50	1098 81	1098-C 78	1098-E 84	1098-F 03	1098-Q 74	1098-T 83	1099-A 80	1099-B 79	1099-C 85	1099-CAP 73	1099-DIV 91	1099-G 86	1099-INT 92	1099-K 10	1099-LS 16
[ ]	[ ]	[ ]	[ ]	[ ]	[ ]	[ ]	[ ]	[ ]	[ ]	[ ]	[ ]	[ ]	[ ]	[ ]	[ ]	[ ]

1099-LTC 93	1099-MISC 95	1099-NEC 71	1099-OID 96	1099-PATR 97	1099-Q 31	1099-QA 1A	1099-R 98	1099-S 75	1099-SA 94	1099-SB 43	3921 25	3922 26	5498 28	5498-ESA 72	5498-QA 2A	5498-SA 27
[ ]	[X]	[ ]	[ ]	[ ]	[ ]	[ ]	[ ]	[ ]	[ ]	[ ]	[ ]	[ ]	[ ]	[ ]	[ ]	[ ]

Return this entire page to the Internal Revenue Service. Photocopies are not acceptable.

Under penalties of perjury, I declare that I have examined this return and accompanying documents and, to the best of my knowledge and belief, they are true, correct, and complete.

Signature ► *Daniel L. Lewis*   Title ► Treasurer   Date ► 1/13/21

Form 1096 is the "cover sheet" or transmittal form that must accompany Forms 1099 and other information forms.

Copies of the forms (or electronic media) must be filed with the IRS by January 31 following the year that the funds were paid or received.

An extension of time to file may be requested by filing Form 8809, Application for Extension of Time to File Information Returns, by the due date of the returns.

Obtaining correct identification numbers

Organizations required to file information returns with the IRS must obtain the correct taxpayer identification number (TIN) to report real estate transactions, mortgage interest paid to or by the organization, and certain other transactions.

Form W-9 (see page 96), Request for Taxpayer Identification Number and Certification, is used to furnish the correct TIN to the organization and in certain other situations:

Remember

If the recipient does not furnish a completed Form W-9, the church or nonprofit organization is required to withhold 24% of the payment for amounts paid, deposit the withholding electronically, and report amounts withheld on Forms 1099, as applicable.

> ➤ to certify that the TIN furnished is correct

> ➤ to certify that the recipient of the income is not subject to backup withholding, or

> ➤ to certify exemption from backup withholding

Failure to obtain a Form W-9 can lead to assessment of penalties to the organization when Form 1099 is filed without the payee's TIN.

It is a very wise practice to obtain W-9 before payment is made to the payee. In a situation where this is not possible, the organization should document all attempts requesting the W-9 information from the payee. A minimum of three attempts are needed to avoid IRS penalties.

Reporting on the Receipt of Funds

Receipt of interest on mortgages

Use Form 1098, Mortgage Interest Statement, to report mortgage interest of $600 or more received by an organization from an individual during the year (including a sole proprietor). There is no requirement to file Form 1098 for interest received from a corporation, partnership, trust, estate, or association. A transmittal Form 1096 (see page 96) must accompany one or more Forms 1098.

Reporting on the Payment of Funds

Payments of interest

File Form 1099-INT, Interest Income, for each person to whom an organization paid interest reportable in Box 1, 3, and 8 of at least $10 in any calendar year. This form is also required if any federal income tax was withheld under the backup withholding rules (24% is the 2020 rate), regardless of the amount of the payment. In certain instances, the $10 limit increases to $600. There is no requirement to file Form 1099-INT for payments made to a corporation or another tax-exempt organization.

9292	☐ VOID	☐ CORRECTED		
PAYER'S name, street address, city or town, state or province, country, ZIP or foreign postal code, and telephone no.	Payer's RTN (optional)	OMB No. 1545-0112		
Lancaster Community Church 1425 Spencer Avenue Logansport, IN 46958	1 Interest income $ 913.00	20**20** Form **1099-INT**	**Interest Income**	
	2 Early withdrawal penalty $		Copy A	
PAYER'S TIN 35-7921873	RECIPIENT'S TIN 307-20-6590	3 Interest on U.S. Savings Bonds and Treas. obligations $	For Internal Revenue Service Center	
RECIPIENT'S name James R. Moore	4 Federal income tax withheld $	5 Investment expenses $	File with Form 1096.	
	6 Foreign tax paid $	7 Foreign country or U.S. possession	For Privacy Act and Paperwork Reduction Act Notice, see the **2020 General Instructions for Certain Information Returns.**	
Street address (including apt. no.) 804 Linden Avenue	8 Tax-exempt interest $	9 Specified private activity bond interest $		
City or town, state or province, country, and ZIP or foreign postal code Wabash, IN 46992	10 Market discount $	11 Bond premium $		
	FATCA filing requirement ☐	12 Bond premium on Treasury obligations $	13 Bond premium on tax-exempt bond $	
Account number (see instructions)	2nd TIN not. ☐	14 Tax-exempt and tax credit bond CUSIP no.	15 State	16 State identification no.	17 State tax withheld $ $

Form **1099-INT**   Cat. No. 14410K   www.irs.gov/Form1099INT   Department of the Treasury - Internal Revenue Service
Do Not Cut or Separate Forms on This Page — Do Not Cut or Separate Forms on This Page

Use Form 1099-INT to report certain interest payments to the recipients.

Payments to annuitants

File Form 1099-R for each person to whom the organization made a designated distribution that is a total distribution from a retirement plan or a payment to an annuitant of $10 or more. If part of the distribution is taxable and part is nontaxable, Form 1099-R should reflect the entire distribution.

> *Example:* ABC Charity makes payments of $1,000 during the year to one of its annuitants, Mary Hughes. (Several years earlier, Mary entered into the charitable gift annuity agreement by giving a check to ABC.)

A portion of each annuity payment is a tax-free return of principal, and the remainder is annuity income for Mary. ABC will generally report the entire $1,000 in Box 1 on Form 1099-R and check Box 2b unless ABC determines the taxable amount for the year.

9898	☐ VOID	☐ CORRECTED			
PAYER'S name, street address, city or town, state or province, country, ZIP or foreign postal code, and phone no. ABC Charity 8049 Riverside Blvd. Sacramento, CA 95831		**1** Gross distribution $ 1000.00	OMB No. 1545-0119 20**20** Form **1099-R**		**Distributions From Pensions, Annuities, Retirement or Profit-Sharing Plans, IRAs, Insurance Contracts, etc.**
		2a Taxable amount $			
		2b Taxable amount not determined ☒	Total distribution ☐		**Copy A For Internal Revenue Service Center**
PAYER'S TIN 35-0179214	RECIPIENT'S TIN • 945-77-2540	**3** Capital gain (included in box 2a) $	**4** Federal income tax withheld $		File with Form 1096.
RECIPIENT'S name Mary Hughes		**5** Employee contributions/ Designated Roth contributions or insurance premiums $	**6** Net unrealized appreciation in employer's securities $		For Privacy Act and Paperwork Reduction Act Notice, see the **2020 General Instructions for Certain Information Returns.**
Street address (including apt. no.) PO Box 942		**7** Distribution code(s)	IRA/ SEP/ SIMPLE ☐	**8** Other $ %	
City or town, state or province, country, and ZIP or foreign postal code El Toro, CA 92609		**9a** Your percentage of total distribution %	**9b** Total employee contributions $		
10 Amount allocable to IRR within 5 years $	**11** 1st year of desig. Roth contrib.	**12** FATCA filing requirement ☐	**14** State tax withheld $	**15** State/Payer's state no.	**16** State distribution $
Account number (see instructions)		**13** Date of payment	**17** Local tax withheld $	**18** Name of locality	**19** Local distribution $

Form **1099-R**   Cat. No. 14436Q   www.irs.gov/Form1099R   Department of the Treasury - Internal Revenue Service

Do Not Cut or Separate Forms on This Page   —   Do Not Cut or Separate Forms on This Page

Use Form 1099-R for retirement or annuity payments.

Form W-4P, Withholding Certificate for Pension or Annuity Payments, should be completed by recipients of income from annuity, pension, and certain other deferred compensation plans to inform payers whether income tax is to be withheld and on what basis.

Payments to nonresident aliens

Payments for personal services made to noncitizens who are temporarily in this country (nonresident aliens) are often subject to federal income tax withholding at a 30% rate. A nonresident alien is a person who is neither a U.S. citizen nor a resident of the United States. Some payments may be exempt from income tax withholding if the person is from a country with which the United States maintains a tax treaty. Salary payments to nonresident aliens employed in the United States are subject to income tax withholding based on the regular withholding tables.

Single, nonrecurring, fixed, or determinable payments to nonresident aliens are generally not subject to withholding. Honoraria paid to visiting speakers usually fit this definition. It is unclear if love offerings are subject to withholding.

All payments to nonresident aliens, other than expense reimbursements and amounts reported on Form W-2, must be reported on Forms 1042 and 1042-S. These forms are filed with the IRS by March 15 for the previous calendar year, and a copy of Form 1042-S must be sent to the nonresident alien.

Payments of nonemployee compensation

A new 1099-NEC form has been introduced by the IRS for 2020. It is actually an old form that hasn't been in use since 1982.

Caution

Prior to 2020, organizations could file one Form 1099-MISC to report nonemployee compensation and miscellaneous income items by February 28 each year. In 2015, the Protecting Americans from Tax Hikes Act (PATH Act) changed the Form 1099-MISC due date to January 31 for reporting compensation. Since some data had a January 31 deadline and other data had a February 28 deadline, some organizations were filing two Form 1099-MISCs and confusion ensued.

There is more misunderstanding about the use of the Form 1099-NEC than many IRS forms. Payments of $600 or more per calendar year to each non-corporate provider of services triggers the filing of this form. This form is generally not used for employee compensation payments, so an organization should not report clergy compensation (or the housing allowance) on this form.

So, the IRS brought back Form 1099-NEC to separate the reporting of the payments. The filing due date for Form 1099-MISC is March 1, 2021, if filed on paper, or March 31 if filed electronically. The due date for filing Form 1099-NEC is February 1, 2021, if filed on paper or electronically.

NEC is the acronym for nonemployee compensation. What is nonemployee compensation? It may sound obvious that nonemployee compensation is the payment an organization makes to nonemployees, but it's more complicated than that. For the purposes of reporting nonemployee compensation on Form 1099-NEC, the IRS explains that payments must be reported if all four of these conditions are met.

- *It is made to someone who is not an employee* (emphasis added).

- It is made for services in the course of an organization's trade or business.

- It was made to an individual, partnership, estate, or a corporation if the corporation is a law firm.

- The payments made to that payee were at least $600 or more for the year.

The most common examples of payments that must be reported on Form 1099-NEC include the following:

- professional service fees paid to attorneys (including law firms established as corporations), accountants, architects, etc.

- payments to independent contractors for services including payment for parts or materials used to perform the services if they were incidental to the service

Payments **not** included in Box 1 of Form 1099-NEC include these:

- Any payment to an employee—see first IRS condition shown above.

- Expense reimbursements paid under an accountable expense reimbursement plan to volunteers of nonprofit organizations. With proper substantiation, unreimbursed volunteer expenses may be claimed as charitable contributions.

- Payments for auto mileage up to the maximum IRS rate for charitable miles (14 cents per mile for 2020) are tax-free for

Remember

Legislation is almost annually introduced to allow tax-free mileage reimbursements to volunteers at the business mileage rate. To date, this provision has not been enacted.

7171	☐ VOID	☐ CORRECTED	

PAYER'S name, street address, city or town, state or province, country, ZIP or foreign postal code, and telephone no.

ABC Charity
110 Harding Avenue
Cincinnati, OH 45963

OMB No. 1545-0116

20**20**

Form **1099-NEC**

Nonemployee Compensation

1 Nonemployee compensation
$ **2400.00**

2

Copy A
For
**Internal Revenue
Service Center**

File with Form 1096.

PAYER'S TIN
35-1148942

RECIPIENT'S TIN
389-11-8067

RECIPIENT'S name
Mark A. Mitchell

3

For Privacy Act
and Paperwork
Reduction Act
Notice, see the
**2020 General
Instructions for
Certain
Information
Returns.**

Street address (including apt. no.)
512 Warren Avenue

4 Federal income tax withheld
$

City or town, state or province, country, and ZIP or foreign postal code
Norwood, OH 45212

FATCA filing
requirement ☐

Account number (see instructions)

2nd TIN not. ☐

5 State tax withheld
$
$

6 State/Payer's state no.

7 State income
$
$

Form **1099-NEC**   Cat. No. 72590N   www.irs.gov/Form1099NEC   Department of the Treasury - Internal Revenue Service
Do Not Cut or Separate Forms on This Page — Do Not Cut or Separate Forms on This Page

Use Form 1099-NEC to report nonemployee services payments.

volunteers. When an organization provides liability insurance for its volunteers, the value of the coverage can be excluded from the volunteer's income as a working condition fringe benefit.

- Payments to or on behalf of volunteers that are not substantiated business expenses are reported on Form W-2 or Form 1099-NEC, depending on whether or not a common law employee relationship exists. When the relationship takes the form of an employer-employee, payments other than accountable expense reimbursements are reported on Form W-2. Payments to nonemployee volunteers for medical, educational, or personal living expenses are reportable on Form 1099-NEC. Tax-free payments to volunteers for lodging, meals, and incidental expenses are limited to actual expenses (including the charitable mileage rate).

- Advances, reimbursements, allowances, or expenses for traveling and other business expenses of an employee. These payments are reported on Form W-2 if they do not comply with the accountable expense plan rules.

- Advances, reimbursements, or expenses for traveling and other business expenses of a self-employed person are not reportable on Form 1099-NEC if made under an accountable expense reimbursement plan. Under this type of plan, expenses are reimbursed only if they are substantiated as to amount, date, and business nature, and any excess reimbursements must be returned to the organization.

- Deceased employee wages paid in the year after death (report in Box 3 of Form 1099-MISC).

- Payments more appropriately described as rent (report in Box 1 of Form 1099-MISC), royalties (report in Box 2 of Form 1099-MISC), other income not subject to self-employment tax (report in Box 3 of Form 1099-MISC), interest (use Form 1099-INT).

- The cost of current life insurance protection (report on Form W-2 or Form 1099-R).

- An employee's wages, travel or auto allowance, or bonuses and prizes (report on Form W-2).

- The cost of group-term life insurance paid on behalf of a former employee (report on Form W-2).

- Cash housing allowance paid to a minister (report on W-2, Box 14 or by other communication to the minister).

- Benevolence payments made to nonemployees. These payments are not reportable on Form 1099-NEC or any other form. Benevolence payments to employees are generally includible on Form W-2.

Example 1: During 2020, an organization pays a contractor, who is a sole proprietor, $5,500 for drywall work at one of the organization's facilities. Since the contractor is a sole proprietor and the amount paid is $600 or more, the contractor should receive a Form 1099-NEC reflecting the $5,500 in Box 1 as nonemployee compensation.

Example 2: During 2020, an organization pays a consultant, who is a sole proprietor, $2,000 of which $800 was a travel reimbursement. The consultant did not substantiate the travel expenses. Since the amount paid is $600 or more, and the travel expenses were not substantiated, Form 1099-NEC should reflect the $2,000 in Box 1 as nonemployee compensation.

Example 3: During 2020, an organization pays a speaker, who is a sole proprietor, $1,000 of which $600 was substantiated and paid by the organization as related travel expenses. After excluding the substantiated expenses of $600, the remaining $400 is less than the annual $600 limit. There is no requirement to issue a Form 1099-NEC to the speaker.

Payments of rents, royalties and more

An organization must file Form 1099-MISC for each recipient (other than corporations) to whom it has paid

- at least $10 in royalties (Box 2)

- at least $600 in:

  - **Rents—Box 1.** Real estate and machine rentals (do not include payments of rent to real estate agents or property managers)

  - **Prizes and awards—Box 3**

  - **Other income—Box 3.** Enter other income of $600 or more required to be reported on Form 1099-MISC that is not reportable in one of the other boxes on the form.

  - **Other specialized forms of payment go in certain other boxes**—few of these boxes apply to churches and nonprofit organizations.

A ministry must also file Form 1099-MISC for each person from whom they have withheld any federal income tax (Box 4) under the backup withholding rules regardless of the amount of the payment.

9595	☐ VOID	☐ CORRECTED	

PAYER'S name, street address, city or town, state or province, country, ZIP or foreign postal code, and telephone no.	1 Rents	OMB No. 1545-0115	**Miscellaneous Income**
ABC Charity 110 Harding Avenue Cincinnati, OH 45963	$	2020	
	2 Royalties $	Form **1099-MISC**	
	3 Other income $ 1800.00	4 Federal income tax withheld $	**Copy A**
PAYER'S TIN 35-1148942	**RECIPIENT'S TIN** 389-11-8067	5 Fishing boat proceeds	6 Medical and health care payments	**For Internal Revenue Service Center**

RECIPIENT'S name Mark A. Mitchell		$	$	**File with Form 1096.**
	7 Payer made direct sales of $5,000 or more of consumer products to a buyer (recipient) for resale ☐	8 Substitute payments in lieu of dividends or interest $	For Privacy Act and Paperwork Reduction Act Notice, see the **2020 General Instructions for Certain Information Returns.**
Street address (including apt. no.) 512 Warren Avenue	9 Crop insurance proceeds $	10 Gross proceeds paid to an attorney $	
City or town, state or province, country, and ZIP or foreign postal code Norwood, OH 45212	11	12 Section 409A deferrals $	
Account number (see instructions)	FATCA filing requirement ☐	2nd TIN not. ☐	13 Excess golden parachute payments $	14 Nonqualified deferred compensation $	
		15 State tax withheld $ $	16 State/Payer's state no.	17 State income $ $

Form **1099-MISC**   Cat. No. 14425J   www.irs.gov/Form1099MISC   Department of the Treasury - Internal Revenue Service
Do Not Cut or Separate Forms on This Page — Do Not Cut or Separate Forms on This Page

Some payments do not have to be reported on Form 1099-MISC, although they may be taxable to the recipient. Payments for which a Form 1099-MISC is *not required* include all the following:

- Generally, payments to a corporation (including a limited liability company, LLC, that is treated as a C or S corporation). This exemption does not apply to reporting payments made to corporations for legal services. These payments are reportable in Box 1 of Form 1099-NEC.

- Payments for merchandise, telegrams, telephone, freight, storage, and similar items.

- Payments of rent to real estate agents or property managers.

- Wages paid to employees (report on Form W-2).

- Business travel allowances paid to employees. These payments are reportable on Form W-2 if they do not comply with the accountable expense plan rules.

Racial nondiscrimination requirements for private schools

Form 5578, *Annual Certification of Racial Nondiscrimination for a Private School Exempt from Federal Income Tax,* must be filed by churches and other nonprofits that operate, supervise, or control a private school. The form must be filed by the 15th day of the fifth month following the end of the organization's calendar year or fiscal period. For organizations that must file Form 990, there is no requirement to file Form 5578 since the information is included in Schedule E.

The "private school" definition includes preschools, primary, secondary, preparatory, and high schools, and colleges and universities, whether operated as a separate legal entity or an activity of a church.

A nonprofit private school, including a school operated or controlled by a church, must have a *racially nondiscriminatory policy,* must properly publicize the policy, and must operate in a racially nondiscriminatory manner. A school that does not have a racially nondiscriminatory policy applying to its students does not qualify as an organization exempt from federal income tax.

A school is an educational organization that normally maintains a regular faculty and curriculum and normally has a regularly enrolled body of pupils or students in attendance at the place where its educational activities are regularly carried on. The term includes preschools, primary, secondary, preparatory, or high schools and colleges and universities.

A *racially nondiscriminatory policy* as to students means that the school admits the students of any race to all the rights, privileges, programs, and activities generally

Form **5578** (Rev. November 2019) Department of the Treasury Internal Revenue Service	**Annual Certification of Racial Nondiscrimination for a Private School Exempt From Federal Income Tax** (for use by organizations that do not file Form 990 or Form 990-EZ) ▶ Go to *www.irs.gov/Form5578* for the latest information.	OMB No. 1545-0047 **Open to Public Inspection** For IRS Use Only

For the period beginning **July 1, 2019** , 20 and ending **June 30, 2020** , 20

1a	Name of organization that operates, supervises, and/or controls school(s).	1b Employer identification number
	Fellowship Church	**73-0896893**

Address (number and street or P.O. box no., if mail is not delivered to street address)	Room/suite
East Main Street	

City or town, state, and ZIP + 4 (If foreign address, list city or town, state or province, and country. Include postal code.)
Lamont, KS 66855

2a	Name of central organization holding group exemption letter covering the school(s). (If same as 1a above, write "Same" and complete 2c.) If the organization in 1a holds an individual exemption letter, write "Not Applicable."	2b Employer identification number

Address (number and street or P.O. box no., if mail is not delivered to street address)	Room/suite	2c Group exemption number (see instructions under *Definitions*)

City or town, state, and ZIP + 4 (If foreign address, list city or town, state or province, and country. Include postal code.)

3a	Name of school. (If more than one school, write "See Attached" and attach a list of the names, complete addresses, including postal codes, and employer identification numbers of the schools.) If same as 1a, write "Same."	3b Employer identification number, if any
	Fellowship Christian School	**Same**

Address (number and street or P.O. box no., if mail is not delivered to street address)	Room/suite
Same	

City or town, state, and ZIP + 4 (If foreign address, list city or town, state or province, and country. Include postal code.)
Same

Under penalties of perjury, I hereby certify that I am authorized to take official action on behalf of the above school(s) and that to the best of my knowledge and belief the school(s) has (have) satisfied the applicable requirements of sections 4.01 through 4.05 of Rev. Proc. 75-50, 1975-2 C.B. 587, for the period covered by this certification.

Ralph Winzeler (Signature)	**Ralph Winzeler, Superintendent** (Type or print name and title.)	**5/26/20** (Date)

For Paperwork Reduction Act Notice, see instructions.   Cat. No. 42658A   Form **5578** (Rev. 11-2019)

accorded or made available to students at that school and that the school does not discriminate on the basis of race in the administration of its educational policies, admissions policies, scholarship and loan programs, and athletic and other school-administered programs.

The racially nondiscriminatory policy must be publicized in one of the following three ways:

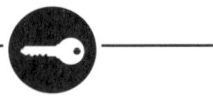

Key Issue

Organizations must publicize a racially nondiscriminatory policy, using one of three approved methods.

1. **Publish a notice** at least once annually in a newspaper of general circulation that serves all racial segments of the community. The notice must appear in a section of the newspaper likely to be read by prospective students and their families, and it must occupy at least three column inches, captioned in at least 12-point boldface type and its text must be printed in at least 8-point type.

2. **Use the broadcast media** to publicize the policy if this use makes the policy known to all segments of the general community the school serves.

3. **Display a notice** of the policy on its primary publicly accessible Internet homepage at all times during its taxable year in a manner reasonably expected to be noticed by visitors to the homepage (a link on the homepage to another page where the notice appears, or a notice that appears in a carousel or only by selecting a dropdown or by mouse-over is not acceptable).

Every organization that claims exemption from federal income tax under section 501(c)(3) of the Internal Revenue Code and that operates, supervises, or controls a private school(s) must file a racial nondiscrimination certification. If an organization is required to file Form 990 or 990-EZ, either as a separate return or as part of a group return, the certification must be made on Schedule E of Form 990 or 990-EZ, Schools. For organizations not required to file Form 990 or 990-EZ, the certification must be on Form 5578, which is due on the 15th day of the 5th month after the organization's year-end.

Federal guidance on complying with racial nondiscrimination requirements for private schools may be found in Revenue Ruling 71-447, Revenue Procedure 75-50, and Revenue Procedure 2019-22. *Note: A school may be able to publicize its racial nondiscrimination policy in certain other ways if it meets certain criteria in Revenue Procedure 75-50 regarding the area(s) from which it draws students.*

Employment eligibility verification

All employers must complete Form I-9 (see page 108) to document verification of the identity and employment authorization of each new employee, both citizen and noncitizen, hired to work in the United States. Both employers and employees are responsible for completing their respective sections of Form I-9.

On the form, an employee must attest, under penalty of perjury, that they are in one of the following categories:

- a U.S. citizen

- a U.S. non-citizen national

- a lawful permanent resident

- an alien authorized to work

The employee must also present the employer with acceptable documents evidencing identity and employment authorization. The employer must examine the employment eligibility and identity document(s) that an employee presents to determine whether the document(s) reasonably appear to be genuine and to relate to the employee, and must record the document information on the Form I-9. The list of acceptable documents is reflected on the last page of the form. Employers may be fined if the Form I-9 is not properly completed.

Employers must retain Form I-9 for a designated period and make it available for inspection by authorized government officers. The Form I-9 is not filed with the U.S. Citizenship and Immigration Services or U.S. Immigrations and Customs Enforcement (ICE).

Employment Eligibility Verification
Department of Homeland Security
U.S. Citizenship and Immigration Services

USCIS
Form I-9
OMB No. 1615-0047
Expires 10/31/2022

▶ START HERE: Read instructions carefully before completing this form. The instructions must be available, either in paper or electronically, during completion of this form. Employers are liable for errors in the completion of this form.

ANTI-DISCRIMINATION NOTICE: It is illegal to discriminate against work-authorized individuals. Employers CANNOT specify which document(s) an employee may present to establish employment authorization and identity. The refusal to hire or continue to employ an individual because the documentation presented has a future expiration date may also constitute illegal discrimination.

Section 1. Employee Information and Attestation (Employees must complete and sign Section 1 of Form I-9 no later than the first day of employment, but not before accepting a job offer.)

Last Name (Family Name)	First Name (Given Name)	Middle Initial	Other Last Names Used (if any)
Hendricks	Fred	W.	

Address (Street Number and Name)	Apt. Number	City or Town	State	ZIP Code
408 Forest Avenue		Cincinnati	OH	45980

Date of Birth (mm/dd/yyyy)	U.S. Social Security Number	Employee's E-mail Address	Employee's Telephone Number
06-12-1959	5 1 4 - 4 2 - 9 0 8 7	fhend@hotmail.com	513-641-5950

I am aware that federal law provides for imprisonment and/or fines for false statements or use of false documents in connection with the completion of this form.

I attest, under penalty of perjury, that I am (check one of the following boxes):

[X] 1. A citizen of the United States
[ ] 2. A noncitizen national of the United States (See instructions)
[ ] 3. A lawful permanent resident (Alien Registration Number/USCIS Number):
[ ] 4. An alien authorized to work until (expiration date, mm/dd/yyyy):
Some aliens may write "N/A" in the expiration date field. (See instructions)

Aliens authorized to work must provide only one of the following document numbers to complete Form I-9:
An Alien Registration Number/USCIS Number OR Form I-94 Admission Number OR Foreign Passport Number.

1. Alien Registration Number/USCIS Number:
OR
2. Form I-94 Admission Number:
OR
3. Foreign Passport Number:
Country of Issuance:

QR Code - Section 1
Do Not Write In This Space

Signature of Employee _Fred W. Hendricks_   Today's Date (mm/dd/yyyy) 01/03/2021

Preparer and/or Translator Certification (check one):
[ ] I did not use a preparer or translator. [ ] A preparer(s) and/or translator(s) assisted the employee in completing Section 1.
(Fields below must be completed and signed when preparers and/or translators assist an employee in completing Section 1.)

I attest, under penalty of perjury, that I have assisted in the completion of Section 1 of this form and that to the best of my knowledge the information is true and correct.

Signature of Preparer or Translator   Today's Date (mm/dd/yyyy)

Last Name (Family Name)	First Name (Given Name)

Address (Street Number and Name)	City or Town	State	ZIP Code

Form I-9 10/21/2019   Page 1 of 3

Employment Eligibility Verification
Department of Homeland Security
U.S. Citizenship and Immigration Services

USCIS
Form I-9
OMB No. 1615-0047
Expires 10/31/2022

Section 2. Employer or Authorized Representative Review and Verification
(Employers or their authorized representative must complete and sign Section 2 within 3 business days of the employee's first day of employment. You must physically examine one document from List A OR a combination of one document from List B and one document from List C as listed on the "Lists of Acceptable Documents.")

Employee Info from Section 1	Last Name (Family Name)	First Name (Given Name)	M.I.	Citizenship/Immigration Status
	Hendricks	Fred	W	Citizen

List A		List B		List C
Identity and Employment Authorization	OR	Identity	AND	Employment Authorization

List A Document Title	List B Document Title	List C Document Title
	Driver's License	Birth Certificate
Issuing Authority	Issuing Authority: Ohio	Issuing Authority: Ohio
Document Number	Document Number: 514-42-9087	Document Number
Expiration Date (if any):	Expiration Date (if any): 6/30/22	Expiration Date (if any):

Additional Information

QR Code - Sections 2 & 3
Do Not Write In This Space

Certification: I attest, under penalty of perjury, that (1) I have examined the document(s) presented by the above-named employee, (2) the above-listed document(s) appear to be genuine and to relate to the employee named, and (3) to the best of my knowledge the employee is authorized to work in the United States.

The employee's first day of employment (mm/dd/yyyy): _____ (See instructions for exemptions.)

Signature of Employer or Authorized Representative	Today's Date (mm/dd/yyyy) 01/03/2021	Title of Employer or Authorized Representative: Business Manager

Last Name of Employer or Authorized Representative: Brown	First Name of Employer or Authorized Representative: David L.	Employer's Business or Organization Name: Fairfield Church

Employer's Business or Organization Address (Street Number and Name): 110 Harding Avenue	City or Town: Cincinnati	State: OH	ZIP Code: 45960

Section 3. Reverification and Rehires (To be completed and signed by employer or authorized representative.)

A. New Name (if applicable) Last Name (Family Name)	First Name (Given Name)	Middle Initial	B. Date of Rehire (if applicable) Date (mm/dd/yyyy)

C. If the employee's previous grant of employment authorization has expired, provide the information for the document or receipt that establishes continuing employment authorization in the space provided below.

Document Title	Document Number	Expiration Date (if any) (mm/dd/yyyy)

I attest, under penalty of perjury, that to the best of my knowledge, this employee is authorized to work in the United States, and if the employee presented document(s), the document(s) I have examined appear to be genuine and to relate to the individual.

Signature of Employer or Authorized Representative	Today's Date (mm/dd/yyyy)	Name of Employer or Authorized Representative

Form I-9 10/21/2019   Page 2 of 3

This form must be completed and retained on file by all employers for employees hired after November 6, 1986. (For more information on completing this form, go to www.uscis.gov.)

Summary of Payment Reporting Requirements

Below is an alphabetical list of some common payments and the forms necessary to report them. It is not a complete list of payments, and the absence of a payment from the list does not suggest that the payment is exempt from reporting.

Types of Payment	Report on Form
Advance earned income credit	W-2
Annuities, periodic payments	1099-R
* Attorneys' fees	1099-NEC
** Auto, personal use of employer-owned vehicle	W-2
Auto reimbursements (nonaccountable plan):	
Employee	W-2
Nonemployee	1099-NEC
Awards:	
Employee	W-2
Nonemployee	1099-NEC
Bonuses:	
Employee	W-2
Nonemployee	1099-NEC
Cafeteria/flexible benefit plan	5500, 5500-C, or 5500-R
Christmas bonuses:	
Employee	W-2
Nonemployee	1099-NEC
Commissions:	
Employee	W-2
Nonemployee	1099-NEC
Compensation:	
Employee	W-2
Nonemployee	1099-NEC
Dependent care payments	W-2
Education expense reimbursement (nonaccountable plan):	
Employee	W-2
Nonemployee	1099-NEC
Employee business expense reimbursement (nonaccountable plan)	W-2

Types of Payment	Report on Form
Fees:	
Employee	W-2
Nonemployee	1099-NEC
Group-term life insurance (PS 58 rates)	W-2 or 1099-R
Interest, other than mortgage	1099-INT
Long-term care benefits	1099-LTC
Medical expense reimbursement plan (employee-funded)	5500, 5500-C, or 5500-R
Mileage (nonaccountable plan):	
Employee	W-2
Nonemployee	1099-NEC
Mortgage interest	1098
Moving expense:	
Employee	W-2
Nonemployee	1099-NEC
Prizes:	
Employee	W-2
Nonemployee	1099-NEC
Real estate proceeds	1099-S
Rents	1099-MISC
Royalties	1099-MISC
Severance pay	W-2
Sick pay	W-2
Supplemental unemployment	W-2
Vacation allowance:	
Employee	W-2
Nonemployee	1099-NEC

* The exemption from reporting payments made to corporations does not apply to payments to a lawyer or a law firm for legal services, even if the provider of the legal services is incorporated.

**The value may also be reported on a separate statement to the employee.

- **Obtaining a completed Form W-9.** The proper completion of forms in the 1099 series all starts with obtaining a completed Form W-9 for the taxpayer identification number (TIN) before the applicable payments are made by the church or nonprofit. Unless the Form W-9 is obtained before payments are made, it may be very difficult to obtain the form at a later date and could complicate the filing of the appropriate Form 1099. Integrity requires having procedures to obtain a Form W-9 at the beginning of the relationship with a recipient of certain payments from a ministry.

- **Reporting of payments to independent contractors.** Because there is generally no tax to withhold, it is easy for a ministry to overlook the filing of Form 1099-NEC. When a ministry fails to file a required Form 1099-NEC, it may be inadvertently giving an independent contractor a license to avoid reporting taxable income. Integrity requires the proper filing of Form 1099-NEC and all other forms in the 1099 series, if applicable.

- **Reporting of payments to noncitizens.** Ministries often make payments to individuals who are not U.S. citizens and are temporarily in the U.S. The proper reporting to the IRS is often overlooked. For example, payments might be made by a church to a national worker (noncitizen) visiting the church to recount the effectiveness of gifts made by a church to an international mission field, triggering the filing of Form 1042-S.

  While reimbursements made under an accountable expense reimbursement plan are not reportable, other payments must be reported on Form 1042-S, and some payments are even subject to federal income tax withholding. Integrity requires organizations understand the rules relating to payments to noncitizens before the payments are made to comply with the law and demonstrate a witness above reproach before a watching world.

Financial Management and Reporting

One does not have to look far to find examples of organizations that have suffered because their financial records and reporting systems were deficient. Sound financial recordkeeping is invaluable to churches and other nonprofit organizations in these three ways:

➢ **Helps board and staff make well-informed decisions.** Only from a quality set of financial records may good reports be prepared which reflect the true financial condition of the organization. These reports are vital to allow the board and staff to assess the overall financial health of the organization, determine financial trends, measure financial outcomes, and project future budgetary needs. Informed decisions may only be made based on solid financial records.

➢ **Helps the organization keep running smoothly.** Without a sound accounting system, it will not be possible for an organization to stay on track financially. Quality financial records keep order from turning into chaos. Imagine the challenges an organization would face if its records did not clearly reflect its liabilities, if it did not know how much had been expended of a giver's restricted gift, or if the accounting records had not been reconciled to the bank statement. Yes, a smoothly running organization requires good accounting records!

➢ **Helps the organization demonstrate financial accountability.** Churches and nonprofit organizations must demonstrate accountability in a variety of ways. Church members anticipate financial data on the church's operations at least annually. Most nonprofit organizations other than churches must file Form 990 and perhaps Form 990-T with the Internal Revenue Service. Grant funders anticipate appropriate reporting on the use of grant funds. Accountability to the organization's board is a given. Good financial records are the basis for accountability to all constituents.

Accounting Records

Accounting systems differ in shape, size, complexity, and efficiency. The objectives of the system should be to measure and track financial activities and to provide financial information to an organization's governing body, a congregation, and givers. When choosing the accounting system for an organization, consideration should be given to budget available to purchase a system, ability of the individual(s) keeping the records, and level of access to technical expertise to keep the infrastructure operating properly.

Basis of accounting

There are three primary methods by which a ministry can account for its finances:

1. **Cash.** The cash basis of accounting will record income and expenses as the money actually comes in and goes out. This is the method that many ministries use on a day-to-day basis. It makes it easy to understand the daily cash balance and is the simplest approach.

2. **Accrual.** The accrual basis of accounting will record income when it is earned and expenses when they are incurred. For example, an expense would be recorded when the ministry receives the new Bible study books they ordered rather than when the invoice is paid. This method also recognizes assets and liabilities to reflect a more long-term approach to finances. U.S. generally accepted accounting principles (GAAP) requires the use of accrual-based financial statements. This "gold standard" of GAAP accrual accounting may be important to outside users of the financial information such as lenders or accreditation bodies such as ECFA.

Idea

Even when obtaining an accrual basis audit, an organization may keep its books on the cash basis during the year and record journal entries on the last day of the year to convert to accrual. Some ministries struggle to keep their books on the accrual basis throughout the year (recording accounts receivable, accounts payable, etc.) when their financial life would be much simpler if the cash basis were used.

3. **Modified cash.** There is a hybrid of the cash and accrual methods. The modified cash basis of accounting considers many things on a cash basis but may include certain assets and

liabilities on the statement of financial position (balance sheet) such as fixed assets or accounts payable. This method may allow the leaders of a ministry to more clearly understand the value of what the ministry owns as well as the amounts that are owed for which resources will need to be available, without the complexity of full accrual accounting.

Depreciation

Cash basis financial statements will not show property and equipment assets and therefore will not show depreciation of those assets. However, accrual statements will require this presentation, and modified cash statements will typically include these assets as well to better reflect what the ministry owns. Depreciation is calculated over the expected useful life of the asset and therefore can be useful from a budgeting perspective to accumulate replacement reserves. If these amounts are set aside in cash, there should not be a need to obtain financing for items such as air conditioning units or roof replacements.

Fund accounting

Fund accounting (or accounting by classes of net assets) provides an excellent basis for stewardship reporting. It is a system of accounting in which separate records are kept for resources donated to an organization that are restricted by givers or outside parties for certain specified purposes or uses.

GAAP requires that net assets be broken down into the following three classes, based on the presence or absence of giver-imposed restrictions and their nature:

Remember

Fund accounting does not necessarily require multiple bank accounts. One bank account is all that is usually necessary. However, it may be appropriate to place restricted funds into a separate bank account to ensure the funds are not inadvertently spent for other purposes.

Net assets

There are two classes of net assets:

➤ **Net assets without donor restrictions.** These assets are not subject to donor-imposed restrictions and may be used for any of the organization's purposes.

➤ **Net assets with donor restrictions.** These assets are subject to donor-imposed restrictions for specific ministry purposes.

Giver-imposed restrictions normally apply to the use of net assets and not to the use of specific assets. Only givers or outside parties may "restrict" funds given to a nonprofit organization. The organization's board may not "restrict" monies—they may only "designate" funds. For example, if a giver donates money for a new building, the funds should be placed in a restricted fund. However, if the church board sets aside funds without donor restrictions in a debt retirement fund, this is a board-*designated* fund, a subdesignation of unrestricted net assets.

Record retention and destruction

Proper maintenance of corporate documents and records is critical from both a management and a legal perspective. An organization's preparedness for a financial or IRS audit, legal action and/or response, public inquiry, and loss by theft or natural catastrophe, among other things, depends largely on keeping accurate records for as long as necessary.

For a sample Record Retention and Destruction Policy, see ECFA's Knowledge Center at *www.ECFA.church.*

Financial Reports

Financial reports should:

> ➢ be easily comprehensible so that any person taking the time to study them will understand the financial picture

> ➢ be concise so that the person studying them will not get lost in detail

> ➢ be all-inclusive in scope and embrace all activities of the organization

> ➢ have a focal point for comparison so that the person reading them will have some basis for making a judgment (usually a comparison with a budget or data from the corresponding period of the previous year)

> ➢ be prepared on a timely basis (the longer the delay after the end of the period, the longer the time before any corrective action can be taken)

Key Issue

"Dashboard" financial reporting is increasingly used by nonprofits. It gets its name because it's like a financial dashboard—with gauges, redlines, and warning lights. It cuts through the barrage of uninterrupted data and delivers a clear view of the organization's performance. It often includes a visualization of historical information and personalized reports from key staff members.

Dashboard reports present a quick, comprehensible overview of an organization's financial status. Dashboard reports can also reflect other critical measures of organizational performance and mission effectiveness. When dashboard reports present key indicators in consistent formats, board members and staff can readily spot changes and trends in these measurements. Like the dashboard inside a car, these reports often display the equivalent of warning lights that only flare up when there is an impending problem or when certain variables are outside of predetermined limits.

In preparing financial reports, there is one basic rule: Prepare different reports for different audiences. For example, a church board would normally receive a more detailed financial report than the church membership. Department heads in a nonprofit organization might receive reports that relate only to their department.

For additional reading, see the eBooks—*10 Essentials of Accounting and Financial Reporting for Ministries, 10 Essentials of Understanding Ministry Financial Statements, 10 Essentials of Church Accounting and Financial Reporting, and 10 Essentials of Understanding Church Financial Statements.*

Statement of financial position

A statement of financial position shows assets, liabilities, and net assets as of the end-of-period date. This statement is also called a balance sheet because it shows how the two sides of the accounting equation (assets minus liabilities equals net assets) "balance" in the organization.

Anything an organization owns that has a monetary value is an asset. Cash, land, buildings, furniture, and fixtures are examples of assets. Anything the organization owes is a liability. Liabilities might include amounts owed to suppliers (accounts payable) or to the bank (notes payable and other amounts due).

Statement of activities

The statement of activities (also referred to as a statement of revenues and expenses) reflects an organization's support and revenue, expenses, and changes in net assets for a certain period of time. It shows the sources of an organization's income and how the resources were used. The form of the statement will depend on the type of organization and accounting method used. But the statement must present the change in net assets with and without donor restrictions as well as total net assets.

Churches and nonprofit organizations will have several lines for support and revenue such as contributions, sales of products, investment income, and so on. Expenses are often listed by natural classification such as salaries, fringe benefits, supplies, and so on.

Organizations desiring to meet GAAP accounting standards must reflect functional expenses (by classes of program services and supporting activities) in the statement of activities, footnotes, or in a separate Schedule 1 statement. Organizations will also show expenses by natural classification in the statement of activities, in the footnotes, or in a separate schedule/statement.

Statement of cash flows

The statement of cash flows provides information about the cash receipts and disbursements of an organization and the extent to which resources were obtained from, or used in, operating, investing, or financing activities. The direct method of presenting a cash flow statement starts by listing all sources of cash from operations during the period and deducting all operating outflows of cash to arrive at the net cash flow. The indirect method begins with the change in net assets and adjusts backwards to reconcile the change in net assets to net cash flows.

Caution

Recent changes in nonprofit accounting standards now require reporting of expenses by natural and functional classification in one location.

Statement of functional expenses

A statement of functional expenses provides information about the nature and amount of costs associated with each of the program services and supporting activities (general and administrative, fundraising, etc.) carried out by the organization.

Budgeting

A budget is an effective tool for allocating financial resources and planning and controlling spending even for smaller organizations. A budget matches anticipated inflows of resources with outflows of resources. Preparing a budget requires considerable effort. It includes looking back at revenue and expense trends. Projected plans and programs must be converted into estimated dollar amounts. Too many organizations budget their expenses with some degree of precision and then set the income budget at whatever it takes to cover the total expenses. This is often a dangerous approach. A list of key considerations is included in the ECFA eBooks—*10 Essentials of Church Budgeting* and *10 Essentials of Ministry Budgeting*.

Separate budgets should be prepared for all funds of an organization. Even capital and debt-retirement funds should be budgeted. Line-item budgets within each fund reflect the projected cost of salaries, fringe benefits, utilities, maintenance, debt retirement, and other expenses. The line-item approach is generally used in reporting to department heads or other responsible individuals.

Program budgets are often presented to the board of a nonprofit organization or a church's board or membership. In this approach, the cost of a program is reflected rather than the cost of specific line-items such as salaries or fringe benefits.

Here are three helpful budget preparation steps: (1) lay the budgeting ground rules, (2) determine your "Big Number," and (3) recognize which expenses are subject to budget allocations:

1. **Lay the budgeting ground rules.** While the ground rules will vary from one ministry to another, it is important to make several decisions before fully launching into the budgeting process:

   A. **Decide whether mid-year budget adjustments will be considered.** When revenues spike or take an unexpected and sharp dip, the two primary options are to:

      a. adjust the revenue and expense budget mid-year or

      b. leave the budget unadjusted.

      Few ministries make formal mid-year budget adjustments. This is not to say that ministries do not make spending adjustments when, for example, revenue projections are not being met. Spending adjustments are different from adjustments to the budget.

   B. **Determine whether multiple budgets should be prepared.** If multiple budgets are prepared, the primary budget takes the most effort to produce. In the next budget scenario, leadership identifies cuts that would be made if the actual results were X% lower than expected. The third budget identifies those activities to be funded if actual results were Y% higher than budgeted. Multiple budgets provide a ministry with enhanced flexibility to move to an optional budget when needed.

Idea

Multiple budgets are often prepared when ministry revenue is unstable. Preparing a primary budget and two others—anticipating higher or lower revenue—are often helpful.

   C. **Determine when the budgeting process will begin for the next year and the timeline for the process.** At a minimum, the budgeting process should begin early enough prior to the new year to allow adequate input from each ministry area and time for analysis of giving and spending trends. Here is a budgeting axiom: The larger the ministry, the earlier the annual budgeting process should begin.

D. **Determine the budget period.** Budgets almost always coincide with the accounting period—either fiscal or calendar accounting period. In other words, if the ministry uses a calendar accounting period, the budget will usually be for the same time period.

A few larger ministries use an annual budget but adjust it on a quarterly rolling basis. A quarterly rolling budget:

   a. allows for real-time future stewardship planning based on the most recent three-month experience,

   b. may be an important approach when a ministry's revenue is significantly rising or falling, and

   c. requires more budget preparation time.

E. **Determine if the ministry will limit the percentage of certain expenses to total expenses.** Most ministries are keenly aware of the percentage of staff costs to the overall operating budget. And some ministries do establish an upper limit for the percentage of compensation and fringe benefits in relation to total operational expenses.

Another factor that is often managed during the budget process is overhead. Some ministries have a target such that the total administration and fundraising expenses do not exceed a certain percentage of total expenses. However, an arbitrary limit on the overhead percentage could result in a loss in competent administrative staffing.

F. **Determine how the budgeting philosophy will impact setting the Big Number for the next year.** Will the ministry approach the new budget year from a very conservative or very aggressive posture or somewhere in between? For example, a ministry without debt may be able to take a more aggressive budgeting philosophy than a ministry with significant debt. A ministry with significant debt will likely be more cautious in its budgeting philosophy because of the need to protect reserves for mortgage payments.

G. **Decide whether to include or exclude depreciation for budgeting purposes.** Is depreciation recorded? If not, depreciation is excluded from the budget by default.

If a ministry records depreciation, it may be included in the operating budget even though it is a non-cash item. Or a ministry may exclude depreciation from the budget perhaps because the removal of this major noncash item makes budgeting simpler.

Whether or not depreciation is included in the budget, it is essential to set aside funds for capital expenditures. HVAC units wear out, parking lots develop cracks, roofs leak, technology equipment becomes outdated, and plumbing breaks down.

Most ministries include depreciation in the budget as a way to set aside funds for capital expenditures and raise funds for special purposes such as a campus expansion or major refreshing of facilities. However, the depreciation amount may or may not be adequate for routine capital expenditures each year.

2. **Determine your "Big Number."** The Big Number for your budget is the total of budgeted expenses for next year. It is often called the Big Number because determining this one number is often the starting point in the budgeting process.

The Big Number is determined in a variety of ways:

- Some ministries arrive at the Big Number by applying a formula, setting the number at 95%, 100% or 105%, for example, of the prior year budgeted expenses.

- Other ministries do not use a formula but arrive at the Big Number based on giving trends, economic indicators, demographics and more.

Idea

The Big Number is often the starting point in the budgeting process. It is the total of budgeted expenses for the next year.

Some ministries calculate the Big Number early in the budgeting process and others a little later. But it is important to determine when the governing board will set the big budget number. It is also important to determine how to obtain buy-in of the Big Number with the leaders of each program area.

The Big Number for projected expenses may not be the same as the projected total revenue number. This is because planned additions to reserves may be budgeted as an excess of revenue over expenses. Therefore, the total revenue projection will often be higher than the total expense budget.

For example, consider this budget data:

Projected revenue	$1,650,000
Big Number projected expenses	1,500,000
Projected addition to operational reserves	$150,000

Or, consider this example:

Projected revenue	$2,400,000
Big Number projected expenses	2,600,000
Projected use of restricted gifts raised in a prior year	$200,000

3. **Recognize which expenses are subject to budget allocation.** The overall budget can seem overwhelming, but the reality is that a major portion, perhaps most, of the budget is locked in for next year. It usually comes down to expenses for people, facilities, and then everything else.

Here are the budget components that typically offer relatively little allocation flexibility:

- Compensation and fringe benefits

- Facility expenses: mortgage and loan payments, rent, insurance, and utilities

- Capital replacements

- Grant commitments to specific projects or ministry fields

When ministries are preparing budgets and viewing the budget holistically, it is also a good time to look at how to cut costs, especially for a cost category that makes up a large percentage of the budget or is increasing. Budget managers can easily identify these trends and determine a plan to reduce costs during the year. For example, it may be time to meet with vendors who supply IT, HVAC, Internet, telephone services, and insurance premiums. Are there ways to reduce? Generate a list from the accounts payable system of the total payments made to each vendor. Contact the vendors receiving the highest aggregate dollars to review their service level and rates for the coming year.

When a ministry lets its people and facility expenses get out of line, there are fewer funds left for direct program expenses. So, let's say a ministry is spending 50% of its operating budget on personnel and 30% on facility expenses, that only leaves 20% of the budget to allocate for other expenses. Leadership must determine if that is reasonable.

The small portion of the budget that is subject to annual allocation becomes the critical issue when revenues take a downturn. In these instances, cuts in the people budget are usually required.

Cash Reserves

The topic of cash reserves for ministries is age-old. One ministry leader observes that setting aside little or no reserves ignores the biblical admonition to plan and set aside resources for lean times (for example, Joseph planning for a famine). Yet another says that establishing ministry cash reserves shows a lack of faith—"God is sovereign, and He will provide." A healthy tension exists between these positions.

Still, most ministry leaders recognize the wisdom of having some cash reserves. So, if it is wise for a ministry to have cash reserves, the first questions are: how much is enough, how can a ministry build cash reserves, and when should a ministry use cash reserves? A key challenge is demonstrating wise stewardship without hoarding.

Why do ministries need cash reserves? Consider these four reasons:

1. **Cash reserves enable a ministry to honor God.** John Wesley is attributed with the statement: "Our primary responsibility is to give the world the right impression of God." Cash reserves allow a ministry to meet its obligations in a timely manner. Otherwise, a ministry will not give the world the right impression of God.

2. **Cash reserves level out the ebb and flow of revenue and expenses.** Recurring digital gifts help minimize revenue fluctuations. Still, some months will reflect higher giving than others. Some expenses will be consistent from month-to-month, like mortgage payments and rent, while most other expenses will fluctuate. Cash reserves level out the ebb and flow of cash and allow a ministry to operate with integrity.

3. **Cash reserves provide a financial buffer for unplanned events.** Consider these examples: A ministry was hoping to get a few more years from the HVAC system, but it quit functioning in the middle of a hot summer. At another ministry, a lawsuit against the ministry is settled out-of-court, but the settlement and the associated legal fees are significant. Adequate cash reserves help weather these and many other types of unplanned events.

4. **Cash reserves provide the financial platform to take advantage of potential opportunities.** Consider some opportunities that may be presented to a ministry. An outstanding leader inquires about employment at a ministry. There is not a budgeted position for the application, but the person would be an outstanding addition to the staff. For another ministry, a parcel of land that the ministry needs for expansion suddenly goes on the market and other buyers will soon secure it unless the ministry can present a cash offer. Since the ministry could not predict that the land would go on the market, the purchase of the land is not in the budget. Even though the budget did not provide for these opportunities, they might be considered if cash reserves are available.

Creating and maintaining cash reserves is not as easy as it seems. It requires thoughtful planning and faithful administration. There may be pressure to pay down debt early, pressure to increase the compensation of staff, pressure for a new program—but these pressures do not discount the importance of creating and maintaining cash reserves.

The manner in which an organization balances these cash liquidity opportunities will speak volumes about how that ministry demonstrates its financial stewardship.

Understand cash reserves philosophies. There is a broad spectrum of cash reserves philosophies. On one end of the spectrum, some say ministries should have few reserves because "God will provide." On the other end of the scale, some take the position that 12 months of operating reserves should be maintained. Most organizations find neither extreme to be ideal for them.

Setting the cash reserves philosophy for a ministry is generally the responsibility of the governing board. The budget approval process may express the cash reserves philosophy based on the reserves built into or not built into the annual budget.

Make a plan to generate cash reserves. Sometimes a ministry leader might say: "We must balance the cash budget and stay within the cash budget." Staying within the cash budget is certainly preferable to operating outside the cash budget, but if cash inflows consistently equal cash outflows, then cash reserves are not being depleted, nor are they being built.

Here are a few ways ministries might build cash reserves:

1. **Project next year's revenue to be lower than current year expenses.** For example, a ministry may project the budget for the following year at 90% of the current year revenue. Then, if the ensuing year's revenue is equal to or greater than the previous year's revenue, the ministry does not spend all of the difference—some of the positive variance is added to cash reserves and some is used to fund other ministry opportunities.

2. **Look for opportunities to reduce corresponding expense budgets to create cash reserves.** Occasionally, an opportunity to significantly reduce expense line items comes along. The savings can be set aside to add to cash reserves.

> *Example:* A program has run its course. Adhering to the old adage, "When your horse is dead, dismount," the ministry discontinues a program, which has a significant budget. While there will be a temptation to simply reallocate the funds to another program, this is an opportunity to save the funds that were being applied to the discontinued program and shore up cash reserves.

3. **Include a cash reserves line in the budget.** Some ministries budget revenue conservatively and include a line-item in the expense budget for "Additions to Cash Reserves." Then if revenue and expenses equal the budget, an automatic excess of revenue over expenses is generated and the portion not used for capital items goes directly to cash reserves.

4. **Add legacy gifts to cash reserves.** Ministries occasionally receive gifts from wills or matured charitable trusts. These are excellent opportunities to add to cash reserves, if the gifts are not specified for a particular purpose.

5. **Budget depreciation.** If a ministry is using the accrual basis of accounting and budgets depreciation, this can be a way to build cash reserves—that is, if the depreciation exceeds expenditures for capitalized items. Also, see page 113.

Here is the bottom line: The only way to create cash reserves is when cash inflows exceed cash outflows. It is the "law of cash reserves." If cash reserves are not planned, they probably won't happen.

Set aside reserves for restricted gifts. The first priority for the use of cash reserves is to be sure that reserves are at least equal to unspent restricted gifts. A restricted gift is one that is for a purpose more specific than the broad limits imposed by the ministry's purpose and nature, such as (1) restricted for a country, (2) restricted for a project, or (3) other time or purpose restrictions.

Without sufficient reserves to cover unspent restricted gifts, a ministry may not have the resources to spend gifts restricted by givers in a timely manner.

> *Example 1:* A ministry has $100,000 of unspent funds restricted for new technology. The ministry should have at least $100,000 of cash on hand related to these gifts. Further, the $100,000 should be excluded when calculating operating cash reserves.

> *Example 2:* A ministry has total cash balances of $200,000. Of this balance, $75,000 represents unexpended restricted gifts. The $125,000 difference represents operational cash reserves.

Example 3: A ministry has total cash balances of $300,000. At the same time, there are unexpended restricted balances of $350,000.

The difference between $350,000 and $300,000 of $50,000 means that the ministry has spent $50,000 of restricted funds for operating purposes. In other words, the ministry has borrowed $50,000 of restricted funds. The ministry should restore the full $350,000 balance as soon as possible to ensure the timely use of restricted gifts.

Note: Gifts restricted by givers are different from unrestricted net assets designated by a board. Only givers can restrict gifts. Boards can designate unrestricted net assets and may remove the designation.

On page 127 is a simplified Statement of Financial Position which illustrates how to measure cash reserves and determine if any of the reserves relating to gifts with donor restrictions have been borrowed for operating purposes.

Adopt a cash reserves policy. A ministry should consider the following in developing its policy on cash reserves:

a. **Restricted gift reserves.** A sound policy requires the ministry to maintain cash reserves at least equal to the unexpended balance of designated or restricted gifts.

b. **Debt service reserves.** If the ministry has debt, the policy should require maintaining reserves in conformity with mortgage reserve requirements—typically enough to cover several months of mortgage payments. Even without mortgage reserve requirements, a ministry should maintain sufficient reserves to ensure that revenue fluctuations will not impair the ability to keep the mortgage payments current.

c. **Capital replacement reserves.** If the ministry owns its facilities, it is important to consider the life cycle of heating/air conditioning systems, roofing, parking lots, and more. A ministry with aging facilities and/or deferred maintenance may need to give a high priority to building reserves to replace and maintain facilities over and above the need for operating reserves. As Tim Cool with Cool Solutions says in the ebook, *5 Intentional Steps to Establish a Capital Reserve Account*: "All buildings deteriorate and deferred maintenance accelerates the deterioration."

Remember

Attentive stewards evaluate the needs of the community alongside God's seasonal provision, to ensure appropriate reserves are available and ministry is not hindered.

A policy guiding the maintenance of capital replacement reserves can be based on projected life cycles.

d. **Ministry opportunity reserves.** Whether starting a new location or pursuing other major ministry opportunities, cash is needed to get started. Building these reserves will probably not occur without setting goals, perhaps guided by a policy.

e. **Operating reserves cap.** A policy establishing a cap on operating reserves communicates that the ministry is being wise in stewardship rather than hoarding. A cap can be set as a percentage of the budget or as a dollar amount.

f. **Operating reserves floor.** After setting a policy on reserves for restricted gifts, debt service, and other specific reserves, a ministry should have a target for an operating reserves floor. The operating reserves floor is the minimum level the ministry hopes to avoid falling below.

Measure cash reserves. How are cash reserves typically measured? There are two basic options for measuring cash reserves:

1. **Specific amount of cash.** Some ministries set their cash reserve goal based on a specific dollar amount. While this may be a convenient way to set the cash reserve goal, it will require adjusting the cash reserve target amount from time to time based on changes in the ministry's revenue or expense levels.

2. **Number of months of cash.** Projecting cash reserve goals based on the number of months of cash is a common practice. Here is the typical calculation (also see worksheet on page 128):

   - Total operating expenses (excluding amounts expended from net assets with donor restrictions)

   - $\dfrac{\text{total operating expenses}}{12}$ = monthly operating expenses

   - $\dfrac{\text{monthly operating expenses}}{\text{available cash}}$ = The number of months of operating cash

Available cash equals total cash and cash equivalents plus investments readily convertible to cash minus cash equal to unexpended restricted gifts and current liabilities. Available cash should be sufficient to cover current liability balances and should be in addition to the months of operating cash deemed appropriate. Otherwise, a ministry with significant current liabilities could be deluded in thinking cash reserves are adequate when, in fact, there is insufficient cash to cover current liabilities.

A BETTER concept to measure church cash reserves. A more effective approach to measure cash reserves combines the typical months of cash concept with carving out |cash balances that are not available for operating purposes. Use the easy 6-step approach shown on the worksheet on page 128 to determine available operating cash and reflect the number of months of operating cash compared to the cash reserves target.

STEP 1—Determine monthly operating expenses based on the ministry's annual operating budget. Exclude releases from net assets with donor restrictions. The significant use (releases) of net assets with restrictions could skew the cash reserves calculation.

STEP 2—Determine total available cash. Include cash in bank, cash equivalents plus investments readily convertible to cash.

- **Subtract unexpended funds with donor restrictions.**

- **Subtract mortgage reserve amounts.** Even if a mortgage does not have cash reserve requirements, it may be wise to include mortgage reserve amounts in the calculation.

- **Subtract major facility maintenance reserves.** Facility maintenance reserves are especially important for ministry facilities with significant deferred maintenance and or aging facilities.

- **Subtract current liabilities.** A ministry should have enough operating cash to cover current liabilities. This is very important if some liabilities are not current and/or if there is significant deferred revenue.

STEP 3—Determine net available operating cash by subtracting the cash reserve set-asides from total cash.

STEP 4—Determine number of months of operating cash.

STEP 5—Reflect the number of months cash reserve goal. This goal could vary depending on the month of the year. For example, the goal might be lower for months when cash is typically lower and higher when cash is generally higher.

STEP 6—Calculate the number of months of cash reserves over or under the target.

For additional reading, see the eBook—*9 Essentials of Cash Reserves for Ministries* at *www.ECFA.org*, or *9 Essentials of Church Cash Reserves* at *www.ECFA.church*.

YOUR MINISTRY
Statement of Financial Position
August 31, 20XX

ASSETS:
    Current assets:

Cash and cash equivalents	$ 181,072	(1)
Deposits	7,400	
Equipment-net	281,916	
Total Assets	$ 470,388	

LIABILITIES AND NET ASSETS:
    Current liabilities:

Accounts payable	$ 51,670	
Accrued expenses	37,857	
Note payable-current portion	50,000	
Total Liabilities	139,527	

Net assets:
    Without donor restrictions:

Net investment in equipment	281,916	
Unrestricted, undesignated	(33,071)	
	248,845	
With donor restrictions – Purpose restricted	82,016	(2)
	330,861	
Total Liabilities and Net Assets	$ 470,388	

Note:
    Cash and cash equivalents of $181,072 (1) is greater than net assets with restrictions of $82,016 (2). Thus, no borrowing of cash related to net assets with restrictions has occurred.

Cash Reserves Worksheet

		Months		
	Jan	Feb	Mar	Apr
Step 1 – Determine monthly operating expenses				
A. Monthly operating expenses divided by 12[1]	200,000	200,000	200,000	200,000
Step 2 – Determine total available cash				
B. Cash and cash equivalents plus investments readily convertible to cash	1,140,000	1,100,000	1,025,000	1,150,000
C. Subtract cash to cover unexpended gifts with donor restrictions	(70,000)	(90,000)	(65,000)	(85,000)
D. Subtract cash needed for any mortgage reserve	(380,000)	(380,000)	(380,000)	(380,000)
E. Subtract cash needed for major facility maintenance or capital replacement reserves	(200,000)	(200,000)	(175,000)	(175,000)
F. Subtract cash equal to current liabilities	(190,000)	(220,000)	(180,000)	(210,000)
Step 3 – Determine net available operating cash				
G. Net available operating cash (B less C, D, E, F)	200,000	210,000	225,000	300,000
Step 4 – Determine number of months of operating cash				
H. Cash (G) divided by monthly operating expenses (A) = Number of months of cash	1.00	1.05	1.12	1.50
Step 5 – Reflect the cash reserve goal				
I. Target number of months of cash reserves	3.00	2.80	2.80	2.70
Step 6 – Calculate the variance between actual and the goal				
J. Over or <under> cash reserves target	<2.00>	<1.75>	<1.68>	<1.20>

[1] In this example, the annual budget is $2.4M.

Audits and Other Related Services

An annual audit, review, or compilation of the financial statements and the disclosure of the financial statements are key components of transparency, both within a ministry and to givers and the public. This flows directly from biblical principles: "This is the verdict: Light has come into the world, but men loved darkness instead of light because their deeds were evil. Everyone who does evil hates the light, and will not come into the light for fear that his deeds will be exposed" (John 3:19–20).

External audits, reviews, and compilations should be performed by an independent CPA who has no impairing relationship to the ministry and has maximum objectivity. Additionally, internal audits may be performed by members or other volunteers closely associated with the organization.

External services

Selecting the level of CPA service for a ministry requires an understanding of the desired outcome. An audit may be necessary because of criteria such as a requirement in the organization's bylaws or a debt covenant. It may also be that the ministry is large enough that an audit is a good internal control and provides more accountability and transparency to the constituents. A review may be helpful for a smaller ministry that desires to have a third party involved but doesn't have the size or complexity to require a full audit. If an organization chooses to have a compilation, it may want to consider including some agreed-upon procedures testing at the same time or at another time during the year. It is a cost-effective way to gain greater confidence in certain areas of operations. See ECFA's eBooks—*7 Essentials of Preparing for an Audit, Review, or Compilation for Ministries* and *7 Essentials of Preparing for a Church Audit, Review, or Compilation.*

An **audit** is a formal examination of financial statements intended to assess the accuracy and thoroughness of financial records. An independent CPA performs this procedure on a set of financial statements in order to render an opinion based on the accounting records provided. An unmodified audit opinion states that the financial statements are in conformity with accounting principles generally accepted in the United States (GAAP). Audits are performed according to auditing standards generally accepted in the United States (GAAS). An audit is generally more expensive than a review or compilation because an opinion on the accuracy of financial statements requires significantly more work than that involved in either a review or a compilation. The result should be an audit report in addition to a management comment letter describing any material weaknesses or significant deficiencies that may exist in the organization's systems or processes.

A **review** is the performance of limited procedures as a basis for expressing limited assurance on financial statements. Although not as comprehensive as an audit, a review provides some assurance. This is compared to no assurance provided with respect to a compilation. A review report states that: (1) the accountants do not express an opinion on the financial statements, and (2) based on their review, they are not aware of any material modifications that should be made to the financial statements. A review is generally less expensive than an audit but more expensive than a compilation. In performing this accounting service, the accountant must conform to the American Institute of Certified Public Accountants (AICPA) Statements on Standards for Accounting and Review Services (SSARS).

RECOMMENDATIONS FOR INTERNAL/EXTERNAL AUDITS AND CPA ENGAGEMENT

TOTAL ANNUAL REVENUE	RECOMMENDATIONS	
↑ 3M	Internal Audit ✚	External audit of financial statements (GAAP/GAAS)
2M to 3M	Internal Audit ✚	External review of financial statements prepared on either the accrual or modified-cash basis of accounting
250K to 2M	Internal Audit ✚	Compiled financial statements prepared on either the accrual or modified-cash basis of accounting
At least 250K	Internal Audit ✚	When possible, compiled financial statements prepared on either the accrual or modified-cash basis os accounting

A **compilation** is the gathering of financial information and the creation of financial statements for an organization. A compilation involves no assurance on the financial statements, as the accountant simply assembles the financial statements for the organization. In performing this accounting service, the accountant must conform to SSARS.

Agreed-upon procedures may be appropriate when an audit, review, or compilation is not required or selected. An independent CPA is engaged to report findings on specific procedures performed on a particular subject matter. For example, an agreed-upon procedures engagement might be performed to evaluate an organization's internal control procedures, cash handling procedures, or worker classification procedures.

A good choice for a CPA firm is one that:

> ➤ is thoroughly knowledgeable about current accounting standards and one that understands the organization's niche of Christ-centered nonprofits

> ➤ routinely prepares value-added management letters for its audit clients

> ➤ helps minimize fees

> ➤ understands the organization's accounting system

Remember

Independence is the cornerstone of the external CPA. The independent CPA should have no ties to management and no responsibility for governance or finance. The public can place faith in the audit or review function because an independent CPA is impartial and recognizes an obligation of fairness.

Preparing for an external CPA service. Any external involvement in an organization's finances causes an additional level of work. It can seem overwhelming, especially the first time. Here are some keys to simplify the process:

• Start earlier than you think is necessary in preparing for a CPA engagement.

• Clear, upfront, and ongoing communication with the CPA will minimize unnecessary work or possible frustration. Ask questions along the way.

• Perform reconciliations throughout the year. Accounts such as cash, investments, contributions, and payroll should be reconciled monthly rather than waiting to do it at year-end.

• Prepare all requested items *before* the CPA begins work. What may take hours to prepare will only take minutes to review.

• Determine what staff will be involved in the engagement and be certain they are available during the scheduled time.

- If a ministry has never gathered information related to its fixed assets, an excellent start is to review the accounting records for the previous five years and gather information on furniture and equipment that has been purchased. For buildings that are older and where invoices may not exist, staff can work with the CPA to determine options, but usually a value can be determined based on information such as previous board minutes or past county assessor's records.

Internal audits

Volunteers or members of the organization may form an audit committee to perform an internal audit to determine the validity of the financial statements. The result may be significant improvements in internal control and accounting procedures. A key concept of an internal audit is to *test* a sample of transactions, not to *review* all the transactions. For more information on internal audits, see ECFA's eBooks—*10 Essentials of Ministry Internal Audits* and *10 Essentials of Church Internal Audits*.

International Financial Activity

Christ-centered ministries are often directly involved in international ministries, including sending or spending money overseas. With those activities come certain additional responsibilities.

2 Corinthians 8:18-21 stresses the importance of being above reproach. As ministries have a global reach, proper accountability and oversight over the funds being received and sent is critical. Fostering accountability is not only good stewardship, it also speaks volumes to those with whom we interact. Givers are also encouraged in generosity when they have a high level of trust in the ministry they support.

Sending or spending ministry funds internationally requires significant attention to legal and other compliance requirements. Ministries should understand the requirements before engaging in international financial activity.

The word "grant" is the term used by the IRS when discussing international activity. A leader might think, "this doesn't apply to our ministry; we do not make grants." However, the IRS uses this term broadly to mean transfer, disbursement, contribution, noncash assistance, stipends, scholarships, reimbursement, and so on. If a ministry sends funds or provides any services internationally, the term "grant" generally applies.

On the other hand, if a ministry partners with other U.S.-based 501(c)(3) organizations to carry out international ministry on their behalf, the essentials outlined here apply to those organizations. Before an organization partners with another to carry out international ministry on their behalf, they should ensure the partner has policies and procedures in place for proper accountability and legal compliance.

Good governance, disclosure, transparency, and financial accountability are hallmarks of responsible ministries. There is, however, no single set of "best practices" for all international grant-making. The board of directors of each ministry is responsible for establishing a culture of compliance with laws and regulations, empowering the ministry to adopt suitable governance practices.

Monitor the use of funds. It is important for a ministry to maintain complete and accurate records of all funds sent internationally. Monitoring the use of funds to ensure they are used for the purpose agreed upon is also important.

The ministry must maintain responsibility for the funds as they are expended. There are four main elements of expenditure responsibility that should be followed. Follow these steps to demonstrate sound grant oversight.

Step 1: Perform a pre-grant inquiry. A pre-grant inquiry should consider identity, prior history, and experience of the grantee organization and its managers. Any knowledge or other information concerning the management, activities, and practices of the grantee organization should also be considered when deciding to provide funding. The scope of the inquiry will vary based on size and purpose of the grant. Also, the inquiry may be waived if there is prior history of compliance or if the individual receiving the funds is an employee of the U.S. ministry.

Step 2: Execute a written grant agreement. It is wise for a grant-making ministry to have written grant agreements for all funds that are sent internationally to foreign organizations and individuals. The grant agreement should be specific as to the overall purpose of the funds and the timing of the grant agreement. The agreement should also commit the grant-making ministry to the following:

Remember

The oversight of funds spent internationally is often a challenging issue. Making an international gift or grant is only the starting point.

- Repaying any funds not used for purposes of the grant

- Submitting full and complete reports at least annually, describing how funds are spent and the progress in completing the purposes of the grant

- Maintaining records of receipts and expenditures

- Making records available to the grant-making ministry at reasonable times

- Not using funds to influence legislation or political outcomes

- Using the funds only for the exempt purpose of the grant-making ministry

Step 3: Require periodic reporting. Proper reporting emphasizes control and accountability over the funds that are provided. Reporting may take on different forms depending on who the funds were sent to and for what purpose. For more specific information on reporting related to international grant-making, ECFA offers the following document: "Guidelines for International Grant-Making" in its Knowledge Center at *www.ECFA.org/KnowledgeCenter*.

If a ministry has an ongoing relationship and sends funds on a regular basis, annual reporting should be required at a minimum. Quarterly reporting is often appropriate for larger grants.

Step 4: Take additional steps to ensure grantees fulfill the grant agreement. Based on the amount of the grant, it may be prudent and necessary to take additional oversight steps. For example, the larger the grant, the more appropriate and necessary are periodic visits to the location where the grant funds are expended. This could be accomplished by personnel from the grant-making ministry or perhaps by a report from a ministry partner working in the same region of the world.

Screen and vet the grant recipients. When a ministry sends grant funds internationally to an organization, it is important to obtain the names of top leadership, board members, and key individuals receiving the funds. Obtain the names in English translation and any other aliases the individual goes by. All the names should be compared against the Office of Foreign Assets Control (OFAC) list: List of Specially Designated Nationals and Blocked Persons. Several commercial tools are also available for vetting, but they can be expensive and will generally require substantial activity to be cost-effective.

Remember

The larger the grant, the higher the level of due diligence should be exercised by the ministry making the grant of funds.

For each separate transaction, it is wise to document the names of each individual and foreign organization that the ministry searched for on the OFAC list, the screenshot image of the search on the OFAC site, and what additional procedures were completed if there was a match.

When screening an organization against the OFAC list, it is recommended that the search is done for all board members, top leadership, and the main contact for the organization who is entrusted with the funds.

A match with the OFAC list could potentially be a false "positive" due to similar names and translations. When a match is identified, it is critical to follow some additional steps to verify whether it is a positive match.

Here is a process to use in searching for false "positives" in the screening process:

- Identify any other characteristics that may be helpful in reviewing. The more identifying information one has, the better.

- Obtain testimonies from other people.

- Visit the Department of Treasury FAQ page.

- Make the best determination possible.

When screening, also consider if the proposed activities will take place in whole or in part in an OFAC-sanctioned country. Even if the activities will be in a non-sanctioned country, consider if there is a high number of sanctioned individuals in the country where activities will take place. This could increase the likelihood of interaction with sanctioned individuals. The ministry might also consider including grant language that the grantee must comply with OFAC sanctions when disbursing funds.

Report on foreign accounts and transporting cash. When operating internationally, there may be a need to establish a foreign bank account to hold funds. This account may have employees or foreign partners that are on the account as signatories.

The FinCEN 114 Report, including a Report of Foreign Bank and Financial Accounts (FBAR), is a required filing for a U.S. person having a financial interest or signatory authority over financial accounts where the aggregate value of the foreign accounts exceeds $10,000 at any time during the calendar year. For purposes of this form, a U.S. person includes an individual, partnership, limited liability corporation, or a corporation—including a nonprofit corporation or church. A U.S. citizen having signing authority on a foreign bank account for business purposes or personal purposes is required to file a FinCEN 114 report. *It is important to remember that both the organization and the individual, if a U.S. citizen, having signing authority must file the FinCEN 114 Report.*

The FinCEN 114 Report is due on April 15th of each year. There is an automatic extension available with no requirement to file an extension form. With the automatic extension, the form is due by October 15th. The form must be filed

Remember

The rules governing the international transportation of currency are often overlooked at the peril of a ministry.

electronically. A third party may prepare and file the form but both the individual and organization must complete a FinCEN 114(a) form giving authorization for a third party to complete.

Transporting cash (FinCEN Form 105). Ministries involved in international activity sometimes ask staff or volunteers to carry significant cash on a trip. When transporting cash, the process must be properly handled in order to reduce the risks of significant fines, jail time, and forfeiture of funds.

There are three main questions that every ministry should consider before asking staff or volunteers to transport cash:

1. Is this absolutely necessary?

2. Does this place staff or volunteers at an elevated security risk?

3. Are there appropriate internal controls to protect both the ministry and the individuals involved?

After analyzing these three questions, if it is determined that the ministry must still transport cash, it is important to understand the potential legal ramifications and reporting requirements. It is not enough to just understand U.S. law; the country of destination may also have legal disclosure requirements.

The FinCEN Form 105 is to report on international transportation of currency or monetary instruments. This form is generally required when carrying more than $10,000 of cash in or out of the U.S. This form applies to either a single individual or entity transporting an aggregate of more than $10,000 of cash.

> *Example:* XYZ Ministry is sending a team of 10 doctors and nurses to visit a local hospital in Haiti. During the visit, the team will provide medical care and provide support to the doctors and nurses onsite. As part of the trip, it is required that the team bring cash to cover the cost of lodging, meals, transportation, and supplies while in country. Due to banking issues, a wire transfer is not possible. Therefore, the team is bringing $15,000 in cash. The team splits the cash between three people in order to not have any one individual carry more than the $10,000 limit. In this example, the team representing the ministry is taking over $10,000. The FinCEN Form 105 **is required** to be completed because the team in aggregate exceeded the $10,000 limit.

For more information on when and where to file, see the instructions printed on the FinCEN Form 105.

Also see ECFA's eBooks—*5 Essentials of International Financial Activity for Churches* and *6 Essentials of International Financial Activity for Ministries.*

Fraud

Internal controls and preventing fraud

Fraud and misuse of ministry resources is the fodder for really sensational news. When this happens, it is generally attributed to all ministries. Sadly, this causes a diminished witness of the Gospel in the sight of skeptics.

An additional perspective in fraud prevention is to consider what happens when a staff member is subjected to inaccurate accusations of fraud. If the organization has not allowed for adequate controls, that person may be without any means to disprove the accusations, resulting in a grave injustice to the staff member.

So why don't we eliminate the possibility of any fraud being committed by utilizing better internal controls? The simple answer is that it is impossible. The processes necessary to eliminate all fraud are nothing short of having a small army of employees rotating through different jobs as they separately review each transaction, with checks and balances that would bring any organization to a grinding halt. This would not be effective stewardship. Therefore, our goal should not be to eliminate all fraud but to find a reasonable balance between preventive efforts and risks.

Idea

Good fraud controls will minimize ministry financial losses *and* protect staff from inaccurate accusations of financial improprieties.

For resources on minimizing fraud, see the ECFA eBooks—*10 Essentials of Church Internal Controls, 10 Essentials of Internal Controls for Ministries, 9 Essentials of Avoiding Church Fraud,* and *9 Essentials of Avoiding Ministry Fraud.*

How to detect fraud

The Association of Certified Fraud Examiners (ACFE) reports that merely relying on one fraud detection tool is ineffective in uncovering fraud. It also highlights the importance of equipping personnel with a means to effectively report suspicions without fear of retribution, especially when the job market is tight. For this reason, each organization should have a whistleblower policy in place.

The frequency of discovering fraud is also higher when an organization has taken proactive steps to look for fraud. Ministry leaders should review systems and transactions, internal audits should be performed, reconciliations should be performed on a timely basis, and other monitoring that senior staff may conduct will help prevent unnecessary steps in operations as well as enhance fraud prevention and detection. It is important that an organization's leadership sets the example in fraud detection from the top down, rather than trivializing these important steps.

Looking for fraud can take a variety of forms, and it is helpful if this process is modified periodically to prevent measures from being easily anticipated. Senior staff will want to:

➢ **Review and check procedures.** In reviewing processes, a leader may find procedures that are antiquated or ineffective to accomplish the goal. A leader should be able to provide a logical reason for any step in the process.

Tip

Consider job cross-training and mandatory vacations for employees as a fraud detection stop.

➢ **Look for uncorrected errors.** If an error goes unnoticed by anyone in an office, this could form the opportunity element for an employee, just waiting for pressure and rationalization. If a leader discovers an uncorrected error, especially a substantial one, then the review process should be evaluated to prevent this from reoccurring.

➢ **Look for trends, abnormalities, or inconsistencies.** A leader should review inconsistencies or changes to see if there are correlations to a certain worker. For example, every time a certain pair of workers count funds, there appears to be a drop in gifts received.

➢ **Look for unwillingness to let others help.** It is fairly common for fraud or errors to be discovered when someone goes on leave or takes a vacation. This is a good reason, among others, to consider job cross-training and mandatory vacations for employees.

How to prevent fraud

The best way to prevent fraud is to look for it. Looking for fraud and internal controls in general should be structured to prevent any person from developing the opportunity to commit fraud undetected.

Tip

Structure internal controls so that no one person has the opportunity to commit fraud undetected.

Surveys show that weaknesses creating an opportunity for fraud mostly relate to either not having sufficient controls in place or a lack of leadership to adequately review, update, and test controls to ensure effectiveness. This equates to a double impact for organizations. First, it indicates a vulnerability to fraud opportunities. Second, it's likely that resources have been ineffectively expended in trying to prevent fraud. It is important for leaders to continually review fraud prevention efforts and to maintain a balance between prevention and program operations. This is a process, not just a one-time event.

What to do when fraud is discovered

When fraud is discovered, time is of the essence since there may be time limitations for pursuing legal recourse or recovering the funds before they or related records disappear. A ministry should consider working through the following steps in a timely manner:

1. Discuss the fraud with the organization's insurance carrier.

2. Contact an attorney with expertise in handling fraud cases.

3. Consider engaging a certified fraud examiner.

4. Investigate the complaint swiftly and thoroughly with expert help.

5. Consider protecting other organizations by notifying law enforcement.

- **Handling incoming funds.** The handling of incoming funds by a church or other nonprofit organization is one of the most critical elements of the financial management process. The potential of embezzlement is often high at the point funds are received.

  Sound policies and procedures should be adopted and followed to ensure no funds are lost at the point of entry. Sound internal controls also protect the staff members or volunteers handling the funds. Pastors and ministry leaders should not be involved in day-to-day financial transactions but should set a strong tone of accountability at the top.

- **Choosing an accounting method.** The choice of an accounting method has many implications. Large organizations generally use the accrual basis of accounting throughout the year and use the same approach for budgeting, while smaller organizations often utilize the cash or modified cash basis of accounting.

  The basis of accounting used for interim financial statements can be changed at year-end by posting a few journal entries. Reverse those entries on the first day of the subsequent accounting year, and the books are back to the previous accounting method.

  To ensure comparative financial data, it is important that the same approach (accrual, modified cash, or cash) be used on the accounting records throughout the year as is used for budgeting purposes.

- **Preventing and detecting fraud.** No ministry is beyond the possibility of being a fraud victim. However, well planned internal controls and ongoing monitoring by ministry leaders will help to prevent many possible opportunities for fraud.

CHAPTER 7 Charitable Gifts

While most givers care more about the reason for giving than about the potential tax implications, the joy of giving should never be reduced by unexpected tax results.

In tax law, a "gift" is an unconditional transfer of cash or property with no personal benefit to the giver. The mere transfer of funds to a church or nonprofit is not necessarily a gift. For example, when a parent pays the college tuition for a child, there is no gift or charitable deduction despite the tax-exempt educational nature of the organization. Yet, a gift restricted for a specific ministry purpose or for a future time period is an unconditional transfer.

If payments are made to a ministry to receive something in exchange (an "exchange transaction"), that transaction is more in the nature of a purchase. The tax law states that a transfer to a nonprofit is not a contribution when made "with a reasonable expectation of financial return commensurate with the amount of the transfer." When one transfer comprises both a gift and a purchase, only the gift portion is tax-deductible to the giver.

The two broad categories of charitable gifts are outright gifts and deferred gifts. Outright gifts require that the giver immediately transfer possession and use of the gift property to the recipient ministry. In deferred giving, the giver also makes a current gift, but the gift is of a future interest. Accordingly, actual possession and use of the gift property by the recipient ministry is deferred until the future.

Charitable contributions are deductible if given "to and for the use" of a "qualified" tax-exempt organization to be used under its control to accomplish its exempt purposes. ("Qualified" organizations are churches and other domestic 501(c)(3) organizations.)

The following are three types of gifts commonly given to churches and other nonprofit organizations:

➤ **Gifts *without* giver restrictions.** Contributions received without giver restrictions (e.g., "use where needed most") are generally tax-deductible.

➤ **Gifts *with* giver restrictions.** Givers often place restrictions on gifts that limit their use to certain purposes or times. These stipulations specify a use for a contributed asset that is more specific than the broad limits relating to the nature of the ministry, the environment in which it operates, and the purposes specified in its articles of incorporation or bylaws (or comparable documents for unincorporated entities). A restricted gift generally results whenever a giver selects a giving option on a response device other than "unrestricted" or "where needed most."

Remember

The practice by nonprofits of raising funds with the gifts *preferenced* for the ministry support of certain employees of the organization is often called deputized or staff-support fundraising. The IRS acknowledges that deputized fundraising is a widespread and legitimate practice, and contributions properly raised by this method are tax-deductible (see Chapter 8).

➤ **Personal gifts.** Gifts made through a ministry to an individual, where the giver has specified, by name, the identity of the person who is to receive the gift, generally are not tax-deductible.

If gifts are *earmarked* for a specific individual, no tax deduction is generally allowed unless the organization exercises adequate discretion and control over the funds and they are spent for program activities of the ministry (see pages 175-78 for a discussion of preferenced gifts).

A ministry does not have a sound position to accept personal gifts. However, if the ministry accepts personal gifts, charitable gift receipts should not be issued to the giver, and the ministry should affirmatively advise givers that these gifts are not tax-deductible.

Charitable Gift Options

Irrevocable nontrust gifts

The following types of gifts may not be revoked by the giver, and they do not involve a trust agreement:

➤ **Cash.** A gift of cash is the simplest method of giving. A cash gift is deductible within the adjusted gross income limitations, depending on the type of the recipient organization. Generally the 60% limit applies; for gifts to certain types of organizations, the limit is 30%, although under the CARES Act there has been a temporary suspension of these limits on charitable deductions. For tax year 2020, individuals may deduct up to 100% of their adjusted gross income.

➤ **Securities.** For stocks and bonds held long-term (12 months or more) the contribution deduction is the mean between the highest and lowest selling prices on the date of the gift where there is a market for listed securities. On the other hand, the contribution deduction is limited to cost for securities held short-term.

> *Example:* An individual taxpayer plans to make a gift of $50,000 to a college. To provide the capital, the taxpayer planned to sell stock that had cost $20,000 some years earlier, yielding a long-term capital gain of $30,000. The taxpayer decides to donate the stock instead of donating the proceeds of the sale. The taxpayer qualifies for a contribution deduction of $50,000, and the unrealized gain on the stock is not taxable.

➤ **Real estate.** The contribution deduction for a gift of real estate is based on the fair market value on the date of the gift. If there is a mortgage on the property, the value must be reduced by the amount of the debt.

➤ **Life insurance.** The owner of a life insurance policy may choose to give it to a charitable organization. The deduction will equal one of the following: the cash surrender value of the policy, its replacement value, its tax basis, or its "interpolated terminal reserve" value (a value slightly more than cash surrender value). However, the deduction cannot exceed the giver's tax basis in the policy.

➤ **Bargain sale.** A bargain sale is part donation and part sale. It is a sale of property to the nonprofit in which the amount of the sale proceeds is less than the property's fair market value. The excess of the fair market value of the property over the sales price represents a charitable contribution to the ministry. Generally, each part of a bargain sale is a reportable event, so the giver reports both a sale and a contribution.

➢ **Remainder interest in a personal residence or life estate.** A charitable contribution of the remainder interest in a personal residence (including a vacation home) or farm creates an income tax deduction equal to the present value of that future interest.

➢ **Charitable gift annuity.** With a charitable gift annuity, the giver purchases an annuity contract from a ministry for more than its fair value. This difference in values between what the giver could have obtained and what the giver actually obtained represents a charitable contribution. The contribution is tax-deductible in the year the giver purchases the annuity.

Idea

The American Council on Gift Annuities suggests a list of charitable gift annuity rates for use by charities and their givers. The latest are available at www.acga-web.org.

➢ **Donor-advised funds.** Donor-advised gifts may be made to a donor-advised fund (DAF). A DAF is defined as a fund or account that is separately identified by reference to contributions of a donor or donors, is owned and controlled by a charitable sponsoring organization, and to which a donor (or any person appointed or designated by the donor) has advisory privileges with respect to the distribution or investment of amounts in the fund.

A donor makes an irrevocable contribution of cash and/or securities to the separate fund or account. The donor is eligible for a tax deduction at the time of the contribution to the DAF even though the DAF may distribute the funds to one or more charities in a subsequent tax year. The donor makes recommendations to the trustees ("advises" the trustees) for grants to be made out of his or her separate fund with the DAF. The representatives of the DAF then review these recommended grants to verify whether the target organization is a qualified charity.

The right of a donor to make recommendations to the trustees of a DAF generally does not constitute a restricted gift. However, if a gift to a DAF is restricted by the donor as to purpose or time, with the right to make recommendations as to the eventual charitable recipient(s) of the funds, this gift is temporarily or permanently restricted, based on the nature of the restriction.

Irrevocable gifts in trust

The following types of gifts involve a trust agreement, and the gift may not be revoked by the giver:

➢ **Charitable remainder annuity trust.** With an annuity trust, the giver retains the right to a specified annuity amount for a fixed period or the lifetime of the designated income beneficiary. The giver fixes the amount payable by an annuity trust at the inception of the trust.

➤ **Charitable remainder unitrust.** The unitrust and annuity trust are very similar with two important differences: (1) the unitrust payout rate is applied to the fair market value of the net trust assets, determined annually, to establish the distributable amount each year, as contrasted to a fixed payment with an annuity trust, and (2) additional contributions may be made to a unitrust compared to one-time gifts allowable to annuity trusts.

➤ **Charitable lead trust.** The charitable lead trust is the reverse of the charitable remainder trust. The giver transfers property into a trust, creating an income interest in the property in favor of the charitable organization for a period of years or for the life or lives of an individual or individuals. The remainder interest is either returned to the giver or given to a noncharitable beneficiary (usually a family member).

➤ **Pooled income fund.** A pooled income fund consists of separate contributions of property from numerous givers. A pooled income fund's payout to its income beneficiaries is not a fixed percentage. The rate of return that the fund earns each year determines the annual payout.

Revocable gifts

The following are other types of gifts that may be revoked by a giver:

➤ **Trust savings accounts.** A trust savings account may be established at a bank, credit union, or savings and loan institution. The account is placed in the name of the depositor "in trust for" a beneficiary, which is a person or organization other than the depositor.

The depositor retains full ownership and control of the account. The beneficiary receives the money in the account when the depositor dies.

➤ **Insurance and retirement plan proceeds.** A ministry may be named the beneficiary of an insurance policy or retirement plan. The owner of the policy

Idea

To set up a charitable remainder trust, a giver places cash or certain assets—such as publicly traded securities or unmortgaged real estate—in a trust that will ultimately benefit a charity. The giver gets an immediate income tax deduction and collects payments from the trust. Before accepting the administration of a charitable remainder trust, a charity should determine if it has the resources to properly administer the trust.

or retirement plan completes a form naming the nonprofit as the beneficiary, and the policy or plan provider accepts the form in writing. The gift may be for part or all of the proceeds.

➢ **Bequests.** By a specific bequest, an individual may direct that, at death, a ministry shall receive either a specified dollar amount or specific property. Through a residuary bequest, an individual may give the estate portion that remains after the payment of other bequests, debts, taxes, and expenses.

Percentage Limitations

Charitable deductions for a particular tax year are limited as follows:

➢ Gifts of cash and ordinary income property to public charities and all private operating foundations and certain private foundations are limited to 60% of adjusted gross income (AGI). Any excess may generally be carried forward up to five years.

Remember

This limit increased temporarily from 50% to 60% under tax reform effective for 2018 and is set to expire after December 31, 2025. *Alert:* This limit has been suspended under the CARES Act and is set at 100% for 2020 only.

➢ Gifts of long-term (held 12 months or more) capital gain property to public charities and private operating foundations are limited to 30% of AGI. The same five-year carry-forward is possible.

➢ Givers of capital gain property to public charities and private operating foundations may use the 50% limitation, instead of the 30% limitation, where the amount of the contribution is reduced by all the unrealized appreciation (nontaxed gain) in the value of the property.

➢ Gifts of cash, short-term (held less than 12 months) capital gain property, and ordinary income property to private foundations and certain other charitable donees (other than public charities and private operating foundations) are generally limited to the item's cost basis and 30% of AGI. The carry-forward rules apply to these gifts.

➢ Gifts of long-term (held 12 months or more) capital gain property to private foundations and other charitable donees (other than public charities and private operating foundations) are generally limited to 20% of AGI. There is no carry-forward for these gifts.

➤ Charitable contribution deductions by corporations in any tax year may not exceed 10% of pre-tax net income (taxable income). Excess contributions may be carried forward up to five years (under the CARES Act, this limitation was suspended and replaced with 25% for 2020).

Gifts That May Not Qualify as Contributions

Some types of gifts do not result in a tax deduction, and no contribution acknowledgment should be provided by the charity in certain situations:

➤ **Earmarked gifts.** When computing one's tax return, most taxpayers know that they cannot count tuition payments as a charitable deduction, even though the check is made out to a charity. In addition, most taxpayers know that their tuition payments are still not deductible if they are paid to another charity with instructions to forward the funds to a certain educational institution. Unfortunately, far too few givers and charities apply the same logic to other similar circumstances.

Warning

Gifts restricted for projects by givers qualify for a charitable deduction. Gifts preferenced for ministry support under the deputized fundraising concept (see Chapter 8) may qualify for a charitable deduction. But when a giver places too many restrictions on a gift, especially when he or she wants the gift to personally benefit a certain individual, it often does not qualify for a charitable deduction.

Some earmarked gifts may qualify for a charitable gift deduction, *e.g.*, a gift earmarked for the building fund. However, other earmarked gifts generally do not meet the requirements of a charitable gift. Here are some examples:

> "I realize they have no connection with your ministry, but if I give the ministry $500, will you pass it through to them and give me a charitable receipt?"

> "I want to give $10,000 to the ministry so the funds can be passed on to a college to cover the tuition for the pastor's daughter. Will the ministry process this gift and give me a receipt?"

Examples like these are donations "earmarked" for individuals. They are also called "conduit" or "pass-through" transactions. These connotations are negative references when used by the IRS and generally denote amounts that do not qualify for a charitable deduction. To be deductible, the ministry must have discretion and control over the contribution without any obligation to benefit a designated individual.

A telltale sign of an earmarked gift is when someone says they want to "run a gift through the ministry," "pass a gift through the ministry," or "process a gift through the ministry." Of course, it is possible the giver will not so clearly signal an earmarked gift and use more general terminology. This is why ministries should clearly understand the concept of earmarked gifts in addition to an awareness of telltale terminology.

Though the concept of earmarked gifts in tax law is well-established, it can be hard to apply to specific situations. Several issues may impact the complexities of these gifts:

☐ The giver's motivation may be loving and charitable in a broad sense; he or she really wants to help, and the only problem is the desire for control.

☐ Many ministries are lax in monitoring this area, and the giver may well say, "If your charity won't process this gift for me, I know of another charity that will handle it."

☐ Sometimes the difference between a nondeductible earmarked gift and a deductible restricted gift is not who benefits but only who determines the beneficiary.

It is wise to establish and follow clear policies to prohibit givers from passing money through a ministry simply to gain a tax benefit.

Though many charitable donations are based on a sense of charity, selflessness, and even love, the IRS believes that people may also have other motivations. The law prevents givers from having undue influence over ministries. It restricts givers from manipulating a ministry into serving noncharitable interests while receiving a deduction for it at the same time.

A special category of earmarked gifts is one in which a giver passes a gift through the ministry for the giver's personal benefit. Such gifts often raise issues beyond the loss of a charitable deduction. Examples include

☐ Scholarship gifts passed through a ministry for the giver's children (instead of paying tuition directly) raise allegations of tax fraud.

☐ A gift to purchase life insurance on the giver benefiting his or her family resulted in a law which can cause substantial penalties for both the giver and organization.

Gifts to a ministry for the support of missionaries or other workers (often called "deputized fundraising") are subject to a different set of guidelines than those generally associated with earmarked gifts. Gifts made under a properly structured deputized fundraising program are generally tax-deductible to the giver (see Chapter 8).

➤ **Strings attached.** A gift must generally be complete and irrevocable to qualify for a charitable deduction. There is usually no charitable deduction if the giver leaves "strings attached" that can be pulled later to bring the gift back to the giver or remove it from the control of the ministry.

> *Example:* An individual makes a "gift" of $10,000 to a ministry. The "gift" is followed or preceded by the sale from the ministry to the giver of an asset valued at $25,000 for $15,000. In this instance, the $10,000 paid to the ministry does not qualify as a charitable contribution. It also raises the issue of private inurement relating to the sale by the ministry.

➤ **Services.** No deduction is allowed for the contribution of services to a charity.

> *Example:* A carpenter donates two months of labor on the construction of a new facility built by a ministry. The time involved in the carpentry work does not qualify for a charitable deduction. The carpenter is entitled to a charitable deduction for any donated out-of-pocket expenses including mileage (14 cents per mile for 2020) for driving to and from the project. If the donated out-of-pocket expenses are $250 or more in a calendar year, the carpenter will need an acknowledgment from the ministry to substantiate the charitable deduction (see page 202 for a sample letter).

Warning

When a person makes a gift of services to a ministry, it may be the highest gift that can be made—a gift of one's time and talents. However, the gift of services does not qualify for a charitable deduction, and it should never be receipted by the ministry— only appreciation should be expressed. A volunteer's unreimbursed, out-of-pocket expenses related to the gift of services may qualify as a charitable gift.

Use of property. The gift of the right to use property does not yield a tax deduction to the giver.

> *Example:* An individual provides a ministry with the rent-free use of an automobile for a year. No charitable deduction is available for the value of that use. If the individual who provided the car also paid the taxes, insurance, repairs, gas, or oil for the vehicle while it was used by

the ministry, these unreimbursed, out-of-pocket expenses are deductible as a charitable contribution.

Charitable Gift Timing

A charitable gift is considered made on the date of delivery. This date is important because it determines the tax year in which the gift is deductible, the valuation date (when applicable), and the date for determining whether the gift qualifies for short-term or long-term property (when applicable).

➤ **Checks.** Under the "delivered-when-mailed" rule, if a giver mails a contribution check to a nonprofit organization, the date of the mailing is deemed the date of delivery, if there are no restrictions on the time or manner of payment and the check is honored when presented.

There are two exceptions:

☐ **Postdated checks.** The date of mailing will not make any difference if the check is postdated. A postdated check is not an immediately payable contribution, but it is a promise to pay on the date shown.

☐ **Checks that bounce.** Generally, if a check is dishonored for insufficient funds, the gift will not be deemed to have been made when it was mailed or delivered.

Normally, the date on a U.S. Mail postmark will conclusively establish the date of mailing. A postage meter date may not be sufficient to establish the date of delivery for a gift that is mailed. The "delivered-when-mailed" rule applies to delivery by the U.S. Postal Service, not to private couriers.

Example 1: A giver mails a check with a postmark of December 31, 2020. The ministry does not receive the check until January 7, 2021. The ministry deposits the check in its bank on January 7, and it clears the giver's bank on January 10. The gift is deductible by the giver in 2020.

Example 2: A giver delivers a check to the ministry on December 31, 2020. The giver asks that the check be held for three months. Complying with the giver's request, the ministry deposits the check on March 31, 2021. This gift is deductible by the giver in 2021.

Example 3: A giver delivers a check to the ministry on January 5, 2021. The check is dated December 31, 2020. The gift is deductible by the giver in 2021.

➤ **Credit cards.** A contribution charged to a credit card is deductible by the giver on the date the charge is reflected by the credit card issuer, even though the credit card bill is not paid until the next year.

➤ **Electronic funds transfers.** IRS Publication 526 (Charitable Contributions) does not provide specific guidance on electronic funds transfers (EFTs) via the internet or mobile devices. It says "pay-by-phone" arrangements are not deductible at the time the giver directs the payment but rather when the payment is made by the financial institution.

➤ **Pledge.** A pledge is not deductible until payment or other satisfaction of the pledge is made.

➤ **Securities.** A contribution of stock is completed upon the unconditional delivery of a properly endorsed stock certificate to a ministry or its agent. If the stock is mailed and is received by the ministry or its agent in the ordinary course of the mail, the gift is effective on the date of mailing. If the giver delivers a stock certificate to the issuing corporation or to the giver's broker for transfer to the name of the ministry, the contribution is not completed until the stock is actually transferred on the corporation's books.

➤ **Real estate.** A gift of real estate is deductible at the time a properly executed deed is delivered to the ministry. However, state law may require that the deed be recorded for delivery to be complete.

Acknowledging and Reporting Charitable Gifts

Contributors to a ministry seeking a federal income tax charitable contribution deduction must produce, if asked, a written receipt from the organization for all gifts of currency and other single contributions valued at $250 or more. Although for the IRS, the burden of compliance with the $250 or more rule falls on the giver, in reality, the burden and administrative costs fall on the ministry, not the giver.

The IRS can fine a ministry that deliberately issues a false acknowledgment to a contributor. The fine is up to $1,000 if the giver is an individual and $10,000 if the giver is a corporation.

For more information on gift acknowledgments, see ECFA's eBooks—*7 Essentials of Cash Gift Acknowledgments for Ministries, 7 Essentials of Cash Gift Acknowledgments for Churches, 7 Essentials of Noncash Gift Administration for Ministries,* and *7 Essentials of Noncash Gift Administration for Churches.*

➢ **Information to be included in the acknowledgment.** All of the following information must be included in the gift receipt:

☐ the giver's name

☐ if cash, the amount of cash contributed

☐ if property, a description, but *not* the value of the property (if the gift is an auto, boat, or airplane, the ministry must generally provide Form 1098-C to the giver—see pages 162-65 for a more detailed discussion)

☐ a statement explaining whether the ministry provided any goods or services to the giver in exchange for the contribution

- if goods or services were provided to the giver, a description and good-faith estimate of their value and a statement that the giver's charitable deduction is limited to the amount of the payment in excess of that value, and if services were provided consisting solely of intangible religious benefits, a statement to that effect

- if no goods or services were provided to the giver, the acknowledgment must so state

☐ the date the donation was made

☐ the date the acknowledgment was issued (recommended, but not required)

➢ **When acknowledgments should be issued.** Givers must obtain their receipts no later than the due date, plus any extension, of their federal income tax return or the date the return was filed, whichever date is earlier. If a giver obtains the acknowledgment after this date, the gift does not qualify for a contribution deduction even on an amended return.

Idea

While a ministry is only required to provide an acknowledgment for single gifts of $250 or more, donors are required to maintain a record of cash contributions of any amount in order to claim a tax deduction (can be done through bank records or written communication from the ministry).

If a ministry issues acknowledgments on an annual basis, it is helpful to provide them to givers at least by January 31 each year, and earlier in January if possible. This will assist givers in gathering the necessary data for tax return preparation.

Form 1098-C must be provided within 30 days after the date that a donated vehicle is sold by the ministry or within 30 days of the donation date if the ministry keeps the property.

Sample Charitable Gift Acknowledgment

Acknowledgment #1

Received from: Howard K. Auburn

Cash received as an absolute gift:

Date Cash Received	Amount Received
1/2/20	$250.00
1/16/20	50.00
3/13/20	300.00
3/27/20	100.00
6/12/20	500.00
7/10/20	150.00
8/21/20	200.00
10/16/20	400.00
11/20/20	350.00
	$2,300.00

Any goods or services you may have received in connection with this gift were solely intangible religious benefits.

> (*Note:* It is very important for a religious organization to use wording of this nature when no goods or services were given in exchange for the gift.)

This document is necessary for any available federal income tax deduction for your contribution. Please retain it for your records.

Acknowledgment issued on: January 10, 2021

Acknowledgment issued by: Harold Morrison, Treasurer
Castleview Church
1008 High Drive
Dover, DE 19901

1. This sample acknowledgment is based on the following assumptions:
   A. No goods or services were provided in exchange for the gifts other than intangible religious benefits.
   B. The acknowledgment is issued on a periodic or annual basis for all gifts whether over or under $250.
2. All acknowledgments should be numbered consecutively for control and accounting purposes.

Sample Letter to Noncash Givers

Charitable Gift Acknowledgment for Noncash Gifts
(other than for autos, boats, or airplanes)

Noncash Acknowledgment #1

RETAIN FOR INCOME TAX PURPOSES

[All acknowledgments should be numbered consecutively for control and accounting purposes.]

Giver's name and address

Thank you for your noncash gift as follows:
    Date of gift:
    Description of gift:
    [Note: No value is shown for the gift. Valuation is the responsibility of the giver.]

Date Acknowledgment Issued

To substantiate your gift for IRS purposes, the tax law requires that this acknowledgment state whether you have received any goods or services in exchange for the gift. You have received no such goods or services. [*Note:* If goods or services were provided to the giver, replace the previous sentence with: In return for your contribution, you have received the following goods or services _ (description)_, which we value at __(good-faith estimate)__. The value of the goods and services you received must be deducted from the value of your contribution to determine your charitable deduction.]

If your noncash gifts for the year total more than $500, you must include Form 8283 (a copy of Form 8283 and its instructions are enclosed for your convenience) with your income tax return. Section A is used to report gifts valued at $5,000 or under. You can complete Section A on your own. When the value of the gift is more than $5,000, you will need to have the property appraised. The appraiser's findings are reported in Section B of Form 8283. The rules also apply if you give "similar items of property" with a total value above $5,000—even if you gave the items to different charities. Section B of Form 8283 must be signed by the appraiser. It is essential to attach the form to your tax return.

You might want an appraisal (even if your gift does not require one) in case you have to convince the IRS of the property's worth. You never need an appraisal or an appraisal summary for gifts of publicly traded securities, even if their total value exceeds $5,000. You must report those gifts (when the value is more than $500) by completing Section A of Form 8283 and attaching it to your return.

For gifts of closely held stock, an appraisal is not required if the value of the stock is under $10,000, but part of the appraisal summary form must be completed if the value is over $5,000. If the gift is valued over $10,000, then both an appraisal and an appraisal summary form are required.

If we receive a gift of property subject to the appraisal summary rules, we must report to both the IRS and to you if we dispose of the gift within three years.

Again, we are grateful for your generous contribution. Please let us know if we can give you and your advisors more information about the IRS's reporting requirements.

Your Nonprofit Organization

➣ **Frequency of issuing acknowledgments.** Receipts or acknowledgments can be issued gift-by-gift, monthly, quarterly, annually, or any other frequency. For ease of administration and clear communication with givers, many charities provide an acknowledgment for all gifts, whether more or less than $250.

➣ **Form of acknowledgments.** No specific design of a charitable gift receipt is required, except for Form 1098-C, used for gifts of vehicles (autos, boats, or airplanes). The IRS has not issued any sample acknowledgments.

An acknowledgment may be in hard-copy or electronic form. An acknowledgment can be issued as a letter, e-mail, or as an attachment to an e-mail. Additionally, a gift acknowledgment may be downloaded from the ministry's website giving platform. There is no requirement for the acknowledgment to be signed. There is also no requirement to include the giver's Social Security number. Although the IRS has not issued any guidance requiring the ministry's Employer Identification Number (EIN) to be included on gift acknowledgments, there are reported instances of the IRS requiring EINs.

➣ **Separate gifts of less than $250.** If a giver makes separate gifts by check during a calendar year of less than $250 each, there is no acknowledgment required since each gift is a separate contribution below the $250 threshold. The canceled check will provide sufficient substantiation. However, many ministries provide a year-end gift summary, including all gifts regardless of whether each gift is under or over $250.

➣ **Donations payable to another charity.** A giver may make a gift of $250 or more payable to a missions organization unrelated to the charity receiving the gift, to

---

Charitable Contribution Substantiation Requirements

	Not more than $75	Over $75 and under $250	At least $250
Canceled check acceptable for giver's deduction?	Yes	Yes	No
Contribution receipt required for deduction?	No *	No *	Yes
Ministry's statement on giver's receipt of goods or services required?	No	Yes **	Yes **

*Generally, no if paid by check, credit card, or wire transfer. Yes, if paid in currency.

**May be avoided if the ministry meets the low-cost items or *de minimis* benefits exceptions described on page 167.

help fund a project. No acknowledgment is required. Since the check was payable to the separate missions organization, that entity (with the check made payable to them) will need to issue the acknowledgment to the giver to document the gift.

➤ **Giver's out-of-pocket expenses.** Volunteers may incur out-of-pocket expenses on behalf of a ministry. Substantiation from the ministry is required if a volunteer claims a deduction for unreimbursed expenses of $250 or more. However, the IRS acknowledges that the ministry may be unaware of the details of the expenses or the dates on which they were incurred. Therefore, the ministry must substantiate (describe) only the types of services performed by the volunteer which relate to out-of-pocket expenses.

➤ **Individuals**. Gifts made by a taxpayer to poor or needy individuals or to employees of a ministry, instead of to or for a ministry, generally do not qualify as charitable contributions and are not the basis for a gift acknowledgment.

➤ **Foreign organizations.** It may be inappropriate to accept gifts restricted for a foreign organization even if the charitable purposes of the foreign charity are consistent with the purposes of the U.S. ministry.

> *Example 1:* An individual offers to make a $5,000 donation to a U.S.-based ministry restricted for the Sri Lanka Relief Outreach (a foreign organization) for its relief and development purposes. While the ministry provides funding for various foreign missionary endeavors, it has no connection with the Sri Lanka Relief Outreach and has no practical way to provide due diligence in relation to a gift to this entity. Based on these facts, the gift has the characteristics of a pass-through gift. The funds should generally not be accepted by the ministry.

> *Example 2:* Same fact pattern as in Example 1, except the U.S.-based ministry regularly sponsors short-term mission trips to Sri Lanka and provides funds to the Sri Lanka Relief Outreach, based on the due diligence performed by the ministry's staff and volunteers on mission trips with respect to this particular foreign entity. Based on these facts, the ministry is generally in a sound position to make a gift of $5,000 to the Sri Lanka-based organization as requested by the giver and provide a charitable receipt for the gift.

Since gifts by U.S. taxpayers to a foreign organization do not produce a charitable deduction, givers may try to convince a U.S.-based ministry to accept a gift restricted for a certain foreign organization and pass it through to the entity. When a U.S.-based ministry is no more than an agent of, or trustee for, a particular foreign organization, or has purposes so narrow that its funds can go only to a particular foreign organization, or solicits funds on behalf of a particular foreign organization, the deductibility of gifts may be questioned by the IRS.

There are some acceptable situations in which a U.S.-based ministry may receive gifts for which a deduction is allowed with the money used abroad.

☐ The money may be used by the U.S.-based ministry directly for projects that it selects to carry out its own exempt purposes. In this instance, the domestic organization would generally have operations in one or more foreign countries functioning directly under the U.S.-based ministry. The responsibility of the donee ministry ends when the purpose of the gift is fulfilled. A system of narrative and financial reports is necessary to document what was accomplished by the gift.

☐ It may create a subsidiary organization in a foreign country to facilitate its exempt operations there, with certain of its funds transmitted directly to the subsidiary. In this instance, the foreign organization is merely an administrative arm of the U.S.-based ministry, with the U.S.-based ministry considered the real recipient of the contributions. The responsibility of the U.S.-based ministry ends when the purpose of the gift is fulfilled by the foreign subsidiary.

☐ It may make grants to charities in a foreign country in furtherance of its exempt purposes, following review and approval of the uses to which the funds are to be put. The responsibility of the U.S. ministry ends when the purpose of the gift is fulfilled by the foreign organization. A narrative and financial report from the foreign organization will usually be necessary to document the fulfillment of the gift.

☐ It may transfer monies to another domestic entity with the second organization fulfilling the purpose of the gift. The responsibility of the first entity usually ends when the funds are transferred to the second organization.

The tax law is clear that money given to an intermediary charity but earmarked for an ultimate recipient is considered as if it has been given directly to the ultimate recipient. It is earmarked if there is an understanding, written or oral, whereby the giver binds the intermediary charity to transfer the funds to the ultimate recipient. The tax law does not allow givers to accomplish indirectly through a conduit (an intermediary charity) what the giver cannot accomplish directly.

➤ **Contingencies.** If a contribution will not be effective until the occurrence of a certain event, an income tax charitable deduction generally is not allowable until the occurrence of the event. Thus, a charitable gift acknowledgment should not be issued until the event has occurred.

> *Example:* A giver makes a donation to a college to fund a new education program that the college does not presently offer and is not contemplating. The donation would not be deductible until the college agrees to the conditions of the gift.

➢ **Charitable remainders in personal residences and farms.** The charitable gift regulations are silent on the substantiation rules for remainder interests in personal residences and farms (a life estate). It should be assumed that the $250 substantiation rules apply to those gifts unless the IRS provides other guidance.

➢ **Charitable trusts.** The $250 substantiation rules do not apply to charitable remainder trusts and charitable lead trusts.

➢ **Gift annuities.** When the gift portion of a gift annuity or a deferred payment gift annuity is $250 or more, a giver must have an acknowledgment from the ministry stating whether any goods or services—in addition to the annuity—were provided to the giver. If no goods or services were provided, the acknowledgment must so state. The acknowledgment should not include a good-faith estimate of the annuity's value.

➢ **Pooled income funds.** The substantiation rules apply to pooled income funds. To deduct a gift of a remainder interest of $250 or more, a giver must have an acknowledgment from the ministry.

In addition to gifts of vehicles (see pages 162-65), certain gifts require IRS reporting, or execution of a form that the giver files with the IRS:

➢ **Noncash gifts in excess of $500.** Noncash gifts in excess of $500 require the completion of certain information on page 1 of Form 8283. For gifts between $500 and $5,000, there is no additional requirement of an appraisal or signature of a ministry representative.

➢ **Noncash gifts in excess of $5,000.** Additional substantiation requirements apply to contributions of property (other than money and publicly traded securities) if the total claimed or reported value of the property is more than $5,000. For these gifts, the giver must obtain a qualified appraisal and attach an appraisal summary to the return on which the deduction is claimed. There is an exception for nonpublicly traded stock. If the claimed value of the stock does not exceed $10,000, the giver does not have to obtain an appraisal by a qualified appraiser.

The appraisal summary must be on Form 8283, signed and dated by a ministry representative and the appraiser, and attached to the giver's return. The signature by a ministry representative does not represent concurrence with the appraised value of the noncash gifts.

Form **8282**
(Rev. April 2009)
Department of the Treasury
Internal Revenue Service

Donee Information Return
(Sale, Exchange, or Other Disposition of Donated Property)

▶ See instructions.

OMB No. 1545-0908

Give a Copy to Donor

Parts To Complete
- If the organization is an **original donee**, complete *Identifying Information*, Part I (lines 1a–1d and, if applicable, lines 2a–2d), and Part III.
- If the organization is a **successor donee**, complete *Identifying Information*, Part I, Part II, and Part III.

Identifying Information

Print or Type	Name of charitable organization (donee)	Employer identification number
	Oneonta First Church	35 : 4829942

Address (number, street, and room or suite no.) (or P.O. box no. if mail is not delivered to the street address)
292 River Street

City or town, state, and ZIP code
Oneonta, NY 13820

Part I Information on ORIGINAL DONOR and SUCCESSOR DONEE Receiving the Property

1a	Name of original donor of the property	1b Identifying number(s)
	Keith E. Chapman	512-40-8076

1c Address (number, street, and room or suite no.) (or P.O. box no. if mail is not delivered to the street address)
504 Church Street

1d City or town, state, and ZIP code
Solvay, NY 13209

Note. Complete lines 2a–2d only if the organization gave this property to another charitable organization (successor donee).

2a	Name of charitable organization	2b Employer identification number
		:

2c Address (number, street, and room or suite no.) (or P.O. box no. if mail is not delivered to the street address)

2d City or town, state, and ZIP code

Part II Information on PREVIOUS DONEES. Complete this part only if the organization was not the first donee to receive the property. See the instructions before completing lines 3a through 4d.

3a	Name of original donee	3b Employer identification number
		:

3c Address (number, street, and room or suite no.) (or P.O. box no. if mail is not delivered to the street address)

3d City or town, state, and ZIP code

4a	Name of preceding donee	4b Employer identification number
		:

4c Address (number, street, and room or suite no.) (or P.O. box no. if mail is not delivered to the street address)

4d City or town, state, and ZIP code

For Paperwork Reduction Act Notice, see page 4.   Cat. No. 62307Y   Form **8282** (Rev. 4-2009)

Form 8282 (Rev. 4-2009)   Page **2**

Part III Information on DONATED PROPERTY

	1. Description of the donated property sold, exchanged, or otherwise disposed of and how the organization used the property. (If you need more space, attach a separate statement.)	2. Did the disposition involve the organization's entire interest in the property?		3. Was the use related to the organization's exempt purpose or function?		4. Information on use of property. • If you answered "Yes" to question 3 and the property was tangible personal property, describe how the organization's use of the property furthered its exempt purpose or function. Also complete Part IV below. • If you answered "No" to question 3 and the property was tangible personal property, describe the organization's intended use (if any) at the time of the contribution. Also complete Part IV below, if the intended use at the time of the contribution was related to the organization's exempt purpose or function and it became impossible or infeasible to implement.
		Yes	No	Yes	No	
A	Real estate/Vacant lot, 82 White St., Oneonta, NY	X			X	
B						
C						
D						

Donated Property

		A	B	C	D
5	Date the organization received the donated property (MM/DD/YY)	9 / 1 / 20	/ /	/ /	/ /
6	Date the original donee received the property (MM/DD/YY)	/ /	/ /	/ /	/ /
7	Date the property was sold, exchanged, or otherwise disposed of (MM/DD/YY)	11 / 10 / 20	/ /	/ /	/ /
8	Amount received upon disposition	$ 3,780	$	$	$

Part IV Certification

You must sign the certification below if any property described in Part III above is tangible personal property and:
- You answered "Yes" to question 3 above, or
- You answered "No" to question 3 above and the intended use of the property became impossible or infeasible to implement.

Under penalties of perjury and the penalty under section 6720B, I certify that either: (1) the use of the property that meets the above requirements, and is described above in Part III, was substantial and related to the donee organization's exempt purpose or function; or (2) the donee organization intended to use the property for its exempt purpose or function, but the intended use has become impossible or infeasible to implement.

Sign Here	▶ Clara Coleman *Signature of officer*	Treasurer *Title*		12/1/20 *Date*
	▶ _____ *Signature of officer*	_____ *Title*		_____ *Date*
	_____ *Type or print name*			

Under penalties of perjury, I declare that I have examined this return, including accompanying schedules and statements, and to the best of my knowledge and belief, it is true, correct, and complete.

Form **8282** (Rev. 4-2009)

This form must generally be filed by a ministry if it disposes of charitable deduction property within three years of the date the original donee received it and the items are valued at $500 or more.

Form **8283** (Rev. December 2020) Department of the Treasury Internal Revenue Service	**Noncash Charitable Contributions** ▶ Attach one or more Forms 8283 to your tax return if you claimed a total deduction of over $500 for all contributed property. ▶ Go to *www.irs.gov/Form8283* for instructions and the latest information.	OMB No. 1545-0908 Attachment Sequence No. **155**
Name(s) shown on your income tax return Mark A. and Joan E. Murphy		Identifying number **392-83-1982**

Note: Figure the amount of your contribution deduction before completing this form. See your tax return instructions.

Section A. Donated Property of $5,000 or Less and Publicly Traded Securities—List in this section **only** an item (or a group of similar items) for which you claimed a deduction of $5,000 or less. Also list publicly traded securities and certain other property even if the deduction is more than $5,000. See instructions.

Part I Information on Donated Property—If you need more space, attach a statement.

1	**(a)** Name and address of the donee organization	**(b)** If donated property is a vehicle (see instructions), check the box. Also enter the vehicle identification number (unless Form 1098-C is attached).	**(c)** Description and condition of donated property (For a vehicle, enter the year, make, model, and mileage. For securities and other property, see instructions.)
A	Endless Mountain Church 561 Maple, Rochester, NY 14623	☐	Used bedroom furniture
B		☐	
C		☐	
D		☐	
E		☐	

Note: If the amount you claimed as a deduction for an item is $500 or less, you do not have to complete columns (e), (f), and (g).

	(d) Date of the contribution	**(e)** Date acquired by donor (mo., yr.)	**(f)** How acquired by donor	**(g)** Donor's cost or adjusted basis	**(h)** Fair market value (see instructions)	**(i)** Method used to determine the fair market value
A	10/1/20	4/15	Purchased	3,400	750	Sales of comparable
B						used furniture
C						
D						
E						

Section B. Donated Property Over $5,000 (Except Publicly Traded Securities, Vehicles, Intellectual Property or Inventory Reportable in Section A)—Complete this section for one item (or a group of similar items) for which you claimed a deduction of more than $5,000 per item or group (except contributions reportable in Section A). Provide a separate form for each item donated unless it is part of a group of similar items. A qualified appraisal is generally required for items reportable in Section B. See instructions.

Part I Information on Donated Property

2 Check the box that describes the type of property donated.

a ☐ Art* (contribution of $20,000 or more)		e ☒ Other Real Estate		i ☐ Vehicles	
b ☐ Qualified Conservation Contribution		f ☐ Securities		j ☐ Clothing and household items	
c ☐ Equipment		g ☐ Collectibles**		k ☐ Other	
d ☐ Art* (contribution of less than $20,000)		h ☐ Intellectual Property			

* Art includes paintings, sculptures, watercolors, prints, drawings, ceramics, antiques, decorative arts, textiles, carpets, silver, rare manuscripts, historical memorabilia, and other similar objects.

** Collectibles include coins, stamps, books, gems, jewelry, sports memorabilia, dolls, etc., but not art as defined above.

Note: In certain cases, you must attach a qualified appraisal of the property. See instructions.

3	**(a)** Description of donated property (if you need more space, attach a separate statement)	**(b)** If any tangible personal property or real property was donated, give a brief summary of the overall physical condition of the property at the time of the gift.	**(c)** Appraised fair market value
A	Residence and two lots:	Good Repair	242,500
B	2080 Long Pond Road		
C	Syracuse, NY		

	(d) Date acquired by donor (mo., yr.)	**(e)** How acquired by donor	**(f)** Donor's cost or adjusted basis	**(g)** For bargain sales, enter amount received and attach a separate statement.	**(h)** Amount claimed as a deduction (see instructions)	**(i)** Date of contribution (see instructions)
A	7/20/14	Purchased	236,900		242,500	10/31/20
B						
C						

For Paperwork Reduction Act Notice, see separate instructions.   Cat. No. 62299J   Form **8283** (Rev. 12-2020)

This form must be completed and filed by the giver with the giver's income tax return for gifts of property valued at $500 or more. There is no requirement of an appraisal or signature of the donee organization for gifts valued between $500 and $5,000.

Form 8283 (Rev. 12-2020)   Page **2**

Name(s) shown on your income tax return	Identifying number
Mark A. and Joan E. Murphy	392-83-1982

Part II   **Partial Interests and Restricted Use Property (Other Than Qualified Conservation Contributions)**—
Complete lines 4a through 4e if you gave less than an entire interest in a property listed in Section B, Part I.
Complete lines 5a through 5c if conditions were placed on a contribution listed in Section B, Part I; also
attach the required statement. See instructions.

4a   Enter the letter from Section B, Part I that identifies the property for which you gave less than an entire interest ▶ _____
   If Section B, Part II applies to more than one property, attach a separate statement.

b   Total amount claimed as a deduction for the property listed in Section B, Part I: **(1)** For this tax year . . ▶ _____
                                                                                                      (2) For any prior tax years ▶ _____

c   Name and address of each organization to which any such contribution was made in a prior year (complete only if different
   from the donee organization above):
   Name of charitable organization (donee)

Address (number, street, and room or suite no.)	City or town, state, and ZIP code

d   For tangible property, enter the place where the property is located or kept ▶ _____

e   Name of any person, other than the donee organization, having actual possession of the property ▶ _____

	Yes	No
5a Is there a restriction, either temporary or permanent, on the donee's right to use or dispose of the donated property?		
b Did you give to anyone (other than the donee organization or another organization participating with the donee organization in cooperative fundraising) the right to the income from the donated property or to the possession of the property, including the right to vote donated securities, to acquire the property by purchase or otherwise, or to designate the person having such income, possession, or right to acquire?		
c Is there a restriction limiting the donated property for a particular use?		

Part III   **Taxpayer (Donor) Statement**—List each item included in Section B, Part I above that the appraisal identifies
as having a value of $500 or less. See instructions.

I declare that the following item(s) included in Section B, Part I above has to the best of my knowledge and belief an appraised value
of not more than $500 (per item). Enter identifying letter from Section B, Part I and describe the specific item. See instructions.

▶ _____

Signature of taxpayer (donor) ▶ *Mark A. Murphy*	Date ▶ **11/28/20**

Part IV   **Declaration of Appraiser**

I declare that I am not the donor, the donee, a party to the transaction in which the donor acquired the property, employed by, or related to any of the foregoing persons, or married to any person who is related to any of the foregoing persons. And, if regularly used by the donor, donee, or party to the transaction, I performed the majority of my appraisals during my tax year for other persons.

Also, I declare that I perform appraisals on a regular basis; and that because of my qualifications as described in the appraisal, I am qualified to make appraisals of the type of property being valued. I certify that the appraisal fees were not based on a percentage of the appraised property value. Furthermore, I understand that a false or fraudulent overstatement of the property value as described in the qualified appraisal or this Form 8283 may subject me to the penalty under section 6701(a) (aiding and abetting the understatement of tax liability). I understand that my appraisal will be used in connection with a return or claim for refund. I also understand that, if there is a substantial or gross valuation misstatement of the value of the property claimed on the return or claim for refund that is based on my appraisal, I may be subject to a penalty under section 6695A of the Internal Revenue Code, as well as other applicable penalties. I affirm that I have not been at any time in the three-year period ending on the date of the appraisal barred from presenting evidence or testimony before the Department of the Treasury or the Internal Revenue Service pursuant to 31 U.S.C. 330(c).

Sign Here	Appraiser signature ▶ *Andrew J. Noble*		Date ▶ **11/20/20**
	Appraiser name ▶ **Andrew J. Noble**	Title ▶ **President**	

Business address (including room or suite no.) **1100 North Adams Street**	Identifying number **541-90-9796**
City or town, state, and ZIP code **Elmira, NY 14904**	

Part V   **Donee Acknowledgment**

This charitable organization acknowledges that it is a qualified organization under section 170(c) and that it received the donated property
as described in Section B, Part I, above on the following date ▶ **8/31/20**

Furthermore, this organization affirms that in the event it sells, exchanges, or otherwise disposes of the property described in Section
B, Part I (or any portion thereof) within 3 years after the date of receipt, it will file **Form 8282**, Donee Information Return, with the IRS
and give the donor a copy of that form. This acknowledgment does not represent agreement with the claimed fair market value.

Does the organization intend to use the property for an unrelated use? . . . . ▶ ☐ Yes ☒ No

Name of charitable organization (donee) **Fairlawn Heights Church**	Employer identification number **35-4029876**
Address (number, street, and room or suite no.) **PO Box 829**	City or town, state, and ZIP code **Oswego, NY 13126**
Authorized signature *James A. Black*	Title **Executive Pastor**	Date **12/15/20**

                                                                                                Form **8283** (Rev. 12-2020)

Section B must be completed for gifts of items (or groups of similar items) for which a deduction
was claimed of more than $5,000 per item or group.

If Form 8283 is required, it is the giver's responsibility to file it. The ministry is under no responsibility to see that this form is filed or that it is properly completed. However, advising givers of their obligations and providing them with the form can produce goodwill.

➢ **Charity reporting for contributed property.** If a noncash gift requiring an appraisal summary on Form 8283 is sold, exchanged, or otherwise disposed of by the ministry within three years after the date of the contribution, the ministry must file Form 8282 with the IRS within 125 days of disposing of the asset.

Caution

The IRS places certain reporting requirements on donors and ministries with respect to many property gifts. The government is suspicious of property valued at one amount on the date of the gift and sold by the ministry for much less. Ministries should never place a value on a gift of property. This is the responsibility of the donor.

This form provides detailed information on the gift and the disposal of the property. A copy of the form must be provided to the giver and one retained by the ministry. A ministry that receives a charitable contribution of property from a corporation valued at more than $5,000 generally does not have to complete Form 8283.

A letter or other written communication from a ministry acknowledging receipt of the property and showing the name of the giver, the date and location of the contribution, and a detailed description of the property is an acceptable contribution receipt for a gift of property.

There is no requirement to include the value of contributed property on the receipt. A tension often surrounds a significant gift of property because the giver may request the ministry to include an excessively high value on the charitable acknowledgment. It is wise for the ministry to remain impartial in the matter and simply acknowledge the property by description and condition while excluding a dollar amount.

> *Example:* A ministry receives a gift of real estate. The receipt should include the legal description of the real property and a description of the improvements with no indication of the dollar value.

➢ **Acknowledging and reporting gifts of vehicles—autos, boats, and airplanes.** Charities are required to provide contemporaneous written acknowledgments containing specific information to givers of autos, boats, and airplanes (see IRS Publication 4302). Taxpayers are required to include a copy of the written acknowledgment (Form 1098-C may be used as the acknowledgment) with their tax returns in order to receive a deduction. The donee organization is also required to provide the information contained in the acknowledgment to the IRS.

The information included in such acknowledgments as well as the meaning of "contemporaneous" depends on what the ministry does with the donated vehicle.

- **Vehicle sold *before* use or improvement.** If the donated auto, boat, or airplane is sold before significant intervening use or material improvement of the auto, boat, or airplane by the ministry, the gross proceeds received by the donee ministry from the subsequent sale of the vehicle will be included on the written acknowledgment. Therefore, for donated property sold before use or improvement, the deductible amount is the gross proceeds received from the sale. A written acknowledgment is considered contemporaneous if the donee ministry provides it within 30 days of the sale of the vehicle. The written acknowledgment provided by the charity should include the following information:

  ☐ the name and taxpayer identification number of the giver

  ☐ the vehicle, boat, or airplane identification number or similar number

  ☐ certification that the property was sold in an arm's length transaction between unrelated parties

  ☐ the gross proceeds from the sale

  ☐ a statement that the deductible amount may not exceed the amount of the gross proceeds

- **Vehicle not sold before use or improvement.** Ministries may plan to significantly use or materially improve a donated auto, boat, or airplane before or instead of selling the property. In such circumstances, the ministry would not include a dollar amount in the written acknowledgment. Instead, the written acknowledgment (prepared within 30 days of the contribution of the vehicle to be considered contemporaneous) should include the following information:

  ☐ the name and taxpayer identification number of the giver

  ☐ the vehicle, boat, or airplane identification number or similar number

  ☐ certification of the intended use or material improvement of the property and the intended duration of such use

  ☐ certification that the property will not be transferred in exchange for money, other property, or services before completion of such use or improvement

The deductible amount for contributed vehicles that will be used or improved by the ministry is the fair market value of the property, as determined by the giver, taking into consideration accessories, mileage, and other indicators of the property's general condition.

7878　　☐ VOID　　☐ CORRECTED

DONEE'S name, street address, city or town, state or province, country, ZIP or foreign postal code, and telephone no. Lamont Community Church 101 East Main Street Lamont, KS 66855	**1** Date of contribution 1/15/20	OMB No. 1545-1959 Form **1098-C**	**Contributions of Motor Vehicles, Boats, and Airplanes**
	2a Odometer mileage 81,980	(Rev. November 2019) For calendar year 20 ____	

		2b Year 2010	**2c** Make Chevy	**2d** Model Colorado	

DONEE'S TIN 35-0189211	DONOR'S TIN 514-41-8007	**3** Vehicle or other identification number 1FAP58923V159753	
DONOR'S name Fred Wilbur		**4a** ☒ Donee certifies that vehicle was sold in arm's length transaction to unrelated party	**Copy A**
Street address (including apt. no.) 512 North Main		**4b** Date of sale 1/25/20	
City or town, state or province, country, and ZIP or foreign postal code Lamont, KS 66855		**4c** Gross proceeds from sale (see instructions) $ 3,000	**For Internal Revenue Service Center**
5a ☐ Donee certifies that vehicle will not be transferred for money, other property, or services before completion of material improvements or significant intervening use			File with Form 1096.
5b ☐ Donee certifies that vehicle is to be transferred to a needy individual for significantly below fair market value in furtherance of donee's charitable purpose			For Privacy Act and Paperwork Reduction Act Notice, see the current **General Instructions for Certain Information Returns.**
5c Donee certifies the following detailed description of material improvements or significant intervening use and duration of use			
6a Did you provide goods or services in exchange for the vehicle? . . . . ▶ Yes ☐ No ☒			
6b Value of goods and services provided in exchange for the vehicle $			
6c Describe the goods and services, if any, that were provided. If this box is checked, donee certifies that the goods and services consisted solely of intangible religious benefits . . . . ▶ ☐			
7 Under the law, the donor may not claim a deduction of more than $500 for this vehicle if this box is checked . . . . . . ▶ ☐			

Form **1098-C** (Rev. 11-2019)　　Cat. No. 39732R　　www.irs.gov/Form1098C　　Department of the Treasury - Internal Revenue Service

In certain instances, a vehicle may be sold at a price significantly below fair market value (or gratuitously transferred) to needy individuals in direct furtherance of the donee ministry's charitable purpose.

For property that meets this definition, the gift acknowledgment must also contain a certification that the donee ministry will sell the property to a needy individual at a price significantly below fair market value (or, if applicable, that the donee ministry gratuitously will transfer the property to a needy individual). Additionally, the ministry must certify that the sale or transfer will be in the direct furtherance of the donee ministry's charitable purpose of relieving the poor and distressed or the underprivileged who are in need of a means of transportation.

Example: On March 1, 2020, a giver contributes a qualified vehicle to a qualified ministry. The ministry's charitable purposes include helping needy individuals who are unemployed develop new job skills, finding job placements for these individuals, and providing transportation for these individuals who need a means of transportation to jobs in areas not served by public transportation. The ministry determines that, in direct furtherance of its charitable purpose, the ministry will sell the qualified vehicle at a price significantly below fair market value to a trainee who needs a means of transportation to a new workplace. On or before March 31, 2020, the ministry provides Form 1098-C to the giver containing the giver's name and taxpayer identification number, the vehicle identification number, a statement that the date of the contribution was March 1, 2020, a certification that the ministry will sell the qualified vehicle to a needy individual at a price significantly below fair market value, and a certification that the sale is in direct furtherance of the organization's charitable purpose.

Generally, no deduction is allowed unless givers receive Form 1098-C within 30 days after the date that the vehicle is sold or within 30 days of the donation date if the ministry keeps the car. If the vehicle is sold, givers must be informed of the gross selling price.

If the ministry keeps the car, the private-party sale price must be used by givers to figure the charitable tax deduction for donations, not the higher dealer retail price.

Quid Pro Quo Disclosure Requirements

When a giver receives goods or services of value approximate to the amount transferred to a ministry, there is no gift. This is because the person received a "quid pro quo" (this for that) of an equivalent amount in exchange for the transfer. If the payment to a ministry exceeds the approximate amount of goods or services provided by the ministry to the giver, the difference qualifies as a charitable gift.

The ministry is required to provide an acknowledgment for all transactions in which the giver makes a payment of more than $75 to the ministry and receives goods or services (other than intangible religious benefits or items of token value).

Form of the acknowledgment

The charitable gift acknowledgment, in quid pro quo situations, must:

> ➤ inform the giver that the amount of the contribution that is deductible for federal income tax purposes is limited to the difference of the amount of money and the

value of any property contributed by the giver over the value of the goods or services provided by the ministry,

➢ provide the giver with a good-faith estimate of the value of goods or services that the charity is providing in exchange for the contribution.

Only single payments of more than $75 are subject to the quid pro quo rules. Payments are not cumulative. It is not a difference of $75 between the amount given and the value of the object received that triggers the disclosure requirements, but the amount actually paid by the giver.

Calculating the gift portion

It is not a requirement for the donee ministry to actually complete the subtraction of the benefit from a cash payment, showing the net charitable deduction. However, providing the net amount available for a charitable deduction is a good approach for clear communication with givers.

When to make the required disclosures

The disclosure of the value of goods or services provided to a giver may be made in the giver solicitation as well as in the subsequent acknowledgment. However, sufficient information will generally not be available to make proper disclosure upon solicitation (for example, the value of a dinner may not be known at the time the solicitation is made).

Warning

A ministry must furnish a disclosure statement in connection with either the solicitation or the receipt of a quid pro quo contribution of over $75. The statement must be in writing and must be made in a manner that is likely to come to the attention of the giver. For example, a disclosure in small print within a larger document might not meet this requirement.

Goods provided to givers

To determine the net charitable contribution, a gift must generally be reduced by the fair market value of any premium, incentive, or other benefit received by the giver in exchange for the gift. Common examples of premiums are books, CDs, DVDs, Bibles, and other resources.

For gifts of more than $75, ministries must advise the giver the fair market value of the premium or incentive and explain that the value of the premium is not deductible for income tax purposes.

Givers must reduce their charitable deduction by the fair market value of goods or services they receive, even when the goods or services were donated to the ministry for use as premiums or gifts or when they were bought wholesale by the ministry. Therefore, ministries cannot pass along to givers the savings realized by receiving products at no cost or buying products at a discount.

In certain circumstances, if givers receive unsolicited free, low-cost articles (free to the giver and low-cost to the distributing ministry) as part of the ministry's stewardship efforts, they are allowed a full tax deduction for the donation:

Remember

Many ministries offer products and suggest a donation amount with respect to the products. For example, a ministry may offer a book with a suggested donation amount of $30. If the fair market value of the book is $30 and the individual sends $30 to the ministry, no charitable donation has been made. However, if the ministry receives $50, a $20 charitable deduction is available.

➤ **Low-cost items.** If an item that has a cost (not retail value) of less than $11.20 (2020 inflation-adjusted amount) and bearing the ministry name or logo is given in return for a donation of more than $56.00 (2020 inflation-adjusted amount), the giver may claim a charitable deduction for the full amount of the donation. Examples of low-cost items are coffee mugs, key chains, bookmarks, and calendars.

➤ *De minimis* **benefits.** A giver can take a full deduction if the fair market value of the benefits received in connection with a gift do not exceed 2% of the donation or $112 (2020 inflation-adjusted amount), whichever is less.

Examples of the quid pro quo rules

Here are various examples of how the quid pro quo rules may apply:

➤ **Admission to events.** Many ministries sponsor banquets, concerts, or other events to which givers and prospective givers are invited in exchange for a contribution or other payment. Typically, the giver receives a benefit equivalent to the payment and no charitable deduction is available.

But if the amount paid is more than the value received, the amount in excess of the fair market value is deductible if the giver intended to make a contribution.

➤ **Auctions.** The IRS has taken the position that the fair market value of an item purchased at a ministry auction is set by the bidders. The winning bidder, therefore, cannot pay more than the item is worth. That means there is no charitable contribution in the IRS's eyes, no deduction, and no need for the ministry to provide any charitable gift substantiation document to the bidder.

Sample Charitable Gift Acknowledgment

Acknowledgment #2

Received from: Charles K. Vandell

Cash received:

Date Cash Received	Gross Amount Received	Value of Goods or Services	Net Charitable Contribution
1/23/20	$80.00	$25.00 [1]	$ 55.00
3/20/20	300.00		300.00
4/24/20	60.00		60.00
6/19/20	500.00	100.00 [2]	400.00
9/04/20	275.00		275.00
10/30/20	200.00		200.00
12/18/20	1,000.00		1,000.00
		Total	$2,290.00

Property received described as follows:

Received on October 22, 2020, 12 brown Samsonite folding chairs.

In return for certain gifts listed above, we only provided you with the following goods or services (our estimate of the fair market value is indicated):

(1) Christian music CDs $25.00
(2) Limited edition art print $100.00

You may have also received intangible religious benefits, but these benefits do not need to be valued for tax purposes.

The deductible portion of your contribution for federal income tax purposes is limited to the excess of your contribution over the value of goods and services we provided to you.

This document is necessary for any available federal income tax deduction for your contribution. Please retain it for your records.

Receipt issued on: January 15, 2021

Receipt issued by: Harold Morrison, Treasurer
                       Castleview Church
                       1008 High Drive
                       Dover, DE 19901

This sample receipt is based on the following assumptions:
  A. Goods or services were provided in exchange for the gifts.
  B. The receipt is issued on a periodic or annual basis for all gifts whether over or under $250.
All receipts should be numbered consecutively for control and accounting purposes.

However, many tax professionals take the position that when the payment (the purchase price) exceeds the fair market value of the items, the amount that exceeds the fair market value is deductible as a charitable contribution. This position also creates a reporting requirement under the quid pro quo rules.

> *Example:* A church youth group auctions goods to raise funds for a missions trip. An individual bought a quilt for $1,000. The church takes the position that the quilt had a fair market value of $50 even though the bidder paid $1,000. Since the payment of $1,000 exceeded the $75 limit, the church is required to provide a written statement indicating that only $950 of the $1,000 payment is eligible for a charitable contribution.

➤ **Bazaars.** Payments for items sold at bazaars and bake sales are not tax-deductible to givers since the purchase price generally equals the fair market value of the item.

➤ **Banquets.** Whether an organization incurs reporting requirements in connection with banquets where funds are raised depends on the specifics of each event.

> *Example 1:* A church sponsors a banquet for missions charging $50 per person. The fair market value of the meal provided is $15 per person. There is no disclosure requirement since the amount charged was less than $75. However, the amount deductible by each giver is still only $35.

> *Example 2:* A church invites individuals to attend a missions banquet without charge. Attendees are invited to make contributions or pledges at the end of the banquet. These payments may not require disclosure even if the amount given is $75 or more if there is only an indirect relationship between the meal and the gift.

➤ **Deduction timing.** The same quid pro quo rule applies to goods and services received in a different year than the one in which payment was given. Thus, a giver's deduction for the year of the payment is limited to the amount, if any, by which the payment exceeds the value of the goods and services received in a previous or subsequent year.

➤ **Good-faith estimates.** A giver is not required to use the estimate provided by a donee ministry in calculating the deductible amount. When a taxpayer knows or has reason to know that an estimate is inaccurate, the taxpayer may ignore the ministry's estimate in determining the fair market value of the goods or services received.

➤ **Rights of refusal.** A giver can claim a full deduction if he or she refuses a benefit from the ministry. However, this must be done affirmatively. Simply not taking advantage of a benefit is not enough. For example, a giver who chooses not to make use of tickets made available by the ministry must deduct the value of the tickets from his or her contribution before claiming a deduction. However, a giver who rejects the right to a benefit at the time the contribution is made (for example, by checking off a refusal box on a form supplied by the ministry) can take a full deduction.

➤ **Sale of products or a service at fair market value.** When an individual purchases products or receives services approximate to the amount paid, no part of the payment is a gift.

> *Example 1:* An individual purchases a set of Bible study guides for $80. Even though the amount paid exceeds the $75 threshold, the church is not required to provide a disclosure statement to the purchaser because the value of the products is approximate to the amount paid to the church.

> *Example 2:* The Brown family uses the fellowship hall of the church for a family reunion. The normal rental fee is $300. The Browns give a check to the church for $300 marked "Contribution." No acknowledgment should be given because no charitable contribution was made. The Browns received a benefit approximate to the amount of their payment. *Note:* It is inappropriate for the church to try to mask a fee by calling it a donation

> *Example 3:* The Smith family uses the church sanctuary and fellowship hall for a wedding and the reception. The church does not have a stated use fee but asks for a donation from those who use the facility. The comparable fee to rent similar facilities is $250. The Smiths give a check to the church for $250 marked "Contribution." No acknowledgment should be given because no charitable contribution was made. The Smiths received a benefit approximate to the amount of their payment.

> *Example 4:* A church operates a Christian school. The parent of a student at the school writes a check payable to the church for his child's tuition. No acknowledgment should be given because a payment of tuition does not qualify as a charitable contribution.

Receipting a taxpayer other than the giver

Givers or prospective givers sometimes present challenging requests to ministries. Some requests relate to the receipting of a gift or potential gift. If a giver asks a ministry to issue a gift receipt to a taxpayer other than the one making the gift, what should the organization do?

➤ Should the ministry automatically issue the receipt as requested by the giver, or should the ministry ask for an explanation?

➤ If the donor provides an explanation that evidences an attempt to understate income or Social Security taxes, what should the ministry do?

➤ If the ministry provides a receipt to a taxpayer other than the giver, is the ministry aiding tax evasion?

➤ Even if the law does not cover these issues, is there a position of "high ground" for the ministry?

> *Example:* Fran Maxwell is the president of a closely-held C corporation, Maxwellian. The corporation is operating at a significant loss for the current year and it is highly unlikely that the financial fortunes of the corporation will turn around anytime soon. Therefore, a charitable gift deduction has no value to the corporation for the current year and potentially into the future. The corporation makes a $20,000 gift to a ministry and requests that a gift acknowledgment be issued in the name of the corporation's president, Fran Maxwell. He says, "Other charities have handled my gifts this way." Mr. Maxwell has enough personal income to put him in the 24% federal tax bracket. So, a gift acknowledgment improperly issued to him personally would save him considerable money. What should the ministry do? Issue the gift acknowledgment in the name of the corporation, Maxwellian. The following policy provides sound guidance on this issue.

Policy on Issuing Acknowledgments to Someone Other than the Giver of the Funds

When the ministry receives requests for an acknowledgment to be issued to a taxpayer other than the remitter of the funds, receipts will be issued only to the taxpayer making the gift.

➤ For a cash gift, the person or entity named on the check (or the individual delivering the cash) is the one to whom the receipt is addressed.

➤ The person or entity transferring ownership of noncash assets to a ministry is the giver.

The following very limited exceptions to this policy may be permitted under certain circumstances:

➤ If the giver documents the appropriateness of issuing a receipt to a taxpayer other than the giver, an exception may be made to the policy.

➤ To facilitate the processing of modest gifts, an exception may be made for small gifts where the risk of significant fraud is diminished.

Sample Giver Privacy Policy

Our ministry is committed to respecting the privacy of our givers. We have developed this privacy policy to assure our givers that their information will not be shared with any third party.

Awareness. This policy is shared to make you aware of our privacy policy and to inform you of the way your information is used. We also provide you with the opportunity to remove your name from our mailing list, if you desire to do so.

Information collected. Here are the types of giver information that we collect and maintain:

- contact information: name, organization/church, complete address, phone number, email address
- shipping information: name, organization/church, complete address
- information concerning how you heard about our ministry
- information you wish to share: questions, comments, suggestions
- your request to receive periodic updates: *e.g.*, to individuals who request them, we will send periodic mailings related to specific fundraising appeals, prayer concerns, and newsletters

How information is used. Our ministry uses your information to understand your needs and provide you with better service. Specifically, we use your information to help you complete a transaction, communicate back to you, and update you on ministry happenings. Credit card numbers are used only for donation or payment processing and are not retained for other purposes. We use the comments you offer to provide you with information requested, and we take seriously each recommendation as to how we might improve communication.

No sharing of personal information. Our ministry will not sell, rent, give, or lease your personal information to other organizations. We assure you that the identity of all of our givers will be kept confidential. Use of giver information will be limited to the internal purposes of our ministry and only to further our ministry activities and purposes.

Removing your name from our mailing list. It is our desire to not send unwanted mail to our givers. Please contact us if you wish to be removed from our mailing list.

Contacting us. If you have comments or questions about our giver privacy policy, please send us an email at info@XYZMinistry.org or call us at (800) 555-5555.

Giver privacy

While giver information is treated with the utmost confidentiality by most ministries, there is no federal law that mandates giver privacy. Is it acceptable for a church pastor, ministry executive, or fundraising consultant to be given a list of givers, identified either within dollar ranges or with actual contribution amounts? This practice is not prohibited or considered unethical if this information is used within a limited context on a "need to know" basis for a specific function within the organization. However, circulating this information outside the ministry is considered unethical.

It is wise and prudent for a ministry to maintain a giver privacy policy to help assure its givers of their privacy in contributing to the ministry (see sample policy on page 172). Ministries should consider including several components in developing giver privacy policies:

> **How the giver information is used.** Common uses are to process contributions, communicate with givers, and update them about ministry events or programs.

> **Who the giver information is shared with.** The privacy policy should specify whether the ministry will share giver information with other organizations. Most ministries have a policy not to share any form of giver information. If, however, a ministry does share giver information with other organizations, it is important that it disclose that fact in the giver privacy policy. Doing so allows givers to be aware that any personal information given may be passed on to another organization.

> **Removal from the mailing list.** A good giver privacy policy will also include instructions that persons may follow to remove their name from the mailing list.

Ministries may communicate their giver privacy policy in several different places. The policy may be included in fundraising appeals, response vehicles, contribution receipts, annual reports, and on the ministry's website. Ministries can publish their entire giver privacy policy or create a simplified giver privacy statement to be used on documents and websites.

Charitable solicitation registration

Most states and the District of Columbia currently have laws regulating the solicitation of funds for charitable purposes. These statutes generally require ministries to register with a state agency before soliciting the state's residents for contributions, providing exemptions from registration for certain categories of nonprofits including churches and religious organizations in some situations. In addition, ministries may be required to file periodic financial reports. State laws may impose additional requirements on fundraising activity involving paid solicitors and fundraising counsel. Before soliciting contributions, ministries may wish to contact the appropriate state agency to learn more about the requirements that may apply in their state. In some states, municipal or other local governments may also require ministries soliciting charitable contributions to register and report.

- **Use the proper year for gift acknowledgment reporting.** The timing of a charitable gift acknowledgment in the appropriate year is a significant integrity issue. Absent clear documentation that a giver is eligible to receive a gift acknowledgment for a prior tax period, a ministry should issue the gift acknowledgment for the year in which the gift was received.

- **The importance of proper receipting for noncash gifts.** When noncash gifts are received by a ministry, it is important to ensure that the ministry provides an appropriate gift acknowledgment. In recent years, a number of major noncash gifts have been disqualified as charitable deductions because the recipient charitable organization's failed to provide an appropriate gift acknowledgment.

- **Transactions which are part gift/part purchase.** These transactions trigger the "quid pro quo" rules and require ministries to demonstrate integrity. Unless the ministry fulfills its responsibility to report to the giver the fair market value of the goods or services provided, the giver lacks the necessary information to claim the correct charitable contribution amount.

- **Use of a gift acceptance policy.** Gifts that may seem at first glance to be a great idea can have unintended consequences, such as a gift of land that also has environmental liabilities that exceed the fair market value of the property. The use of a gift acceptance policy is an important tool to protect the interests of the ministry and outlines how gifts with restrictions should be handled to ensure that giver intent is honored.

Special Charitable Gift Issues

In This Chapter

- Gifts with giver restrictions
- Contributions to support missionaries and other workers

- Contributions to support short-term mission trips
- Other special charitable contribution issues

There are a few charitable gift topics that require special attention from churches and nonprofits to ensure compliance and model integrity. As discussed in this chapter, these include restricted gifts, contributions to support missions, and more.

Gifts with Giver Restrictions

Properly handling gifts with giver-imposed restrictions can be challenging for many churches or ministries. This is because these gifts present a complex combination of accounting, tax, legal, ethical, and other issues.

The two fundamental concepts relating to giver-restricted gifts are (1) ministry discretion and control, and (2) giver preferences:

> **Ministry discretion and control over giver-restricted gifts.** A common misconception is that the control a ministry board must exercise over any giver-restricted gift is in conflict with, or contradictory to, stipulations by givers. *This is not true.*

> Some believe that organizations should not follow giver restrictions, from time to time, to demonstrate their control. *This is inappropriate.*

> Board control and giver restrictions are really a hand-in-glove concept. It is not *either/or* but *both/and*! Restricted gifts must be used for a specific exempt purpose, whereas unrestricted gifts may be used for any exempt purpose.

> The board must control all contributions to a ministry, unrestricted and restricted, to be used exclusively for its exempt purposes. In addition, the board must provide

reasonable measures to assure that giver-restricted gifts are used for the intended exempt purpose(s).

Notifying the giver on the gift acknowledgment that the ministry will exercise discretion and control over the gift does not remove the giver's restriction placed on a gift. Ministries must exercise discretion and control over *all* charitable gifts, whether unrestricted (may be used for any exempt purpose) or restricted (must be used for a specific purpose).

Giver restrictions arise, for example, when a ministry accepts contributions that are solicited for or restricted by a giver for a specific program, project, or a location of missionary work (versus missionary work anywhere in the world). Contributions without donor restrictions have no implicit or explicit giver restrictions and are available to be used in any exempt operations of the ministry.

Givers often like to retain some control over their gifts. However, if too much control is retained, the giver's income tax deduction may be endangered.

The preferencing of a gift does not determine for accounting purposes whether the gift is with or without donor restrictions. When a gift is preferenced to support the ministry of a particular worker, the preferencing may qualify the gift for a charitable tax deduction, but other factors must be reviewed to determine whether the gift is with or without donor restrictions for accounting purposes.

> *Example 1:* Accompanying a gift, a giver communicates: "My preference is that the gift be used for scholarships. However, I give the ministry permission to use the gift for any exempt purpose consistent with the ministry's mission statement." This gift is an unrestricted gift because it is only preferenced and the ministry has full discretion as to the use of the gift.

> *Example 2:* A prayer letter or appeal letter from a ministry that conducts work in several countries describes the need for religious workers in India. The request is for funds preferenced to enable a particular worker employed by the ministry to carry out certain work in India. A gift in response to this appeal is restricted for the ministry's program in India (a geographical restriction), and the gift is preferenced to support a particular worker.

A giver's restriction on a gift limits the ministry's use of the funds to the purposes specified by the giver; *e.g.*, "This gift is made on the condition that," or "This gift is restricted for XYZ project." This type of gift is generally tax-deductible as a charitable contribution.

It may be inappropriate for a ministry to accept a gift if the restrictions accompanying a gift:

☐ prevent the ministry from using the donation in the furtherance of its charitable purposes. For example, if a giver restricts a gift for the benefit of a specific individual and the ministry is prevented from exercising discretion and control over the gift (such as a gift restricted for a particular benevolent recipient, an employee of the charity, etc.), the gift is generally not deductible as a charitable contribution.

☐ are incompatible with the mission of the ministry. Even though a restricted gift is exclusively charitable, it is generally inappropriate for a ministry to accept a gift requiring the expenditure of funds outside the mission of the ministry. For example, if a ministry whose sole purpose is international child sponsorship is offered a gift restricted for inner-city evangelism in the U.S., the gift should generally not be accepted by the ministry because it is inconsistent with the mission of the ministry (the overall mission of the ministry is generally described in the ministry's governing documents).

☐ are at odds with the best interests of the ministry. A restricted gift could be exclusively charitable and compatible with the mission of the ministry and still not be in the best interests of the ministry. A ministry might not have the capacity to comply with gift restrictions. For example, the amount of funds raised for a particular disaster may exceed the ministry's capacity to effectively spend the funds in a reasonable period of time.

Alternatively, the administrative requirements of a restricted gift could consume an inordinate amount of the ministry's resources. For example, the gift of a time share property could be offered to a ministry. However, the ministry may decide the time share is not in the best interest of the ministry because (1) time shares are often unmarketable properties laden with annual costs, and (2) even when sales are made, the low resale market prices can minimize or erase profits.

A giver's *preference* communicates a desire or suggestion which is advisory in nature. A desire or suggestion does not restrict the use of the gift and allows the ministry full discretion to use the gift in relation to the desire or suggestion, or use the funds for any other purpose. Factors that imply a ministry has received a giver preferenced gift and not a restricted gift include:

☐ **Giver intention.** The giver intends only to express a desire or make a suggestion with respect to a gift.

☐ **Ministry communication.** Both the solicitation letter and response form (and perhaps the gift acknowledgment) from the ministry clearly communicate to the giver that preferenced gifts are sought. Materials include statements such as "We appreciate your desire or suggestion as to the use of the funds. While we will endeavor to use the funds as you desire or suggest, we may use the gift for another purpose." This is very different from the statement "Gifts made to our ministry are under the discretion and control of the ministry." All gifts must be under the discretion and control of the ministry, so making that statement does not turn an otherwise giver-restricted gift into an unrestricted gift.

☐ **Giver communication.** The giver communicated in writing or verbally a desire or suggestion regarding the use of the funds, but the giver did not restrict the funds for a certain purpose.

If the giver preferences a gift, even when the preference is for the funds to go to a particular individual, the gift may qualify for a charitable tax deduction if the ministry exercises adequate due diligence with respect to the gift. For example, a gift restricted for missions and preferenced for the missionary endeavors involving a certain identified individual or a gift for benevolence preferenced for a particular benevolent recipient may qualify for a charitable tax deduction if the ministry exercises adequate due diligence related to the gift.

Some ministries request that givers not place the name of a preferenced worker on the memo line of the giver's check. This request may send an inappropriate message to givers—*i.e.*, implying that hiding information from the IRS is an acceptable and/or desirable practice. If a giver wants to use the memo line on the check to indicate a preference to support the work of a particular individual ("preferenced for the ministry of Jill Smith"), this should be no more problematic for IRS purposes than checking a box on the response form which contains preferenced wording.

For more information on giver-restricted gifts, see ECFA's eBooks—*10 Essentials of Giver-Restricted Gifts to Ministries* and *10 Essentials of Giver-Restricted Gifts to Churches*.

Contributions to Support Missionaries and Other Workers

Donations may be received, payable to a ministry, for the support of a particular missionary (often called deputized fundraising). These gifts generally qualify as a charitable contribution if the ministry exercises sufficient discretion and control over the gift. If so, the ministry should include the amounts in gift acknowledgments issued to givers.

The IRS has acknowledged that deputized support-raising is a widespread and legitimate practice, and the contributions properly raised by this method are tax-deductible.

In Technical Instruction Program materials, the IRS outlined two general tests to determine whether a tax-deductible contribution is made to or for the use of a ministry, or whether a gift is a nondeductible pass-through gift to a particular individual who ultimately benefits from the contribution. These two tests, the intended benefit test and the discretion and control test, are explained below.

➤ **Intended benefit test.** The giver's intention must be to benefit the ministry. While the giver's intention is often only in his or her mind, communication provided by the ministry when the gift is solicited and the gift receipt is provided may help clarify giver intent:

☐ **Solicitation.** The best time for the giver to understand that a ministry will have complete discretion and control over a gift is at the point of solicitation—before the gift is ever made—underscoring the principle of truthfulness in fundraising. And using the suggested wording below at the point of solicitation is the best way to communicate the pertinent facts to the prospective giver before the donation is made.

The IRS formally indicated that the following language in solicitations for contributions, with no conflicting language in the solicitations and no conflicting understandings between the parties, will help show that the qualified donee has exercised the necessary control over contributions, that the giver has reason to know that the qualified donee has the necessary discretion and control over contributions, and that the giver intends that the qualified donee is the actual recipient of the contributions:

"Contributions are solicited with the understanding that [insert name of donee organization] has complete discretion and control over the use of all donated funds."

☐ **Gift receipt.** The IRS has provided the following suggested language for use in gift acknowledgments to help clarify the true intentions of a giver at the time of the contribution:

"This contribution is made with the understanding that [insert name of donee organization] has complete control and administration over the use of the donated funds."

Thus, use of this language should provide strong evidence of both giver intent and organizational control in the deputized fundraising context.

➤ **Discretion and control test.** The IRS uses the phrase "discretion and control" with respect to a charity's obligation over deputized funds. Informally, the IRS has stated that discretion and control may be evidenced by such factors as adequate selection and supervision of the self-supported worker (a worker who raises part or all of his or her support) and formalizing a budget that establishes the compensation limit and expenses of each deputized individual. Establishing compensation limits and expense reimbursements with reference to considerations other than an amount of money a deputized fundraiser collects is very important. For a complete list of the factors indicating adequate discretion and control, see the box on page 181.

> *Example 1:* When Worker A leaves the employment of Ministry B, the worker may mistakenly believe that the balance in his or her preferenced account should be transferred to Ministry C, where the worker will be employed. While a transfer to Ministry C may be made if it furthers the charitable purpose of Ministry B, it is not required.

> *Example 2:* When Worker D leaves the employment of Ministry E after completing a two-year missionary term, there is a substantial excess of funds raised for the ministry by Worker D above what was spent for the ministry of this worker. The worker may mistakenly believe the excess in his or her account should be paid to the worker. While a modest severance payment might be made to the worker in conformity with the ministry's policies, the excess is an asset of the ministry and subject to the ministry's discretion and control.

But how does a ministry know if the "intended benefit" and "control" tests have been met? Unfortunately, the IRS provides little guidance for these tests. Ministries, with advice from their CPAs and attorneys, must design their action plan based on applicable law and informal IRS guidelines. The following is a review of issues that should be considered by ministries using the deputized fundraising approach:

> ➤ Ministries should determine how to put givers on notice that they will exercise discretion and control over the donations. Using the IRS-recommended language in solicitations—written or verbal—*and* on receipts is prudent.

> ➤ Ministries should be sure to communicate consistently with givers. Eliminating written conflicts between solicitation emails/letters (including prayer letters), giver response forms, deputized worker training materials, receipts, and other related documents can be accomplished by a careful review of the ministry's current documents. It is also important to establish procedures to ensure

Caution

Prayer or support letters should clearly communicate that gifts are being solicited for the ministry. It is permissible to request that the gift be designated for the ministry of John Doe, who is a missionary employed by the charity. But letters should not request gifts "for a certain missionary" because of the implication that it is a nondeductible conduit transaction.

Factors Demonstrating Discretion and Control over the Deputized Fundraising Process

According to the IRS, ministries that receive revenues through deputized fundraising—through individual missionaries, staff members, or volunteers conducting grassroots fundraising to support the organization—can demonstrate discretion and control by the following factors:

➣ Control by the governing body of donated funds through a budgetary process

➣ Consistent exercise by the ministry's governing body of responsibility for establishing, reviewing, and monitoring the programs and policies of the organization

➣ Staff salaries set by the ministry according to a salary schedule approved by the governing body (Salaries should be set by reference to considerations other than an amount of money a deputized fundraiser collects. There can be no commitments that contributions will be paid as salary or expenses to a particular person.)

➣ Amounts paid as salary, to the extent required by the Internal Revenue Code, reported as compensation on Form W-2 or Form 1099-NEC

➣ Reimbursements of legitimate ministry expenses approved by the organization, pursuant to guidelines approved by the governing body (reimbursements must be set by considerations other than the amount of money a deputized fundraiser collects)

➣ Thorough screening of potential workers pursuant to qualifications established by the ministry that are related to its exempt purposes and not principally related to the amount of funds that may be raised by the workers

➣ Meaningful training, development, and supervision of workers

➣ Workers assigned to programs and project locations by the ministry based upon its assessment of each worker's skills and training, and the specific needs of the ministry

➣ Regular communication to givers of the ministry's full discretion and control over all its programs and funds through such means as newsletters, solicitation literature, and giver acknowledgments

➣ The financial policies and practices of the ministry annually reviewed by an audit committee, a majority of whose members are not employees of the organization that the reviews are ongoing. The more daunting task is the proper training and continuing reinforcement to self-supported workers of the need to clearly and consistently communicate the discretion and control concept to givers.

➢ Use appropriate terminology when communicating with givers. Since the ministry should not infer that contributions will be paid as salary, fringe benefits, and expense reimbursements to a particular person, communication to givers from the ministry or self-supported workers should consistently underscore the ministry's discretion and control over donations. A giver may indicate a preference that a gift to a ministry be used to support the ministry of a certain individual, and the ministry may track the dollars based on the preference. But the ministry and the deputized worker should refrain from any inference that the contributions will be paid as salary or expense reimbursements to the worker. This is a fine line but one that should be observed.

Clear communication with givers about the discretion and control issue not only places givers on notice but also serves to reinforce this concept in the mind of deputized workers. Too often, self-supported workers assume they have an element of personal ownership of funds that they raise for the ministry. For example, when the worker leaves the employment of Ministry A, he or she may mistakenly believe that the balance in his account will be transferred to Ministry B, where he or she will be employed. While a transfer of funds to Ministry B may be appropriate, it is not required.

For more information on this topic, see *The Guide to Charitable Giving for Churches and Ministries* published by ECFAPress (*ECFA.org/books*).

Contributions to Support Short-Term Mission Trips

Many ministries sponsor individuals and/or teams of individuals that serve on short-term mission trips, domestically and internationally. The proper handling of funds raised and expended for short-term mission trips often presents challenging tax, finance, and legal issues for trip participants and sending organizations alike.

The definition of "short-term" varies from one sponsoring organization to another. For church-sponsored trips, a short-term mission trip often means a trip of a week or two in duration. However, for a missions organization, a short-term trip may last as long as two years. Short-term mission trips sometimes only involve adults. Other times, participants are minors supervised by adults, or some combination of adults and minors.

Funding options for short-term mission trips. Short-term mission trips may be funded in a variety of ways. For example, the sponsoring ministry may pay part or all of the expenses of the trip from the ministry's general budget. Or a donor may give funds restricted for short-term mission trips without any preference for particular mission trip participants—the donor simply wishes to support the program of sending short-term missionaries. However, most ministries sponsoring short-term mission trips seek gifts that are preferenced for the ministry of particular trip participants.

➤ **Funding from the sponsoring ministry's general budget.** Expenses relating to short-term mission trips may be funded in full by the sponsoring ministry. This use of funds from the sponsoring ministry's general budget is appropriate if short-term mission trips are consistent with its tax-exempt purposes.

➤ **Funds directly expended by the trip participant with no financial involvement of the sponsoring ministry.** A participant in a short-term mission trip may partially or totally fund trip expenses by making direct payments for airfare, lodging, meals, and other expenses. If a trip is sponsored by a ministry, consistent with the tax-exempt purposes of the ministry, and there is no significant element of personal pleasure, recreation, or vacation, then expenses related to the trip are generally deductible as charitable contributions on the taxpayer's Schedule A, Itemized Deductions. The deduction will not be denied simply because the taxpayer enjoys providing services to the charitable organization. Personal expenses relating to "side-trips" or vacation days unrelated to the mission trip but included during the trip are generally not deductible.

➤ **Funding based on giver-restricted gifts for the trip but with no preference in relation to any trip participant.** Givers may make gifts restricted for a short-term mission trip project. Gifts for the project could be solicited by the ministry or the giver might make an unsolicited gift. These gifts generally qualify as charitable contributions, and it is appropriate for the sponsoring ministry to provide a charitable gift acknowledgment.

If a ministry accepts gifts that are giver-restricted for a short-term mission trip project, the ministry is obligated to spend the funds for the intended purpose.

A giver could change the gift restriction by redirecting the gift to another project. This scenario presumes the donated funds have not already been expended or obligated for the mission trip.

Additionally, a ministry can establish, and disclose with gift solicitation information, a board policy regarding the possible redirection of giver-restricted gifts if a mission trip event is canceled or oversubscribed (more funds are received than needed).

➤ **Funding based on gifts preferenced for particular trip participants.** Generally, mission trip participants are responsible for soliciting gifts to cover part or all of the expenses necessary for the particular trip (see pages 187-88 for a sample letter from a potential short-term mission trip participant to a potential giver).

When mission trip participants raise part or all of the funds required for a trip, the sponsoring ministry generally identifies the amounts preferenced for particular participants to monitor whether sufficient funds have been raised to cover the expenses for each individual's trip.

There is generally no basis for refunding gifts if the preferenced individual does not go on the trip. Refunding gifts demonstrates that the sponsoring ministry does not have adequate discretion and control over the gifts and may raise a question of the tax-deductibility of the gifts given in relation to the particular trip.

When a worker or a volunteer (a short-term mission trip participant typically qualifies as a "volunteer") raises some of his or her own support, the IRS has proposed the following two general tests to determine whether a tax-deductible contribution was made to or for the use of a charitable organization, or whether the gift was a nondeductible, pass-through gift to a particular individual who ultimately benefited from the contribution.

1. **The intended benefit test.** The purpose of this test is to determine whether the contributor's intent in making the donation was to benefit the ministry or the individual.

   The IRS has formally indicated that ministries should avoid the use of conflicting language in their solicitations for contributions and conflicts in understandings between the parties. This is to demonstrate that:

   a. the ministry has exercised the necessary control over contributions.

   b. the giver has reason to know that the ministry will have the necessary discretion and control over contributions.

   c. the giver intends for the ministry to be the actual recipient of the contributions.

   The following statement is recommended for use in solicitations for contributions:

   > *Contributions are solicited with the understanding that [insert name of sponsoring ministry] has complete discretion and control over the use of all donated funds.*

2. **The discretion and control test.** The IRS uses the phrase "discretion and control" to indicate a ministry's obligation regarding charitable gifts. The IRS has stated that ministries receiving funds for the support of mission endeavors can demonstrate discretion and control with the following factors:

a. Reimbursement of legitimate program expenses are approved by the ministry, consistent with the governing body's guidelines. Reimbursement should be set by considerations other than the amount of money collected by the individuals who raise funds.

b. Potential trip members are screened according to qualifications established by the ministry.

c. Trip members are given meaningful training, development, and supervision.

d. The ministry assigns trip members to programs and project locations based upon its assessment of each individual's skills and training, and the specific needs of the ministry.

Remember

Gifts preferenced for particular trip participants should generally not be refunded to givers if the preferred individual does not go on the trip.

e. Giver acknowledgments communicate the ministry's full discretion and control over its programs and funds.

f. Since the ministry should not commit to restricting the use of contributions to a particular person, potential trip participants should not imply the opposite, verbally or in writing. A giver may indicate a preference that the ministry use a gift to support the trip of a certain individual, and the ministry may track the dollars based on that preference. However, the ministry and the potential trip participant should refrain from any inference that the contributions will be paid as expenses to or for a particular worker.

Even if the intended benefit and discretion and control tests are met, there may be charitable tax-deductibility issues based on age of trip participants (see Example 2 below), ministry authorization, and the pursuit of pleasure or personal gain. Two potentially tax-deductible scenarios follow.

> *Example 1:* **Trip participants are adults.** The following two scenarios illustrate different funding patterns when trip participants are adults:
>
> > a. **Participants contribute to the ministry to cover part or all of the trip expenses.** The payments by the participants to the ministry are deductible as charitable contributions if the trip involves no significant element of personal pleasure, recreation, or vacation. These trip contributions may be acknowledged by the ministry as charitable contributions.

b. **All trip expenses are paid by the ministry, and non-participants make contributions to cover trip expenses.** If the ministry has preauthorized the mission trip, the trip furthers the exempt purposes of the ministry, and if the trip involves no significant element of personal pleasure, recreation, or vacation, gifts to cover the trip expenses are generally tax-deductible, even if the givers indicate a preference that gifts be applied to the trip expenses of a particular participant.

Example 2: **Trip participants are minors.**

If a trip participant is a minor, the minor must actually provide services to carry out the tax-exempt purposes of the trip. The age of the minor and the minor's development may be important factors in determining the minor's capability of providing services to the ministry.

If parents, relatives, and/or friends contribute to the ministry with a preference for a child's trip expenses and the ministry pays the trip expenses, these contributions are generally tax-deductible, if the minor significantly contributes to the trip purposes.

➤ **Funding based on gifts restricted for particular trip participants.** A giver may express a *preference* for a particular trip recipient, but if a giver expresses a *restriction* for a certain trip recipient, the gift is generally an earmarked gift. If so, the gift may not qualify for a charitable deduction and should generally not be accepted (or not acknowledged as a charitable gift if accepted).

Sponsors of short-term mission trips generally should not accept gifts earmarked for individuals because the gifts are not consistent with the ministry's tax-exempt purposes. An earmarked gift is a transfer that is intended to benefit an individual, not the ministry ("for Joe Smith's trip costs"). It is a transfer over which the ministry does not have sufficient discretion and control.

Caution

Earmarked gifts (for personal benefit of missionaries) should generally not be accepted by a ministry sponsoring a mission trip.

For example, in the short-term mission trip context, if the ministry accepted a gift restricted for a particular trip participant, the ministry would not have the freedom to use the funds given for another trip participant who fell short of the financial goal for the trip.

Sample Short-Term Mission Trip Fundraising Letter

This short-term mission trip fundraising letter demonstrates elements consistent with IRS guidance. The notes in the letter relate to accounting for the gift and qualifying it for a tax deduction.

1232 Main Street
Yakima, WA 98904
509/248-6739

Date

Dear Mr. and Mrs. Giver,

> This paragraph confirms it is a church-sponsored mission trip.

This summer, I have an exciting opportunity to serve the Lord on a mission trip sponsored by our church, Yakima Fellowship, to East Africa. Fifteen members of my church youth group plan to participate in a 10-day trip. We will fly into Nairobi, Kenya on July 21.

Our ministry during this trip is in Nairobi at an orphanage where most of the children have AIDS. Our team will lead a Vacation Bible School, distribute clothes we will take with us, and be

> This paragraph confirms that ministry will be performed on the trip.

available to work with and support the children in the orphanage. Sponsors from our church will accompany our team and provide ministry oversight.

One of the ways you can help me is to pray for the trip, the ministry we will perform, and for me personally. Only with prayer support will I be able to bless the children in the orphanage.

> This paragraph confirms that gifts are preferenced for Jodi's trip expenses. (For accounting purposes, gifts are temporarily restricted for the mission trip.)

Yes, there are financial needs. The cost of the trip is $2,100, which each team member is responsible to raise in gifts for our church. Please pray with me that the funds to cover my trip expenses will be provided.

Gifts to the church, with an expression of a preference for my trip expenses, are tax-deductible to the extent allowed by law.

If you will commit to pray, please check the appropriate box on the enclosed card. If you are able to make a gift to the church to assist with my expenses, please check the appropriate box, indicating your interest in helping fund my portion of the trip expenses, and make your check payable to the sponsoring church, Yakima

> This paragraph confirms the church will exercise discretion and control over the funds, implied in: "There are no refunds to givers if I don't go."

Fellowship. If I am unable to participate in the trip, your gifts will still be used to support the short-term missions program of the church.

May God bless you richly as you consider your involvement in this mission trip!

Sincerely,

Jodi Hunter

Sample Short-Term Mission Trip
Response Form (Trip Expenses Paid by the Ministry)

We want to support the missions outreach of Yakima Fellowship and are sending our gift of $_____.

Our preference is that this gift be used to support the short-term mission trip of Jodi Hunter. We understand that the use of the gift is subject to the discretion and control of Yakima Fellowship.

> These paragraphs make it clear that the giver's intent is to benefit the charity. Their financial support of Jodi Hunter is simply a desire.

Donor(s):

Bill and Karen Smith
2315 Main
Wenatchee, WA 98801

Sample Short-Term Mission Trip
Gift Acknowledgment (Trip Expenses Paid by the Ministry)

Gift Acknowledgment • Please keep this acknowledgment for your tax records

		Total Amount	Gift Amount	Other Amount
Acknowledgment #2675 Gift Date: 01/02/XX Acknowledgment Date: 01/15/XX Bill and Karen Smith 2315 Main Wenatchee, WA 98801	Preferenced for the mission trip of: Jodi Hunter	$100.00	$100.00	0

Thank you for your contribution which is tax-deductible to the extent allowed by law. While every effort will be made to apply your gift according to an indicated preference, if any, **Yakima Fellowship** has complete discretion and control over the use of the donated funds. We thank God for you and appreciate your support.

Yakima Fellowship
PO Box 4256
Yakima, WA 98904
509/248-5555

No goods or services were provided in exchange for this contribution.

Sample Short-Term Mission Trip
Gift Check (Trip Expenses Paid by the Ministry)

Bill and Karen Smith
2315 Main
Wenatchee, WA 98801

DATE: December 1, 20XX

PAY TO
THE ORDER OF: Yakima Fellowship $ 200.00

Two Hundred and no/100-- -------------------------- DOLLARS

FOR Missions Work

Bill Smith

Note: If a giver wishes to identify the preferenced participant on the check, the "preferential" or "to support the trip of" terminology should be used to avoid communicating the gift is earmarked for a particular participant. It is generally preferable for the giver to check an appropriately worded box on the response form indicating a preference to support the ministry of a particular trip participant.

Sample Short-Term Mission Trip
Gift Acknowledgment (Trip Expenses Paid by the Participant)

Gift Acknowledgment • Please keep this acknowledgment for your tax records

Acknowledgment #4575 Gift Date: 01/02/XX Acknowledgment Date: 01/15/XX Bill and Karen Smith 2315 Main Wenatchee, WA 98801	Description of Services Provided	Build church building in Nairobi, Kenya, on July 21-28, 20XX

Thank you for your contribution which is tax-deductible to the extent allowed by law. While every effort will be made to apply your gift according to an indicated preference, if any, **Yakima Fellowship** has complete discretion and control over the use of the donated funds. We thank God for you and appreciate your support.

Yakima Fellowship
PO Box 4256
Yakima, WA 98904
509/248-5555

No goods or services were provided
in exchange for this contribution..

Sample Short-Term Mission Trip and
Mission Field Assessment Visit Policy

ABC Church occasionally sponsors short-term mission trips. While these trips may provide essential ministry services and encouragement in the field, the visits are primarily intended to introduce trip participants to missions.

Additionally, it is occasionally desirable for church staff and/or volunteers to visit a supported missionary (national or expatriate) in the field, assess a potential field of service for potential future missionary support, or assess a potential field of service for a future short-term mission trip. Visits to missionaries currently supported by the church are to (1) demonstrate the church's commitment to their ministry, (2) provide face-to-face encouragement, and (3) assess the effectiveness of the ministry.

The church desires that God will be honored in every aspect of these trips. Therefore, this policy has been developed and adopted by the church governing board to provide general guidance for these trips.

Trip approval. All short-term mission trips and field assessment visits are recommended by the Missions Committee and approved by the church governing board to be considered under these policies. (*Note:* The trip approval process will vary based on the governance structure of a particular church. In some instances, the governing board may delegate trip approval responsibility to the executive pastor, for example.)

Approval, training, supervision, and assignment of trip participants. Potential non-staff trip members will be screened according to qualifications established by the church, and trip participants are given meaningful training and adequately supervised.

Non-staff trip participants are assigned to programs and project locations based on the assessment of church leaders of each individual's skills and training.

Funding trips. Based on the funding method approved by the church governing board for a particular trip, the following funding approaches may be used:

A. Trip expenses may be fully or partially funded by the church. Funds from the mission or other budget line-items may be identified for this purpose.

B. Trip expenses may be fully or partially funded through resources raised by the trip participants. Funding may be raised to cover direct and indirect trip costs, based on the approval by the governing board of the funding plan. While the church will accept gifts preferenced for the trip of a particular participant, the church will not accept gifts restricted or designated for a particular trip participant. (Reason: Gifts restricted or designated for a particular gift participant do not qualify to receive a charitable gift acknowledgment, and such gifts are not consistent with the tax-exempt status of the church.)

If trip expenses are fully or partially funded by resources raised by the trip participants, all communication to givers—sample text for letters, websites, and blog posting and talking points for the verbal communication about the trip—will be approved by the church.

If resources are raised beyond the goal for a particular trip participant, the excess may be used to provide resources for a trip participant who is under-funded.

If the resources raised by a potential trip participant are less than the financial goal established by the church, the church will determine whether to assign funds sufficient to allow the individual to participate in the trip. The additional funds could come from the church's mission or general funds. Or the additional funds could come from resources raised beyond the goal to fund other potential trip participants.

Issuing charitable gift acknowledgments. At the discretion of the church, charitable gift acknowledgments will be prepared by the church and provided for all gifts that conform with this policy, including gifts from family members and trip participants. However, gifts will not be acknowledged if the trip participant is unable to, or for any reason does not plan to, significantly perform services to carry out the purposes of the trip (for example, a child of age three).

The church will determine the appropriateness of issuing charitable gift acknowledgments when trip participants pay their own expenses for a church-sponsored trip. No charitable gift acknowledgments will be issued for short-term mission trips that have not been approved by the church.

Charitable gift acknowledgments issued by the church will include the following wording:

- An indication that the church has discretion and control over the gifts.
- A statement indicating "no goods or services were provided in exchange for the gifts," if this is true.

In determining whether a gift is preferenced or restricted for a potential trip participant, the church will use the following principles for guidance:

- A preferenced gift merely comes with a preference or a desire that the gift be used to support the trip expenses of a particular trip participant.
- Preferenced gifts generally may be accepted with a gift acknowledgment provided.
- An earmarked gift is a transfer that is intended to benefit an individual, not the church. It is a transfer over which the church does not have sufficient discretion and control. For example, if accepted, the church would not have the freedom to use the funds for a trip participant who fell short of the financial goal for the trip.

  Earmarked gifts generally should not be accepted; therefore, a gift acknowledgment is a moot issue.

Refunding of gifts related to trips. Gifts preferenced for particular gift recipients will not be refunded to givers except in unusual circumstances, such as the cancellation of a trip. Funds preferenced for the trip of a particular participant could be carried forward for a future trip at the discretion of the church.

Discretion and control over gifts. All gifts given to support trips are the property of the church and will be expended under the discretion and control of the church.

Accounting records. The church will separately record revenue and expenses related to each short-term mission trip.

Determining accountable expenses related to trips. Expenses will be reimbursed under the church's accountable expense reimbursement plan. Allowable volunteer expenses include transportation expenses and reasonable expenses for meals and lodging necessarily incurred while away from home. Expenses will not be reimbursed for individuals who have only nominal duties relating to the performance of services for the church or who for significant portions of the trip are not required to render services.

While "a significant element of personal pleasure" is not defined by the tax code or regulations, the current edition of IRS publication 526 provides the following guidance (adapted):

> Generally, trip participants can claim a charitable contribution deduction for travel expenses necessarily incurred while they are away from home performing services for a charitable organization only if there is no significant element of personal pleasure, recreation, or vacation in the travel. This applies whether the participant pays for the expenses directly or indirectly. Expenses are paid indirectly if a payment is made to the ministry and the ministry pays for the travel expenses.
>
> The deduction for travel expenses will not be denied simply because the participant enjoys providing services to the ministry. Even if he or she enjoys the trip, the participant can take a charitable contribution deduction for travel expenses if he or she is on duty in a genuine and substantial sense throughout the trip. However, if the participant has only nominal duties, or if for significant parts of the trip he or she does not have any duties, travel expenses cannot be deducted.

To prove the extent and duration of services, each trip participant will keep an hour-by-hour itinerary of the entire trip. The itinerary should separate those times when the trip participant is on duty for the church from those times when the participant is free to choose his or her own activities.

Church staff participation in trips. Church staff are encouraged to participate in mission trips by providing them with one week of paid time for one trip per year subject to the approval and staff member's supervisor.

Staff members are responsible to raise the same financial support as other trip participants. (*Note:* The church may determine it is appropriate for a staff member who is leading a team to raise support for the team as a whole, whereby the funding for the leader is paid from the overall trip budget.)

> If a staff participant is a non-exempt employee for purposes of the Fair Labor Standards Act and the mission trip responsibilities are not clearly outside the scope of their position description, the church will define the hours on and off duty during the trip to clearly determine any overtime hours. (*Note:* The church may determine staff members participating outside the scope of their position description must use leave time instead of receiving their regular pay.)

Other Special Charitable Contribution Issues

Payments to private schools

Tuition payments to private schools are generally nondeductible since they correspond to value received. The IRS has ruled that payments to private schools are not deductible as charitable contributions if

Remember

Tuition payments are personal expenses. However, taxpayers sometimes attempt to construe tuition payments as charitable deductions. The IRS is particularly alert to arrangements that require a certain amount of contributions from a parent in addition to some tuition payments or arrangement in which education is provided "tuition-free."

> ➤ a contract exists under which a parent agrees to make a "contribution" and that contract contains provisions ensuring the admission of the child

> ➤ there is a plan allowing a parent either to pay tuition or to make "contributions" in exchange for schooling

> ➤ there is the earmarking of a contribution for the direct benefit of a particular individual (student)

> ➤ there is the otherwise unexplained denial of admission or readmission to a school for children of individuals who are financially able to, but do not contribute

Some churches operate related private schools on a "tuition-free" basis. These churches typically request that families with children in the school increase their contributions by the amount that they would otherwise have paid as tuition. In reviewing "tuition-free" situations, the IRS often questions the deductibility of gifts to the church if:

> ➤ contributions of several families increased or decreased markedly as the number of their children enrolled in the school changed

➤ the contributions of parents of students dropped off significantly in the summer months when the school was not in session

➤ the parents were not required to pay tuition

Generally, contributions to a church by parents are not deductible as charitable contributions to the extent that the church pays the parents' tuition liabilities for their children.

Gifts to staff

Ministries often make gifts to employees to show appreciation for their dedicated service. These payments may take several forms and have important implications to the organization, to staff members, and to givers:

➤ **Gifts made by an individual directly to a staff member with no church involvement in the transition.** When the payer of the funds makes the payment directly to a staff member of the church or nonprofit, this is a gift which is not tax-deductible to the giver and is generally not taxable to the recipient. A personal gift of this nature does not raise any tax issues for the ministry.

➤ **Gifts made by an individual to the church but earmarked by the giver for a particular staff member and not intended for use by the ministry.** If contributions are earmarked by the giver and treated as being gifts to the designated individual, they are not tax-deductible as charitable gifts. The earmarking of gifts by givers prevents a ministry from using the funds to carry out its functions and purposes at its discretion. The use of terminology such as a "love gift for [an individual]" or a "[desire to bless an individual]" does not impact the nondeductibility of the gift.

➤ **Gifts to staff members from church or nonprofit funds.** Often gifts are made from ministry funds which are not required by contract or a typical employment plan. The gifts may be given in appreciation near a holiday, a birthday, or an employee anniversary. The gifts may be given in relation to personal, medical, or financial crises.

Gifts to staff members from ministry funds are taxable and subject to payroll tax treatment and reporting unless they meet one of the following exceptions:

1. *De minimis* **gifts.** These gifts are impracticable of specific valuation and are generally less than $25 in value. IRS rulings have emphasized that the difficulty in valuing a *de minimis* gift is just as important as the small value. Cash, gift cards, or other cash equivalents are not *de minimis* gifts, regardless of how small the value.

2. **Employee achievement awards.** To avoid taxation, achievement awards must meet specific tax law requirements. The law generally requires a written, non-discriminatory achievement award program, which provides awards either upon attaining longevity goals or safety standards and meets other requirements for type of gift and limits on amounts.

3. **Staff member is a church attender.** If the staff member is also a church attender, it is possible for the staff member to receive benevolence assistance in the capacity of a church attender without the assistance being taxable. The benevolence need must be handled and paid through the normal benevolence process. While dual status of being both church attender and employee does not require taxation of assistance provided to the person as church attender, it does require careful documentation to ensure the employee is treated just like nonemployees. Due to the challenge of documenting that the staff member would have received a benevolence payment, and in the same amount if the individual had not been a staff member, many churches adopt policies prohibiting the payment of benevolence funds to employees.

➢ **Gifts to "bless" a particular staff member by raising a "love offering."** In the typical love offering scenario, the funds are received by the ministry (payments directly to an individual are discussed above). When the giver knows that a gift will go to a specific person, tax law generally treats the gifts as if they were made to the specific person and the gifts are not deductible as charitable contributions. The payment of the love offering is taxable and subject to payroll tax treatment and reporting with respect to the staff member.

➢ **Gifts to "bless" multiple staff members by raising a "love offering."** When an occasional love offering is raised for more than one staff person (*e.g.*, when an offering is received for a Christmas gift or for a Pastors' Appreciation gift and the funds will be distributed to more than one staff member), if the ministry leadership determines the recipients and the allocation of the offering among staff members, then donations to the love offering are generally tax-deductible. The payment of the love offering is taxable as compensation and subject to payroll tax treatment and reporting with respect to the staff member.

➢ **Gifts to an educational institution to pay tuition for a staff member's dependent.** There is no charitable tax deduction for a gift to a ministry which is designated for the educational expenses of a staff member's dependent. If the ministry uses the funds to pay the tuition of a staff member's dependent, even if the funds are paid directly to the educational institution, the amount is taxable and subject to payroll tax treatment and reporting with respect to the staff member.

Contributions that benefit specific individuals other than staff members and other than the needy

Occasionally individuals give money to a ministry but request that it be sent to a particular recipient who is not on the staff of the ministry, is not a missionary related to the ministry, and does not qualify as a "needy" individual. When told that this "conduit" role is improper, the giver usually responds, "But I can't get a tax deduction otherwise!" The giver is absolutely correct.

In a conduit transaction, the giver is making a gift to the ultimate beneficiary. The IRS will look to the ultimate beneficiary to decide whether the gift qualifies for a charitable contribution deduction.

There are certain limited circumstances in which a ministry may appropriately serve as an intermediary with respect to a gift that will be transferred to another ministry or to a specific individual. In such circumstances, it is essential that the ministry that first receives the monies has the right to control the ultimate destination of the funds.

Caution

An area of frequent abuse involves a monetary donation that the donor specifies must go to a particular individual (or family) to assist their financial needs. Before accepting such a gift, a ministry must determine if it can exercise due diligence to ensure the transaction does not actually constitute earmarking of the funds by a donor, which is not deductible as a charitable contribution.

Giver intent is also a key factor. If the giver intends for a gift to benefit a specific individual instead of supporting the mission of the ministry, the gift is generally not deductible.

> *Example:* Frank Lee makes a gift of $5,000 to Shady Lane Church. Mr. Lee stipulates that the gift must go to a particular music group of which his son is a member. The money will be used to purchase sound equipment. The group will go on tour to present religious music in churches. The group is not an approved ministry of Shady Lane Church. This gift would generally be termed a personal gift to the music group and would not be deductible as a charitable contribution. It is best if the church does not accept or returns the gift to Mr. Lee. If the church accepts the gift and passes the money on to the music group, the church should advise Mr. Lee that the gift is not deductible and should not provide a charitable acknowledgment.

Contributions to needy individuals and benevolence funds

Personal gifts made directly by a giver to needy individuals are not deductible. To qualify for a charitable deduction, contributions must be made to a qualified charitable organization. However, contributions to benevolence funds may be claimed as charitable deductions if they are not earmarked for particular recipients.

Sample Benevolence Fund Policy

Whereas, New Haven Church has a ministry to needy individuals; and

Whereas, The church desires to establish a Benevolence Fund through which funds for the support of needy individuals may be administered; and

Whereas, The church desires to operate the Benevolence Fund according to the highest standards of integrity;

Resolved, That New Haven Church establish a Benevolence Fund to help individuals in financial need and will develop written procedures to document the need, establish reasonable limitations of support per person during a specified time period, and obtain external verification of the need; and

Resolved, That the church will accept only contributions to the Benevolence Fund that are "to or for the use" of the church, and their use must be subject to the control and discretion of the church board. Givers may make suggestions but not designations or restrictions concerning the identity of the needy individuals; and

Resolved, That the church will provide a charitable contribution receipt for gifts that meet the test outlined in the previous resolution. The church reserves the right to return any gifts that do not meet the test.

A gift to a ministry involved in helping needy people marked "to aid the unemployed" is generally deductible. Yet if the gift is designated or restricted for the "Brown family" and the ministry passes the money on to the Browns, the gift is generally not tax-deductible.

If a giver makes a suggestion about the beneficiary of a benevolent contribution, it may be deductible if the recipient ministry exercises proper control over the benevolence fund. The giver's suggestion must be only advisory in nature, and the ministry may accept or reject the suggestion. However, if every "suggestion" is honored by the ministry, the earmarking could be challenged by the IRS.

A ministry may want to help a particular individual or family that has unusually high medical bills or other valid personal financial needs. To announce that funds will be received for the individual or family and acknowledge the monies through the ministry makes the gifts personal and not deductible as charitable contributions. One option is for the ministry to set up a trust fund at a local bank. Contributions to the trust fund are not deductible for tax purposes, but payments from the trust fund do not represent taxable income to a needy individual or family. This method of helping the needy person or family represents personal gifts from one individual to another.

Granting of scholarships

When scholarship assistance is provided by a ministry, it requires careful compliance with tax laws and regulations. Three distinct areas of the tax law must be addressed:

➤ **Protecting the contributor's tax deduction.** The contribution deduction requires the gift be "to or for the use of" a charitable entity, not an individual. To qualify, the gift must be to a ministry or other qualified nonprofit organization, knowing it will be used for scholarships, but without knowing who will receive the scholarship. A gift designated for a specific individual will not qualify.

The group of individuals that may properly receive scholarship assistance from a church is called a charitable class. A charitable class must be large or indefinite enough that providing aid to members of the class benefits the community as a whole. Examples of broad charitable classes may include low-income students or students with specific interests.

Five guidelines for protecting the contribution deduction are as follows:

1. The ministry determines all scholarship recipients through the use of a scholarship committee.

2. The ministry has a well-published policy stating that it determines the recipients according to its own policies and that it expressly rejects any effort to honor a giver's recommendation(s).

3. All scholarship policies contain the following statement: "Scholarships are awarded without regard to sex, race, nationality, or national origin."

4. Recipients of scholarships and the amount they are to receive will be based on funds already received.

5. The criteria for scholarship qualification are in writing.

Key Issue

Too often, well-meaning people want to help a relative or a friend pay their school bills, plus they want a tax deduction for the assistance. So instead of making a personal non-deductible gift to the intended beneficiary, they make a "gift" to a ministry with a request to provide a scholarship for a designated individual. This transfer of funds is not a charitable contribution, and the funds should not be accepted by the ministry.

➢ **Protecting the status of the payments to the scholarship recipient.** Only a candidate for a degree can exclude amounts received as a scholarship. A qualified scholarship is any payment to or for the student if it is for "tuition and fees" or for enrollment or "fees, books, supplies, and equipment" required for specific courses. Amounts used for room and board and non-required expenses (computers and travel) are not tax-exempt. It is not necessary for a ministry granting a scholarship to confirm that it will be expended only for qualified uses. The person receiving the scholarship must report excess amounts as taxable income.

➢ **Employee dependent scholarship programs.** Generally, scholarships for an employee's dependents will be considered taxable compensation to the employee unless they meet the following precise guidelines. A few of the requirements include the following:

1. The existence of the program must not be presented as a benefit of employment by the ministry.

2. Selection of beneficiaries must be made by an independent committee.

3. Selection must be based solely upon substantial objective standards that are completely unrelated to the employment of the recipients or their parents and to the employer's line of business.

4. Generally, not more than 25% of eligible dependents may be recipients of scholarships.

Donated travel and out-of-pocket expenses

Unreimbursed out-of-pocket expenses of a volunteer performing services for a ministry are generally deductible. (Volunteer reimbursements using the per diem method triggers taxable income to the volunteers for the reimbursements in excess of actual expenses.) The expenses must be directly connected with and solely attributable to the providing of the volunteer services.

The type of expenses that are deductible include transportation; travel (mileage at 14 cents per mile for 2020); meals and lodging while away from home if there is no significant element of personal pleasure, recreation, or vacation associated with the travel; postage; phone calls; printing and photocopying; expenses in entertaining prospective givers; and required uniforms without general utility.

It is generally inappropriate to provide a volunteer with a standard charitable receipt, because the ministry is usually unable to confirm the actual amount of a volunteer's expenses. But a letter of appreciation may be sent to the volunteer thanking the individual for the specific services provided. The burden is on the volunteer to prove the amount of the expenses.

Volunteers who incur $250 or more in out-of-pocket expenses in connection with a charitable activity are subject to the acknowledgment rules. The acknowledgment should identify the type of services or expenses provided by the volunteer and state that no goods or services were provided by the ministry to the giver in consideration of the volunteer efforts (see page 202 for a sample letter to volunteers).

When a giver requests a refund or transfer of gift funds

Occasionally, givers request a refund of a charitable gift they have made. Since contributions must be irrevocable to qualify for a charitable deduction, there generally is no basis to return a charitable gift to a giver. In the rare instances where a refund is justified, legal and tax advice should be sought (at least for refunds of significant amounts).

In another instance, after a giver makes a restricted gift to a ministry, but instead of a refund, the giver requests that the funds be transferred to a second ministry. It is within the discretion of Ministry A to determine whether it retains the restricted funds or a gift/grant is made to Ministry B. A gift/grant by Ministry A to Ministry B is appropriate only if Ministry B is qualified to carry out the giver's restrictions and is consistent with Ministry A's exempt purposes.

A few preventive steps may be helpful in this area:

➤ **Adopt a proactive policy.** Start from a position of generally providing no refunds of charitable gifts. Include guidance relating to how the ministry will communicate with givers relating to situations where a restricted project may be overfunded, underfunded, or cancelled. Provide guidance on how the ministry will communicate with givers concerning gift preferences.

➤ **Clearly communicate with givers.** Particularly when accepting gifts with giver preferences (see pages 178-82), clearly communicate that the ministry has discretion and control over the gift. This does not suggest that giver preferences will be ignored. It simply means that the ministry has the right to expend the funds for similar purposes if the preferences are not honored.

Warning

Ministries should have policies and procedures in place to address requests for the return of charitable donations. Significant gifts should be returned only after consulting with legal and tax counsel and after approval by the governing board.

Sample Letter to Volunteers

Date _____

Dear Volunteer:

We appreciate the time, energy, and out-of-pocket costs you devote to our cause as follows:

Description of Services/Expenses Provided/Date Provided

_____

_____

_____

No goods or services were provided to you by our church, except intangible religious benefits, in consideration of your volunteer efforts.

You may deduct unreimbursed expenses that you incur incidental to your volunteer work. Transportation costs (travel from home to our church or other places where you render services), phone calls, postage stamps, stationery, and similar out-of-pocket costs are deductible.

You can deduct the IRS approved charitable mileage rate (14 cents per mile for 2020) in computing the costs of operating your car while doing volunteer work as well as unreimbursed parking and toll costs. Instead of using the cents-per-mile method, you can deduct your actual auto expenses, provided you kept proper records. However, insurance and depreciation on your car are not deductible.

If you travel as a volunteer and must be away from home overnight, reasonable payments for meals and lodging as well as your travel costs are deductible. Your out-of-pocket costs at a convention connected with your volunteer work are deductible if you were duly chosen as a representative of our church.

You cannot deduct travel expenses as charitable gifts if there is a significant element of personal pleasure, recreation, or vacation in the travel.

You cannot deduct the value of your services themselves. For example, if you devote 100 hours during the year to typing for us and the prevailing rate for these services is $8.00 per hour, you can't deduct the $800 value of your services. Although deductions are allowed for property gifts, the IRS doesn't consider your services "property." Nor is the use of your home for meetings a "property contribution."

Finally, you may be required to substantiate your deduction to the IRS. Be prepared to prove your costs with canceled checks, receipted bills, and diary entries. If your expenses total $250 or more for the calendar year, you must have this acknowledgment in hand before you file your income tax return.

Again, thank you for furthering our cause with that most precious commodity: your time.

Castleview Church

When raising or accepting gifts with giver restrictions, it is often wise to communicate to givers that if gift restrictions cannot be met by the ministry, the ministry will use the funds for another project or make a grant to another ministry that is able to fulfill the giver's restrictions.

Avoid duplicity in communicating with givers. *Example:* A church offering envelope provides an opportunity to check a box for a gift for the building fund, the missions fund, or to use where needed most. The following sentence is added: "The church may use this money for any purpose at the discretion of the board." Wording of this nature is very confusing to givers at the very least. It suggests to them that a gift the donor intends to restrict for missions might be used to pay the pastor's salary.

➤ **Make wise administrative decisions.** When gifts with giver restrictions cannot be spent for the intended purpose, make a decision within a reasonable period regarding how the funds will be expended. While there are no hard and fast rules on how quickly restricted gifts must be used, the longer the time it takes the ministry to expend the funds, the greater the risk of creating a public relations issue with givers.

Child adoption gifts

It is not surprising that ministries and givers often seek ways to provide financial support to couples involved in the adoption process. The cost to adopt a child often exceeds the financial resources of the adopting couple.

While there are a few ways ministries can legitimately assist adoptive parents, these options are very limited. A ministry should carefully scrutinize any gifts that are designated for a particular adoptive family. The IRS may consider such gifts as conduit or pass-through transactions which do not qualify for a charitable receipt by a ministry or a charitable deduction by a giver and could endanger the tax status of a ministry.

The following are some considerations for providing support for adoptive parents:

➤ **Personal gifts to the adoptive parents.** An individual may make a personal gift to adoptive parents to assist with adoption expenses. Personal gifts are not deductible as charitable gifts but are not taxable to the adoptive parents.

➤ **Gifts for adoptive parents by a ministry whose purpose and nature are not consistent with such gifts.** If gifts by a ministry to adoptive families are not consistent with the broad limits imposed by the ministry's purpose and nature, the gifts are generally not a proper use of tax-exempt funds.

➤ **Gifts for adoptive parents from the operating fund of a ministry.** If adoption assistance is consistent with the ministry's purpose and nature, a ministry generally has a sound basis to provide assistance for adoptive parents from the ministry's general funds (budgeted or unbudgeted). Payments for adoptive families are often made on the basis of financial need and paid directly to the adoption agency to assure that the funds are properly used. These payments are tax-free to the adoptive parents.

➤ **Gifts to a ministry's adoption fund not preferenced for a particular adoptive family and gifts for an adoptive family from the fund.** If adoption assistance is consistent with the ministry's purpose and nature, a ministry generally has a sound basis to establish a restricted fund (either temporarily restricted or permanently restricted) to accept gifts that are not designated by a giver for a particular adoptive family. Gifts to such a fund will generally qualify as charitable gifts. Payments for adoptive families are often made on the basis of financial need. Payments should typically be made directly to the adoption agency or reimbursed to the adoptive parents based on adequate documentation to assure that the funds are properly used.

➤ **Gifts to a ministry preferenced for a particular adoptive family and gifts for the adoptive family from the fund.** Even if adoption assistance is consistent with the ministry's governing documents, gifts that are preferenced by a giver for a particular adoptive family may raise conduit or pass-through transaction issues. To be deductible, the ministry must generally:

- have discretion and control over the contribution without any obligation to benefit a preferenced individual;

- obtain adequate information about the potential recipient of the funds (including financial resources);

- avoid refunding gifts to givers if a particular adoption is not completed; and

- avoid conflicts of interest between those approving and receiving a loan or a grant.

Before considering accepting gifts of this nature and making related gifts to adoptive parents, a ministry should seek qualified legal counsel.

Providing Assistance to or for Adoptive Parents Implications for Charitable Deduction Purposes	
Type of Gift	**Qualifies as a Charitable Deduction**
Gift from a ministry to/for an adoptive family based on need[1,2]—not based on gifts designated by the giver(s), *e.g.*, from the ministry's general fund.	Yes
Gift from a ministry to/for an adoptive family based on gifts restricted for the ministry's adoption fund but not restricted or preferenced for a particular adoptive family.	Yes
Personal gifts from one individual to/for another individual to assist in an adoption.	No
Gift from a ministry to/for an adoptive family based on gifts preferenced for a particular adoptive family and the *giver's intent* is to benefit the adoptive family, not the ministry.	No
Gift from a ministry to/for an adoptive family based on gifts restricted for a particular adoptive family. *The ministry is unable to provide adequate discretion and control over the payment because of the giver(s) restriction.*	No
Gift from a ministry to/for an adoptive family based on gifts restricted for a particular adoptive family—the adoptive family and the giver are the same taxpayer.	Generally, no (and this may be tax fraud because of the circular nature of the transaction)
Gift from a ministry to/for an adoptive family based on gifts preferenced for a particular adoptive family. *The ministry exercises adequate discretion and control over the gift.*	Based on facts and circumstances

[1] As a best practice, the payments should either be made directly to the adoption agency or reimbursed to the adoptive parents based on adequate documentation to assure that the funds are properly used.

[2] Personal gifts from an individual to another individual may have estate tax implications if the gifts to an individual exceed the annual gift tax limitation.

- **Crossing the line from a restricted to an earmarked gift.** Givers may restrict gifts either as to purpose or to time. When the restriction only relates to a project (such as a capital campaign, the mission budget of a church, or the benevolence fund), the issue of earmarked gifts does not arise. When gifts are preferenced for the support of a particular missionary or a benevolent recipient and the preferencing is only an expression of a desire, not a restriction, the gift is restricted for accounting purposes and the earmarking line generally has not been crossed.

  However, when the gift is not preferenced, but restricted for an individual, the earmarked issue arises. Charitable gift deductions are generally not available for earmarked gifts. Integrity requires carefully monitoring the restricted, preferenced, and earmarked gift issues.

- **Raising money for a mission trip.** The deputized fundraising concept applies to raising money for career and short-term missionaries. When an organization accepts gifts under this concept, it assumes the responsibility for the discretion and control of the gifts. Additionally, the ministry must be precise in its proper communication with the supported missionary and the givers. It is very easy to cross the line from a gift restricted for missions, perhaps even in a particular region of the world or a specific country, to a gift earmarked for a particular missionary.

  Sponsors of short-term mission trips may face the issue of perhaps making refunds for individuals who planned to go on a mission trip but were unable to make the trip. These refunds should be avoided.

- **Gifts to assist others.** Gifts to assist others, such as benevolence and scholarships, are a wonderful way to provide for those with needs. A ministry must make it clear that such gifts cannot be for a specific person, but rather are made to a ministry fund which then is under the discretion and control of the ministry in alignment with giver intent; *e.g.*, a gift for benevolence will be used by the organization to assist a person in need in alignment with its benevolence policy.

Projected 2021 Employer Tax Filing Dates

January

15 Monthly deposit of Social Security, Medicare, and withheld income tax

31 Distribute Form 1099 to recipients and file with the IRS

31 Distribute Form W-2 to recipients and file with the IRS

31 Mail or electronically file Copy A of Form(s) W-2 and W-3 with the SSA

31 File Form 940 for unemployment tax

31 File Form 941 due for Social Security, Medicare, and withheld income tax

February

15 Monthly deposit of Social Security, Medicare, and withheld income tax

15 Federal tax withholding deductions reset for anyone who has not given their employer an updated Form W-4

March

15 Monthly deposit of Social Security, Medicare, and withheld income tax

April

15 Monthly deposit of Social Security, Medicare, and withheld income tax

30 Quarterly Form 941 due (can be filed by May 10 if taxes for quarter were deposited timely, properly and in full)

May

15 Form 990 and 990-T due for calendar year-end organizations (other year-ends on the 15th day of the 5th month after your year-end)

15 Monthly deposit of Social Security, Medicare, and withheld income tax

June

15 Monthly deposit of Social Security, Medicare, and withheld income tax

July

15 Monthly deposit of Social Security, Medicare, and withheld income tax

31 Quarterly Form 941 due (can be filed by August 10 if taxes for quarter were deposited timely, properly and in full)

August

15 Monthly deposit of Social Security, Medicare, and withheld income tax

September

15 Monthly deposit of Social Security, Medicare, and withheld income tax

October

15 Monthly deposit of Social Security, Medicare, and withheld income tax

31 Quarterly Form 941 due (can be filed by November 10 if taxes for quarter were deposited timely, properly and in full)

November

15 Monthly deposit of Social Security, Medicare, and withheld income tax

December

15 Monthly deposit of Social Security, Medicare, and withheld income tax

Policy Checklist

Ministry policies that are distinct from personnel or accounting policies are needed and useful in a church or ministry. Below is a checklist to assess the types of documentation that may be helpful in a particular ministry. Most of these sample policies are free in ECFA's Knowledge Center, *www.ECFA.org/KnowledgeCenter*.

➤ Conflict of interest policy

➤ Policy on suspected misconduct, dishonesty, fraud, and whistleblower protection

➤ Document retention/destruction policy

➤ Gift acceptance policy

➤ Accountable reimbursement plan

➤ Compensation approval policy

➤ Cell phone usage policy

➤ Intellectual property policy

➤ Honoraria policy guidelines

➤ Endowment policy

➤ Investment policy

➤ International activities policy

➤ Benevolence policy

➤ Joint venture policy

➤ Giver privacy policy

➤ Policy of issuing receipts to non-givers

➤ Policy on personal use of ministry-owned vehicles

➤ Board ethics policy

➤ Staff and volunteer ethics policy

Index

Must-Read Lessons for Nonprofit Board Members!

Read Lesson 38, "Great Boards Delegate Their Reading," and consider deputizing a "Leaders Are Readers Champion" on your board. Learn how that person can inspire all board members to be lifelong learners in effective board governance. Leaders are readers!

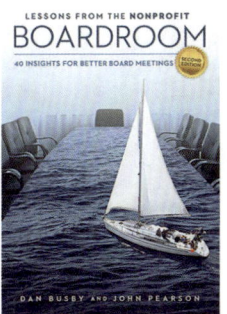

❏ **Lesson 1: Wanted: Lifelong Learners**
Would you trust a surgeon who stopped learning?

❏ **Lesson 4: Do Unwritten Board Policies Really Exist?**
Can't find that 10-year-old policy? You need a BPM.

❏ **Lesson 6: Eliminate Hallway Whining**
The 5/15 report to the board takes just five minutes to read and 15 minutes to write.

❏ **Lesson 19: Never Throw Red Meat on the Board Table**
Boards need advance preparation to fully address complex issues.

❏ **Lesson 23: Focus on Mission Impact and Sustainability**
The "dual bottom line" equips boards to address dead horses and sacred cows (or goats).

❏ **Lesson 24: Ministry Fundraising 101 for Board Members**
Could your board pass a pop-quiz on fundraising practices?

❏ **Lesson 34: Envision Your Best Board Member Orientation Ever**
Equip new board members to serve from day one.

❏ **Lesson 35: Is Your Board Color-Blind to Hazardous Conditions?**
What color is your boardroom flag?

❏ **Lesson 36: Decrease Staff Reporting and Increase Heavy Lifting**
Consider the good, the bad, and the ugly.

❏ **Lesson 40: A Board Prayer**
"Dear God…Let me tell stories and provide statistics that represent accurately."

More Must-Read Lessons for Nonprofit Board Members!

Leverage the insights in this book at your next board retreat. Inspire 10 people (board and staff) to each prepare a 10-minute summary of their assigned chapter. Allocate five minutes for the content, and five minutes for discussion in groups of two or three. Leaders are readers!

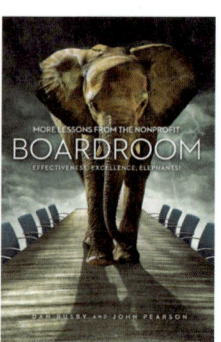

❑ **Lesson 1: Big Blessings Abound When Governance Faithfulness Flourishes**
Two stories: "The Board and the Bachelor Farmer" and "$1.5 Billion Worth of Burger Blessings!"

❑ **Lesson 5: Dashboards Are Not a Secret Sauce for Sound Governance**
Too often the use of dashboards does not clearly communicate the past and give signals for the future.

❑ **Lesson 7: Eliminate Fuzziness Between Board and Staff Roles**
Keep your leaders on track with a one-page Prime Responsibility Chart.

❑ **Lesson 17: Botched Executive Sessions Are Not Pretty**
Don't assume that your executive sessions will automatically be excellent.

❑ **Lesson 22: Whopper Mistakes Can Unravel Your Ministry**
If stupidity got us into this mess, then why can't it get us out?

❑ **Lesson 25: Compensating the CEO—It's About More Than Money**
Getting the compensation-setting process right must be a priority.

❑ **Lesson 26: Big Rocks, Pebbles, and Sand**
Ministry boards have a natural gravitational pull toward issues that should be reserved for the staff.

❑ **Lesson 28: Defending Risks Everywhere Is Not a Strategic Plan**
You must discuss the risk elephant in the boardroom.

❑ **Lesson 30: Are You Competing Based on Overhead— Really?**
Boards should know the back-story on a ministry's overhead.

❑ **Lesson 39: Identify Your Key Assumptions**
An inaccurate premise may lead to a colossal flop!

Must-Read Lessons for Church Board Members!

Read Lesson 40, "A Board Prayer," and learn why some boards read this prayer at every board meeting. As one executive pastor said, "The first time I read Dan Bolin's prayer, I instantly wondered if he had somehow secretly been listening in on every board meeting I ever attended." Leaders are readers!

❑ **Lesson 1: Wanted: Lifelong Learners**
Would you trust a surgeon who stopped learning?

❑ **Lesson 4: What Could Possibly Go Wrong?**
Prepare your board now for the possibility of future accusations and investigations.

❑ **Lesson 5: Do Unwritten Board Policies Really Exist?**
Can't find that 10-year-old policy? You need a BPM.

❑ **Lesson 18: Never Throw Red Meat on the Board Table**
Boards need advance preparation to fully address complex issues.

❑ **Lesson 22: Big Rocks, Pebbles, and Sand**
Church boards have a natural gravitational pull toward issues that should be reserved for the church staff.

❑ **Lesson 23: Pastor Pay—It's About More Than Just Money**
Getting the compensation-setting process right must be a priority.

❑ **Lesson 30: 7 Ways to Avoid a Financial Train Wreck**
Financial derailment of a church is usually a collective failure, but the finger almost always points back to the governing board.

❑ **Lesson 37: Is Your Board Color-Blind to Hazardous Conditions?**
What color is your boardroom flag?

❑ **Lesson 39: Don't Stretch Credulity With BHAGs and Stretch Goals**
The actual achievement of audacious goals is very uncommon.

❑ **Lesson 40: A Board Prayer**
"Dear God . . . Grant us the joy of arriving at adjournment closer to one another because we are closer to You."

Download the Lessons and Share Them With Your Board Members!

Board Enrichment Idea: Once-a-month, email one lesson to board members.
Links to the lessons are posted in the ECFA Knowledge Center under "Governance."

www.ECFA.org/KnowledgeCenter

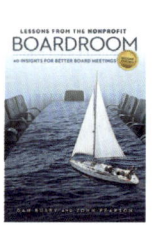

Blogs on all 40 lessons	*nonprofitboardroom.blogspot.com/*
Download all 40 lessons	*www.ECFA.org/KnowledgeCenter*

Blogs on all 40 lessons	*churchboardroom.blogspot.com/*
Download all 40 lessons	*www.ECFA.org/KnowledgeCenter*

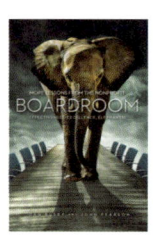

Blogs on all 40 lessons	*morelessonsnonprofitboardroom.blogspot.com/*
Download all 40 lessons	*www.ECFA.org/KnowledgeCenter.aspx*

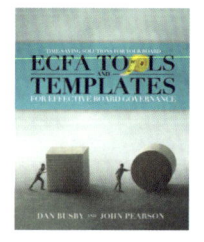

Blogs on all 22 tools	*ecfagovernance.blogspot.com/2020/03/index-to-22-time-saving-governance.html*
Download the templates	See the link in ECFA Tools and Templates

Biggest Tax and Financial Mistakes Made by Churches and Nonprofits

1. Not setting up and adequately monitoring an accountable expense reimbursement plan for employees. (Chapter 3)

2. Failure to comply with the Fair Labor Standards Act for churches and other nonprofits. (Chapter 3)

3. Not reporting taxable fringe benefits and Social Security reimbursements as additional compensation to employees. (Chapter 3)

4. Deducting FICA tax from the salary of qualified ministers, whether employed by a church or other nonprofit. (Chapter 4)

5. Failing to file Form 1099-NEC for independent contractors. (Chapter 5)

6. Weak controls over revenue, including failing to have offerings and other cash and checks controlled by two individuals until the funds are counted. (Chapter 6)

7. Inadequate controls over disbursements, leaving the ministry at risk for embezzlement. (Chapter 6)

8. Failure to issue a proper receipt (including the fair market value of the goods or services provided) when a donor makes a payment of more than $75 and receives goods or services. (Chapter 7)

9. Providing receipts for the donation of services and the rent-free use of property. Receipting contributions designated for individuals without proper discretion and control exercised by the donee organization. Placing values on noncash gifts. (Chapter 7)

10. Accepting earmarked gifts with the ministry exercising inadequate control when the gift is disbursed to another ministry or benevolent recipient. (Chapter 8)

Tax and Finance Questions Most Frequently Asked by Churches and Nonprofits

1. **Tax exempt status.** Should our church or nonprofit file for tax exemption with the Internal Revenue Service? Are we required to annually file Form 990? (Chapter 2)

2. **Unrelated business income exposure.** Do we have any filing requirements for unrelated business income? If we have some unrelated business income, will we lose our tax-exempt status? (Chapter 2)

3. **Public disclosure.** Is our organization required to disclose any documents to the public based on appropriate requests for them? If so, which documents? (Chapter 2)

4. **Political activities.** Are the activities of our organization consistent with the political activity law? (Chapter 2)

5. **Housing allowance.** How do we determine whether a minister qualifies for a housing allowance designation? Are the rules for qualifying for the housing allowance identical for churches and other nonprofits? (Chapter 3)

6. **Reporting compensation.** Which payments to employees are taxable and must be reported on the annual Form W-2? (Chapter 5)

7. **Internal and external auditing.** Should we have an audit, review, or compilation by an independent CPA? If not, how can we perform a valid internal audit of our financial processes? (Chapter 6)

8. **Handling gifts.** What steps can we take to ensure the highest integrity in processing gifts, especially cash offerings, and providing acknowledgments to givers? (Chapter 7)

9. **Noncash gifts.** How do we handle noncash gifts? Should we ever place a value on a noncash gift, including gifts of services? (Chapter 7)

10. **Giver-restricted gifts.** When a giver restricts a gift, how do we determine whether we should accept the gift and whether it qualifies as a charitable contribution? (Chapter 8)